Politics, Policies, and Economic Development in Latin America

Politics, Policies, and Economic Development in Latin America

Robert Wesson
Editor

122078

Hoover Institution Press

Stanford University, Stanford, California

Hoover Press Publication 306

Copyright © 1984 by the Board of Trustees of the
   Leland Stanford Junior University

First printing, 1984

Manufactured in the United States of America

88 87 86 85 84   9 8 7 6 5 4 3 2 1

Library of Congress Cataloging in Publication Data
Main entry under title:

Politics, policies and economic development in Latin America.

  (Hoover Press publication 306)
  Includes bibliographies and index.
    1. Latin America—Politics and government—1948–
—Addresses, essays, lectures. 2. Economic development—
Political aspects—Addresses, essays, lectures. 3. Latin
America—Economic policy—Addresses, essays, lectures.
I. Wesson, Robert G., 1920– .
JL960.P65 1984   320.98   84-19236
ISBN 0-8179-8061-X
ISBN 0-8179-8062-8 (pbk.)

Design by P. Kelly Baker

Contents

Preface

One of the gravest problems of the modern world is the gap between a few rich nations and the many poor to very poor ones. The difference in per capita income is as much as a hundred to one, with all that this means in terms of deprivation, compressed and degraded lives, cultural and material loss, hunger and poor health, as well as lack of the paraphernalia and amenities of modernity. The implications for the international order, and even for the well-being of the more prosperous parts of the world, are ominous. No country can separate itself from the problems of the world's majority. Consequently, there has been an enormous amount of discussion of the problem of economic growth or economic development of the Third World. This discussion, however, is usually particular—controversy over certain policies—or diffuse and ideological. It is, moreover, carried on largely by economists in economic terms. Thus, in the extensive publications of the World Bank, one may search in vain for a reference to political conditions, and countries of the most varied political complexion are added together indiscriminately.

Yet it would seem intuitively obvious that political institutions have a large effect on the kind of policies adopted, that policies create the climate and conditions for productive enterprise and economic development. Political leaders take this proposition as axiomatic, urging support for this or that candidate or program in order to increase jobs and prosperity. Usually, the promises of the politicians are unfulfilled, and the policies advocated do not have the expected results, but no one doubts their significance. Governments inevitably receive blame for hard times or take credit for good, even though factors beyond their control, from world prices to the weather, may have been largely responsible. There is, withal, no broad logical analysis linking politics, policies, and economic development generally in the Third World, but as many approaches as there are political tendencies.

The essays that follow offer no theory to fill this need but seek to approach the subject by considering the recent experience of a number of

Latin American countries. Limiting our investigation to this region is appropriate because the nations share much cultural background and mores are similar in most of these countries. There is something of a community of political culture; Latin Americans generally have more or less democratic aspirations along with a susceptibility to military dictatorship, and an individualistic ethos along with much state interventionism. Yet there is quite a variety of political systems. At the same time, except in the Central American–Caribbean region, their situation has been little complicated by extraneous conflicts. Moreover, Latin American countries have been relatively free of the ethnic, religious, and linguistic divisions that have plagued most Asian and African countries and have led in many to violent conflict. Latin Americans have been much freer to concentrate on economic problems, which have been the chief meat of politics throughout the region. Yet policies applied to those problems have varied strikingly.

Consequently, quite apart from the inherent interest of Latin America for the United States, that area is especially suited for a study of the problem indicated by the title of this volume. Within it, ten countries have been chosen for attention, mostly on grounds of the interest of their economic experiments. Chile had a most remarkable, almost unique program in the monetarist direction, under the auspices of a stern military dictatorship. Uruguay and Argentina, in some ways parallel to Chile, illustrate the efforts of a military regime to reconstruct badly disordered economies, with little success. Mexico has a quite different governmental system, which until recently was markedly successful. Brazil is perhaps the clearest case of a government instituted (by the coup of 1964) primarily for economic reasons; the results of authoritarianism and, since 1974, of relaxation are most instructive. Colombia is a somewhat qualified democracy, which has been called a two-party dictatorship; its economic experience has been rather different from that of its neighbors. Peru had, uniquely for Latin America, a leftist military regime, which came to grief largely for economic reasons; the shaky democracy that came to power in 1980 is threatened by the same fate. The most interesting aspect of Venezuelan development is the management of oil wealth by a democratic government. Costa Rica, as the most democratic of Latin American states, is of interest much beyond its size, for the results of popular democracy. Jamaica is included even though, as an English-speaking, former British colony, it does not strictly belong to Latin America. It is frequently considered with Latin America on grounds of geography; for our purposes, it offers close parallels to Latin American politico-economic experience. It is almost a laboratory of contrasting approaches, statist and free enterprise, within a democratic framework.

On the other hand, Cuba, although unequivocally Latin American, has been omitted because it is too variant to offer useful comparisons with the other countries. It is not a member, for all practical purposes, of the hemispheric trading community, 70 percent of its foreign trade being with the Soviet Union. The Cuban economy is as politicized as the leadership can make it, and it is constrained not only by internal planning but by the requirements of the Council for Mutual Economic Assistance, the Soviet bloc economic agency. The chief pillar of the Cuban economy is the Soviet subsidy equivalent to $4–5 billion per year. The Cuban experience consequently seemed irrelevant for the purposes of this volume.

It is not to be expected that a relatively brief survey of these countries, each immensely complex, will give any clear answers to the questions posed about politics and development. However, to look even cursorily and through different eyes at the varied experience of these Latin American lands, with their different approaches to rather similar problems of insufficiency, should at least help to clarify thinking and provide a basis for further inquiry.

Robert Wesson

Hoover Institution

Introduction

It is difficult to envision Latin American countries surmounting grave problems of indebtedness, inflation, and unemployment unless they can find means of assuring stable and sound economic development and growth—of increasing the national output of goods and services by improved technology, greater investment, better management, higher productivity, more effective marketing, and better allocation of the factors of production. Only through economic growth can the less affluent countries hope to overcome present troubles and achieve economic independence, or balanced interdependence. Economic growth is almost equivalent to modernization. It not only gives material welfare—the necessities, amenities, luxuries, and toys that people covet; it also makes possible improved health care, better education, a more active cultural life, and wider freedom of choice. Perhaps even more important from the point of view of political and military leaders, economic modernization and growth are prerequisites for national strength and prestige. Many lament that economic growth and correlated social changes undo traditional virtues, set people unhappily adrift, and cause social disorder and inequality; but hardly anyone, despite these unfortunate by-products, seems to doubt the value in principle of increasing the national product. If it is a goal of capitalists, communists claim to achieve it better, and those seeking a third way are looking to the same end.

Agreement ends when discussion turns to the kind of policies or political and economic system that will bring about economic growth. Obviously many nations, all desirous of becoming more productive and richer, adopt quite different approaches; and if any one has the answer, others either will not or cannot apply its magic formula. Hardly anything is the subject of more controversy than the proper way to prosperity.

In historical perspective, however, the picture seems rather clear. The great modern economic upsurge began in the Netherlands in the seventeenth century and continued even more strongly in Britain of the eighteenth century; both were outstanding for a great deal of individual freedom. Ever since then, constitutional government and latitude for free enterprise have usually corresponded fairly closely to the degree of industrialization and prosperity. At present, no politically unfree country ranks near the top in per capita income, except for some to which petroleum has brought essentially accidental revenues thanks to technologies invented elsewhere. The prosperous advanced countries of the West, including Japan, are all democratic, and all rely basically on private ownership and market guidance, despite substantial state sectors in a number of them, such as Britain and France.

This appears logical and understandable. Modernization and economic development seem to imply the abundant and unhampered circulation of information, the rule of law, predictability of authority, and responsibility of government to the governed, which together practically amount to a definition of constitutional democratic government. Industrialization also entails encouragement of innovation and efficiency and a society in which status comes not from birth or political relationships but from productive achievement. This rather clearly implies an economy with minimal governmental-bureaucratic controls and much competition—or a market economy. A corollary of modernization and industrialization is the relative autonomy of individuals and groups and the development of independent classes without regard to birth—such as merchants, lawyers, teachers, journalists— classes that have traditionally been the backbone of most democratic societies.

Hence, the way to economic growth seems reasonably clear: a country should adopt a democratic form of government, with freedom and legality, while opening the economy to the free play of market forces. The result ought to be rapid growth, the more rapid as the country was only awaiting the large-scale application of available technology and skills. Foreigners and foreign capital will cooperate because of their desire to share in the ensuing prosperity of modernization, taking advantage of (and thereby raising) the relatively low wage rates of the poorer land and putting to use the unexploited opportunities of its markets and resources. As imported knowledge and ways are assimilated, the country should become increasingly capable of progressing on its own.

Reality is by no means so clear-cut. A country like Peru may be at least outwardly democratic and more or less dedicated to a market economy, but this does not guarantee a happy ending. For several decades, India and Sri Lanka have been democratic and have had legality and freedom to a degree unusual in the Third World. Although their policies have been more or less socialistic-interventionist, they have certainly not excluded private wealth-seeking. Yet their record of economic growth has lagged behind the world average. On the other hand, the spectacular achievers have been the nondemocratic Asian "gang of four," South Korea, Taiwan, Hongkong, and

Singapore, which have increased production by 10–20 percent annually for many years. These countries provided a suitable environment of stability, social order, low taxes, and a relatively free market in which people were invited to enrich themselves and thereby enrich the state. Yet they are all quite authoritarian, and there is no guarantee of any freedom in them (except Hongkong, governed under British authority and British law).

The phenomenal growth record of the "gang of four" complicates understanding the relationship between democracy and economic growth, although it seems to confirm the importance of state nonintervention in the economy. Yet despite the recent success of these four states, and despite the historical leadership of lightly governed Britain and the contemporary correlation between productivity and economic freedom, it has been widely, almost generally, believed that the state has a large, positive role to play in promoting modernization. Perhaps theoretically the marketplace can best allocate resources, and the state should do no more than enforce general rules and ensure that the market is free and competitive. But states have seldom been satisfied to behave that way, especially when they felt that they had to catch up with earlier industrializing powers. Even the United States, for example, subsidized early railroad building with huge land donations and protected its infant industries with high tariffs. Various European countries in the nineteenth century were even more inclined to apply state power to industrialization; the tradition of mercantilism never died, despite the success of the liberal approach. Germany in particular fostered a powerful heavy industry for military purposes by tariff protection and government patronage in the late nineteenth century. The Japanese state, after the Meiji Restoration of 1868, undertook to promote modernization on a broad scale, importing technology and building not only infrastructure but industrial plants. These were generally sold to private ownership, but there remained a custom of government coordination and support for economic enterprise within the framework of entrepreneurial risk-taking, a tradition that has given rise to the notion of "Japan, Inc."

The industrialization policies of Germany and Japan were strictly pragmatic. An ideological challenge to laissez-faire was posed by socialism, which from the early nineteenth century rejected private ownership and individual wealth-making in principle. This doctrine gained strength, especially in the European labor movement, in the last decades of the nineteenth century and the first part of the twentieth. It became the official creed of a great state after a Marxist party seized power in Russia in November 1917.

It was appropriate that Russia should propound an alternative to the prevalent Western economic as well as political model because Russia was desperately anxious to catch up with the industrialized countries and wanted a new and better approach instead of merely copying the leaders. The Russians were in any case disposed by centuries of autocratic rule to accept governance in all aspects of life. The Bolsheviks were able to combine Russian tradition and Western socialist theory to claim that their state represented a historic leap ahead to the utopian state, infinitely superior to Western capitalism. State control of the economy, or socialism, was held up as the means to modernization, not only more just but more effective and rapid than the anarchic ways of the capitalist countries.

This vision of the socialist future was inspiring to many in the West, especially in times of economic disruption and disorder ensuing after World War I. In Russia, however, the state-managed economy was only a qualified success. Controls were extended, in the heat of civil war, to practically the entirety of transactions; money became almost worthless. If this worked reasonably well during the conflict, afterwards it broke down. Lenin saved the communist state by making a far-reaching retreat, allowing private enterprise to function freely in trade and small- and medium-scale production, reserving for the state the "commanding heights."

Lenin thus inaugurated a mixed economy of overall state control and direction and mostly private production. From roughly 1922 to 1928, this policy was very successful in restoring the devastated Soviet economy, giving the Soviet Union the highest rate of growth it has ever registered. This model became ineffective, however, as unused capacity was returned to production and massive new investment became necessary for further progress. Probably more important, however, in the abandonment of this approach were political considerations. Stalin's assault on the independent peasantry, the collectivization of agriculture, and his grandiose industrialization program under first one, then a series of five-year plans, amounted to imposing a new system of total dictatorship, soon to be climaxed by the great purges. Stalin's success in giving the Soviet Union a heavy industrial base at unprecedented speed (considerably exaggerated by propaganda) greatly reinforced the idea of massive state action to modernize a backward economy; and this idea was further bolstered by the Soviet victory in World War II—which was partly credited to Stalinist industrialization. After the war, the Stalinist model was imposed on Eastern Europe, and again it resulted in a statistically impressive industrial growth rate in the satellite countries, especially in the poorest of them, Romania and Bulgaria. The Soviet model also seemed to result in extremely rapid industrial growth in China for about a decade after the establishment of the People's Republic in 1949.

Many economists have hence accepted that a large measure of state intervention is desirable, necessary, or unavoidable for the rapid industrialization of Third World countries (for example, A. H. Hansen, *Public Enterprise and Economic Development* [London, 1965]). Many reasons aside from the communist example have been urged for this thesis. There is a severe shortage of capital, and what may be available goes preferentially into unneeded investment, such as real estate, or may be shifted abroad for safety; hence it is up to the state to mobilize needed investment funds. Private capital is simply uninterested in many necessary undertakings, especially infrastructural. Where markets do not function well or fully, the state should manage and coordinate investment. Not least, private capital is, in practice, likely to mean foreign capital; even states dedicated in principle to free enterprise are apt to prefer state to foreign control of important enterprises, especially in mining or utilities. The state is also called on to intervene to provide services at reduced, perhaps uneconomic, prices. Finally, the state should take over unprofitable or failing enterprises in order to maintain production and avoid unemployment. There may also be less legitimate political reasons for state intervention, especially to create jobs to be filled by politically deserving persons.

The arguments for an active state role in the economy are strong, or at least very persuasive, and state enterprises abound in most Third World countries, not only in those dedicated more or less to socialistic ideology but also in more conservatively oriented states, such as Argentina and Brazil. The principle that the state should not interfere is hardly known. Even where, as in Sri Lanka or Jamaica, a party devoted to market economics comes to power after a socialistic period, it can make only limited progress toward extricating the government from the economy. A government, such as that of Chile after 1973, that makes a strong effort to destatize the economy is a rarity, and the Chilean regime could not have done so without dictatorial powers.

Yet skepticism about the general utility of interventionism is considerably stronger at present than it was a decade ago. One reason is the striking success of the small, free-market Asian powers. Their example has become hard to ignore. Equally important is that the communist model has become much less convincing. The Soviet growth rate has slowed continually—even judged by presumably optimistic Soviet statistics—to a quite unimpressive level, and the Soviet Union continues to depend on imported Western technology and grain. China no longer boasts of "great leaps forward"; indeed, it appears that China under communism has seen growth well below the world average, not to mention that of the formidably successful Taiwan. East European states have similarly proved that the planning commission is no panacea for economic woes, as all have experienced slack times and some have undergone crises resembling the worst of the capitalist business cycle. Poland and Vietnam are only the most notable of a list of communist economic disasters.

Noncommunist socialism has also been a severe disappointment in the Third World (see Réné Dumont, *Socialism and Development* [New York, 1973]). For example, Burma's military socialism has pushed that country decades backward. Tanzania, despite very generous foreign assistance, has floundered in stagnation with its unprofitable state enterprises and inefficient collectivized villages.

Thus the relationship between state interventionism and economic growth is cloudy, as is the related question of the utility or disutility of democracy for economic management. There are many arguments in favor of the democratic order; most convincing, as already noted, is that a democratic state has seemed to be a necessary (but certainly not a sufficient) condition for a highly modernized society.

On the other hand, it may be argued that if democracy were favorable for development in the Third World, it would not be so uncommon. There must be reasons for this fact beyond the shortcomings of Third World political cultures. Perhaps it is more difficult to implement concerted purposes when all decisions are subject to the trammels and haggling of democratic processes. A considerably stronger argument against the democratic system is that the majority in poor countries may well want more benefits than the state can afford or than the ruling classes are prepared to concede and may use political power to the detriment of the economy. This seems almost axiomatic. If the less affluent masses are mobilizable and power comes from their votes, politicians are sure to bid for their support, without necessarily considering the costs of fulfilling their promises. This easily leads to economically questionable subsidies, as for food or transportation, to labor legislation raising production costs, to uneconomic make-work projects, and most of all to deficit financing. The last, with consequent inflation and monetary problems, is a problem almost everywhere. But in a country with many poor and few rich citizens, if the state is responsive to the desires of the majority, strong and farseeing leadership is necessary to avoid economic policies of short-term or superficial benefit and long-term economic harm.

The authoritarian regime suffers corresponding disadvantages. It lacks input, is likely to be poorly informed about the wants and needs of the people, easily becomes isolated from all but a few, and lacks sound legitimacy. Serious, perhaps, is the corruption, the bane of all authoritarian states, that thrives in the absence of free criticism. On the other hand, the state not subject to democratic responsibility should be able to call in experts and decide on clear-cut rational policies—assuming it can pick experts rationally and repress factionalism. Then it can implement laws designed to bring long-term benefits even if in the short term they are injurious to the majority. Military governments have often boasted that they could straighten out the economy by carrying through austerity programs a democracy could not undertake. In a poor and deeply divided country, the treasury may well need protection from spoilation by the masses.

This is more or less theoretical. But theory is gray, and life is a shimmering melange, and reality is much more complex. Latin American countries have experimented with varying degrees of authoritarian or liberal-democratic government, conducting policies oriented toward or away from state intervention in the economy. Their experiences can be highly instructive, although the reader, after perusing the case studies that follow, may well wonder just what can be concluded about the thematic questions of this book.

Robert Wesson

Hoover Institution

1 Chile

Free-Market Authoritarianism

Paul E. Sigmund

Economic policy makers often complain that political considerations prevent their recommendations from being followed. Since the 1973 coup in Chile that overthrew the Marxist-dominated government of Salvador Allende, however, a small group of devotees of the free-market policies of Milton Friedman and Arnold Harberger of the University of Chicago, the so-called Chicago boys, have had almost complete control of the economy. Like Plato's philosopher-king, they could remold their society to conform to their vision of wise policy, and until 1982 they were assured of support by President Augusto Pinochet. Repression, a controlled press, radio, and television, "intervened" universities, a ban on political activity, and the imprisonment, exile, or expulsion of opposition leaders helped to assure that they could reorganize the Chilean economy with little or no criticism or political interference.

Faced in September 1973 with a bankrupt economy reeling from an inflation rate of 700 percent, these free-market devotees were able to carry out a complete transformation of Chilean economic life. After an initial lag, their policies produced in the late 1970s a spectacular expansion of the economy, a reduction of the inflation rate to 9 percent (with a negative rate in the wholesale price index), and a material prosperity unprecedented in Chilean history. Just as spectacular, however, was the bust that followed in 1982. Industry and agriculture were destroyed by foreign competition, high interest rates, and the paralysis of economic activity; a third of the population was either unemployed or earning a pittance in government make-work programs; the gross domestic product contracted by 14 percent; and the nation's debt soared to $17 billion, making Chile, along with Costa Rica and Israel, one of the most heavily indebted countries in the world on a per capita basis.

Why did the Chilean economic miracle turn sour? And what lessons for other developing countries can be drawn from the Chilean experience? In particular, what are the attractions and the dangers of the free-market approach to economic growth demonstrated by the Chilean case—and to what degree are the problems that Chile developed related to the application of that approach by an authoritarian government? And finally, what does Chile tell us about the relationship between economic and political freedom?

The Rise of the Chicago Boys

In the mid-1950s, the School of Economics of the Catholic University of Chile began sending its best students to the University of Chicago for their doctorates. A few of the "Chicago boys," as they were already being called, entered the reformist government of Christian Democratic president Eduardo Frei (1964–1970), but most returned to join the faculty of their alma mater, giving the economics school a community of ideological outlook—a commitment to the efficacy of the free market—and a high level of expertise and familiarity with the latest advances in economics unmatched elsewhere in Chilean intellectual and academic life. When Salvador Allende, at the head of the Marxist-dominated Popular Unity coalition, gained the presidency in 1970 with 36.3 percent of the vote, a group of professors and former students of the Catholic University formed an economic research institute that published a newsletter analyzing and criticizing the errors of economic policy that ultimately led to the galloping inflation of 1973 and to Allende's downfall.

Those errors included a variety of exchange rates, which in 1973 ranged from 30 escudos to the dollar for certain transactions to 3,000 on the black market, price controls that made the official price of a full sack of flour lower than the price of an empty sack, subsidies to the state sector in industry and agriculture amounting to 175 billion escudos in 1973, deficit financing of 53 percent of the national budget, and a moratorium on the payment of most foreign debts. These factors resulted in widespread shortages, panic buying and hoarding, and a runaway inflation of 323 percent at official figures and an estimated real rate of over 700 percent. Long lines formed for essential commodities, the government used its control over distribution to favor its supporters, and in early September Allende himself admitted that Chile only had a few days' supply of wheat. Allende's finance minister, Pedro Vuskovic, frankly stated that economic policy was subordinate to political goals—the rapid seizure of control of the economy through a policy of faits accomplis (*hechos consumados*) and increased political support from the lower classes by keeping prices of essential commodities low and expanding the number of government jobs.

In the confusion that followed the September 1973 coup, many observers predicted that the military junta would opt for a nationalist, corporatist economic policy, not unlike that then being pursued by the military government of Gen. Juan Velasco Alvarado in neighboring Peru. However, this view underestimated both the aversion to statism that three years of Allende's "transition to socialism" had produced among the military and the clarity and persuasiveness with which the Chicago-trained economists presented their case for the free market. The military initially appointed a noneconomist, Fernando Leniz, as minister of economics, but the Chicago economists took over the Central Bank and the Office of Planning (ODEPLAN) immediately. Their influence over economic policy expanded in mid-1974 when Sergio de Castro, former head of the economics school at the Catholic University, became economics minister—and even more two years later when he became minister of finance. The military government removed price controls from most of the 3,000 items regulated by the previous government, freed interest rates from government controls, replaced the complicated exchange rates of the Allende government first by three rates and then by a single one, and returned industrial and agricultural holdings that had been seized or taken over on a dubious legal basis to their original owners. The government announced its intention to lower tariffs, and within a year they had been reduced from an average rate of nearly 100 percent to an average of 67 percent. By 1977, they had dropped to 22 percent. Negotiations began on the payment of compensation to the former U.S. owners of nationalized copper mines, and foreign investment was encouraged by favorable regulations on taxation and the repatriation of profits.

The Shock Treatment

In 1974, the inflation rate dropped to 376 percent, but the government still ran a large deficit. When Chile was hit by the double blow of a sharp drop in the price of copper, its principal export, and the OPEC-imposed 500 percent increase in imported oil prices, more drastic measures were adopted. Milton Friedman, flown in from Chicago, recommended a "shock treatment" similar to that imposed by Ludwig Erhard in Germany in 1948. His former students followed his advice, cutting government employment, reducing the money supply drastically, and selling off government enterprises or mandating nonsubsidized prices for their services. Under the new finance minister, Jorge

Cauas, a currency reform was introduced, and his successor, Sergio de Castro, announced a program for reduction of tariffs over several years to a targeted across-the-board rate of 10 percent. More important, the new Chilean peso was linked to the dollar in a series of programmed mini-devaluations, whose goal was to reduce inflationary expectations by achieving complete exchange rate stability.

The overall philosophy behind these measures was what the government's Statement of Principles (March 1974) called the "principle of subsidiarity"—the doctrine that the state should intervene only in areas in which the private sector could not act—as well as the belief that opening Chile to the outside world would produce efficiency in resource allocation and enable it to become prosperous on the basis of the principle of comparative advantage. But first, the distortions produced by protectionism and state intervention had to be removed by the bitter medicine of an abrupt reduction in the government's role in the economy and a shakeout of inefficient enterprises.

The result was an 11 percent drop in the gross national product, a rise in unemployment to 16 percent, a wave of bankruptcies, and a reduction in real wages of nearly 40 percent. However, the government deficit dropped to 3 percent of the gross domestic product, and the balance of payments showed a surplus for the first time in a decade. Small and medium-size businesses protested—while the increasingly concentrated financial sector, which had access to lower-interest foreign loans, was able to buy government enterprises at very low prices, thus establishing the dominance of *los grupos financieros* over Chilean economic life. Yet despite criticism of the "social cost" of the shock treatment from church groups and from moderate Christian Democratic sectors (the party was officially placed "in recess" by government decree but continued to be influential), Pinochet, who by now had consolidated his personal power within the junta, supported the Chicago policies and refused to interfere with their implementation.

The Chilean Economic Miracle

Just at the time that the lessening of political repression as a result of the replacement of the dreaded National Intelligence Directorate (DINA) by the National Information Center (CNI) in mid-1977 allowed more public expression of dissent, the Chicago program began to show significant results. The inflation rate dropped to 174 percent in 1976, then to 63 percent in 1977, and to 30 percent in 1978. The economy turned around, with growth rates of 9.9 percent in 1977, 8.2 percent in 1978, 8.3 percent in 1979, 7.5 percent in 1980, and 6 percent in 1981 (Source: ODEPLAN, *Cuentas Nacionales*). Critics could point out that these rates were only bringing Chile back to the levels it

Table 1.1

Basic Economic Statistics, 1973–1982

Year	Inflation (percentage)	Unemployment in Greater Santiago (percentage)	GDP (annual percentage change)	Net External Debt (U.S.$ millions)
1973	508.1	4.7	−3.6	$ 4,048
1974	376.0	9.7	5.0	4,774
1975	340.0	16.2	−11.3	5,263
1976	174.0	16.8	4.1	5,195
1977	63.5	13.2	8.6	5,434
1978	30.3	14.0	7.3	6,911
1979	38.9	13.6	8.3	8,463
1980	31.2	11.8	7.8	9,413
1981	9.5	11.0	5.7	12,553
1982	20.7	21.9	−14.1	13,892

SOURCES: CORFO, *Chile Economic Profiles*, and *Memoria Anual del Banco Central de Chile*.

had reached in the early 1970s, but there was no denying the outward signs of prosperity in the Chilean "economic miracle." Fueled by foreign borrowing from banks awash with OPEC dollars (private sector external debt rose from $430 million in 1977 to over $1 billion in 1979 with a further increase to $2.4 billion in 1980 and 1981), Chileans went on a buying spree of foreign goods, including Japanese cars, color televisions, electronic gadgets for the upper and middle classes, modish foreign clothes, and whiskey. Circular shopping centers, called *caracolas* from their resemblance to overgrown snails, high-rise apartments, and modern banks and mutual funds proliferated in Santiago, and Pinochet and the Chicago boys took the credit.

Having solved the economic problem to their satisfaction, the young economists turned their attention to social policy. In rapid succession, a series of "modernizations" were introduced. The government privatized large sectors of the national health service, stripped the semi-official professional associations of their power to set fees and regulate conduct, permitted labor union organization at the plant level but severely restricted wider federations and confederations, and set the ground rules for establishing a system of private universities and professional schools to supplement, and in some cases replace, Chile's public university system. The government began to transfer control over primary education to appointive local advisory councils and mayors and gave them some tax and licensing powers as well. The most significant reform was a total reorganization of Chile's antiquated and complex social security system, replacing most of the public insurance programs with contributory retirement programs run by banks and financial institutions.

The authors of these programs spoke of them with the same ideological zeal that the advocates of Allende's "transition to socialism" had used earlier in the decade. In their view, they were laying the foundations of a new decentralized and privatized libertarian society that would maximize individual choice and freedom and eliminate the evils of statism, bureaucratization, and politicization. Thus to the free-market economics of Milton Friedman was added the libertarian politics of Friedrich Hayek (who was also brought to Chile to preach the new gospel of freedom).

There was only one problem—Chile was not politically free, and President Augusto Pinochet seemed determined to hold on to his absolute power for as long as possible. In 1979–1980, the Constitutional Commission, which had been working at a snail's pace since 1973, finally produced a draft constitution, and the advisory Council of State forwarded to the president a slightly amended version that provided for a five-year transition period with an appointive Congress between 1980 and 1985. Pinochet hastily rewrote the draft to add "transitional" features. One provided for his election as president for an eight-year term in the same September 1980 plebiscite in which the constitution was to be approved. He even added a clause allowing his reelection by plebiscite for another eight-year term in 1989 when the first congressional elections were to be called. Other "transitional" provisions gave him power to detain anyone for periods of up to twenty days, to expel Chileans from the country or sentence them to internal exile without judicial review, and to extend indefinitely the state of emergency in existence since 1973. After a brief debate in which critics were limited to one public meeting and denied access to television, Pinochet won the September 1980 plebiscite by a two to one margin and took office as "constitutional" president for an eight-year term in March 1981.

In his inaugural address, Pinochet took personal credit for Chile's economic policies. As unemployment dropped under 10 percent and inflation at 9.8 percent was lower than it had been for two decades, it seemed that the Chicago prescriptions had worked. Critics like Professor Paul Samuelson of the Massachusetts Institute of Technology called the Chilean programs "market fascism," citing in particular, the limits on political criticism and workers' rights to organize and to strike. But as more and more Chileans—especially the powerful middle class—benefited from the economic prosperity, limitations on political expression and the exclusion of the poor from the country's prosperity (see Table 1.2) did little to lessen enthusiasm for what was now called the "Chicago model."

Table 1.2

Income Distribution, Household Monthly Consumption
(1981 dollars)

Households	1969	1978
20% Poor	$164	$ 113
20% Lower Middle Class	255	203
20% Middle Class	337	297
20% Upper Middle Class	443	456
20% Wealthy	862	1,112

Sources: National Statistical Institute (INE), Household Budget Surveys, as analyzed in René Cortazar, "Chile: Distributive Results 1973–1982," presented at the University of California, Davis, November 1982.

The Collapse of the Model

Enthusiasm quickly dimmed, however, in 1981 and 1982 as a series of economic reverses revealed the fragility of Chile's economic prosperity. Part of the problem was exogenous. Like many other Third World producers of primary products, Chile was caught between the decline of international prices for its exports (especially a 50 percent drop in the price of copper, which despite the diversification of Chile's exports in the 1970s still provided about half of its foreign exchange) and higher import costs since the 1979 OPEC price increase, along with a sharp rise in international interest rates. Chilean foreign indebtedness rapidly escalated while its export income declined, producing a $4 billion gap in the balance of payments in 1981.

External factors alone, however, did not account for the magnitude of the gap. In June 1979, as part of the effort to decrease inflation and to control the money supply, Finance Minister de Castro had tied the Chilean peso to the dollar and announced that there would be no further changes in the official rate of 39 pesos to the dollar. In the next two years, as the dollar appreciated against European currencies, Chilean inflation for the first year and a half exceeded the U.S. rate by about 18 percent. As a result, the pegged Chilean peso became substantially overvalued, foreign goods became very cheap, and Chilean exports correspondingly expensive, producing a spectacular decline in domestic sales and employment and an economic contraction. Imports of consumer goods other than food rose from $600 million in 1978 to $2 billion in 1981, and Chilean industry and agriculture were unable to compete with foreign imports, which were subject only to a very low uniform tariff of 10 percent.

In the havoc wreaked by the fixed exchange rate and the lack of tariff protection, the shakiness of the largely unregulated private financial structure (the government eliminated controls on foreign borrowing in 1979) soon became apparent. In violation of its principles of nonintervention in the private sector, the government took over the Viña del Mar Sugar Refining Company in May 1981 to prevent its bankruptcy, and in November it rescued eight banks and financial institutions from the same fate. Many, including members of the government itself, called for a devaluation of the peso, but de Castro, with Pinochet's support, argued that the current imbalances would be rectified by a process of "automatic adjustment"—reduced availability of foreign exchange and cutbacks in wages to make Chile competitive again. In fact, imports declined because Chile was slipping rapidly into a deep depression and bankruptcies were escalating (over 400 in the first half of 1982). Pinochet finally removed de Castro as finance minister in April 1982 and, after insisting to the last minute that no devaluation would take place, allowed his economics minister, Gen. Luis Danus, to announce the first of several devaluations in June.

In subsequent months, the government adopted a dizzying succession of economic policies to revive Chile's ailing economy—each one introduced by a new finance minister. Within six months, Chile tried a maxi-devaluation, programmed mini-devaluations, a floating exchange rate, a "dirty float" (with government intervention), and a preferential exchange rate. None of them worked. By January 1983, the gross national product had dropped by 14 percent, unemployment had reached 21 percent with another 10 percent of the work force in various government work programs, Chile's foreign reserves had dropped from $4 billion to $1.5 billion, and a rescue team from the International Monetary Fund had arrived to arrange for help on the condition that Chile adopt an austerity program of additional sharp reductions in what was already a stripped-down budget. Pinochet, criticized by his former right-wing supporters because of his identification with policies that had brought economic disaster, further alienated them by taking over, dissolving, or "intervening" most of Chile's major private banks—a move that his critics ironically described as the "Chicago way to socialism" since, as they pointed out, even Allende had not been able to seize the major banks that the government now controlled. The government negotiated foreign loans (at interest rates 2.5 percent over the U.S. prime rate), doubled tariffs to 20 percent, and assumed some of the defaulted debts of banks and private industry—despite its earlier insistence that private loans would never receive government guarantees.

The Chicago boys fought back in the media, defending their policies and blaming external factors. They even argued that the automatic adjustment policy would have worked if it had been allowed to operate a little longer, but one of their critics, Sebastián Pinera (an economist trained at Harvard, not Chicago), argued that the economy would have had to contract by 45 percent and unemployment rise to 40 percent for the policy to work as the Chicago economists hoped.

There were political effects too. Pinochet had so staked his prestige on the Chicago policies that their failure undermined one of the principal bases for his civilian support. Criticisms of government economic policy were linked to demands for a genuine political opening. In March 1983, leading right-wing politicians joined the Christian Democrats and most of the Socialist leadership to form a *multipartidaria* similar to the one in Argentina and called for a return to democracy and a change in economic policy. By mid-1983, copper workers and truckers had joined opposition politicians in sponsoring a monthly day of protest that was supposed to escalate until the tenth anniversary of the coup on September 11. Pinochet responded with a combination of carrot-and-stick tactics, buying off the truckers with promises to assume many of their debts and imprisoning the leader of the copper workers and (for four days) the president of the Christian Democrats, former foreign minister Gabriel Valdés. Only the continuing loyalty of the army (or its fear of reprisals in any democratic opening) and Pinochet's skill in using his powers of promotion and retirement to remove or undercut potential rivals kept him in power. He continued to appeal to the constitution as the basis of his legitimacy and to reassert his determination to follow the constitutional timetable by remaining in power until 1989, but few believed that he could survive that long.

The Lessons of Chile

It is easy to criticize the Chilean model after the fact, but any evaluation should begin with an acknowledgment of the positive accomplishments of the Chicago economists. They reformed the collection of taxes, streamlined the bureaucracy, rationalized the price system, abandoned expensive and inefficient subsidies, and targeted social expenditures to areas such as early medical and nutritional care rather than to the previous pattern of across-the-board subsidies. There is no doubt that the Chilean economy had been hyperpoliticized, inefficient, excessively centralized, and protected by absurdly high tariff walls. The new economic policies led to a great increase in nontraditional exports such as fruits, wines, cellulose, and fish meal, reducing Chile's dependence on copper as the single source of foreign exchange (as high as 80 percent in the late 1960s). Foreign oil exploration on a service-contract basis lessened Chile's dependence on imported oil from 80 percent to 50 percent. Inflation was brought down—although at considerable costs to the rest of the economy—and the decentralization and regionalization of government decisionmaking (only partially implemented) were long overdue.

The problem, however, was that these long-needed reforms were imposed with minimal public discussion by a group of ideologues who refused to listen to any criticisms of their policies—in one case attacking a critic of the policies as having no more than a "plumber's" knowledge of the "science of economics." De Castro's obsession with reducing inflation and his belief in automatic adjustment led him to maintain the fixed exchange rate for at least a year too long, thus undermining confidence in the economy, decreasing foreign reserves, and bankrupting industry and agriculture. More fundamentally, the gap left by the virtual elimination of government investment in the economy was not filled by private investors, who devoted their energies to speculation on interest rate spreads and other types of financial manipulation. Foreign investors did not flock to Chile as hoped, because the market was too small, although there was considerable interest in the mining and minerals sector. (The turndown in the world economy at the end of the 1970s delayed a number of multibillion-dollar investments in the copper sector, but this was not the fault of Chilean policymakers.) The drop in savings and investment, in the former case from 15 percent of GNP in the 1960s to 11.5 percent in the 1974–1982 period and in the latter case from 20 to 15 percent, will have a lasting effect on the productivity of the Chilean economy. "External savings," that is, foreign borrowing, were used not to fill the gap but to finance speculation and consumption and left Chile with a crushing debt-service bill—amounting, in the absence of renegotiation, to 80 percent of its foreign exchange earnings. (Debt renegotiation in 1983 lightened its immediate impact, but also stretched out for many years the debt-payment overhang on the balance of payments and limited the foreign exchange available for capital and intermediate imports.)

Far from reducing the state's role in the economy, the Chicago policy had concentrated 85 percent of bank credit in the hands of the government, and military opposition had prevented the privatization of the nationalized copper mines and several other state enterprises. The effort to apply free-market prescriptions in an uncompromising fashion caused a reaction against the whole policy that could lead to a reversion to the old statist protectionism of the pre-1973 period. In 1983, debt bailouts escalated, and the necessity of negotiating international agreements with the International Monetary Fund, the consortia of private banks, and the Bank of International Settlements vastly expanded the role of the state.

Possible Alternatives

Would an alternative policy have worked more effectively? The Christian Democratic opposition suggested an economic program in late 1982, basing it on research carried out for many years at CIEPLAN, an independent economic policy institute directed by Alejandro Foxley. While acknowledging the effectiveness of the market in the efficient allocation of resources, the program argued for an increase in protectionism to an average level of 30–35 percent, for public expenditure to create jobs even at the risk of heightened inflation, and for a tax on consumption with special tax benefits to promote savings and investment. It also called for a "social pact" involving capital, labor, and government in an agreed-upon recovery program, to be arrived at by negotiation. Fundamental to the program was a political opening that would involve public discussion of the distribution of the necessary sacrifices and the appropriate redistributive measures, from the point of view of both social justice and economic reactivation. The basic model was a democratic mixed economy with an important role for the market, but also involving state encouragement of investment, economic growth, and social expenditures.

This brings us to one of the questions with which this essay began—the relationship between economic policy and democracy. The defenders of Pinochet argued for years that economic and social modernization was a necessary prerequisite for a stable democracy. Otherwise, in an underdeveloped economy Marxist demagogues like Salvador Allende would delude the populace into supporting the Left and destroying the economic preconditions of a free society. Now, however, that they have been unsuccessful in creating these preconditions, they argue for the continuation of Pinochet in power in order to impose the hard decisions necessary during a period of economic adversity, an argument that would seem to justify indefinite postponement of the return to democratic government.

Yet, other Latin American countries that have been compelled to make similar adjustments, such as the democracies of Peru, Ecuador, and Colombia, enjoy the self-correcting mechanisms of representative democracy and a free press that were so notoriously absent in Chile under the Chicago boys. They have avoided policy rigidity but produced policies that have worked as well as, or better than, those of more authoritarian regimes.

Democratic governments have not been able to make the same brutal policy shifts or to repress wages to the same degree, but they have cut back on government spending, reduced protectionism, and opened the economy to the outside world without being overthrown or destroyed by popular opposition. In addition, like other successful advocates of the free market such as Brazil and South Korea, they have also retained a role for the state in encouraging national development by tax, tariff, and investment policies.

This has been accomplished without the kind of short-term populism that Pinochet's economic advisers insisted would be inevitable under a democratic system. With responsible leadership and technical competence, democratic governments are capable of taking the restrictive measures required for economic stabilization. Just because a government is responsive to the popular will does not mean that it must destroy the economy.

In the Chilean case it was Marxist ideology—not democratic competition—that led Allende's policymakers to fuel inflation by printing money to subsidize the burgeoning state sector in industry and agriculture. And it was the lack of democratic checks and free expression that permitted the Friedmanite ideologues to do even more damage to the Chilean economy under Pinochet.

The defenders of the Chicago school maintain that the fixed exchange rate was a departure from its teachings, but Friedman's Chilean pupils argue that it is one of several possible ways to control the money supply, a central tenet of the Friedman approach. In any case, the doctrine of automatic adjustment is an article of faith of the Chicago school. The Chilean example seems to demonstrate that a small economy cannot be opened in a doctrinaire and abrupt manner to the vagaries of the world market without negative effects on productive infrastructure and employment that may be short-term in theory, but are long-term in fact.

The "magic of the market" and the principle of comparative advantage should not blind policymakers, as they seem to have done in Chile, to the importance of achieving a balance between inflation and unemployment, between efficiency and national economic development, and between the promotion of private enterprise and overall government responsibility for the country's position in the international economy. Chile's openness to worldwide fluctuations and the fixed exchange rate accentuated and exaggerated its vulnerability to changes in the world economy, with devastating consequences.

It is not necessary to abandon the market and return to the statism of the 1960s and early 1970s in order to pursue a development policy based on a reasonable conception of the national economic interest and the use of state power to further it. A mixed economy and a democratic political system are possible in the developing world, as Chile may demonstrate when it returns to the democratic traditions that have characterized it for most of its history.

Bibliography

Surprisingly little has been written in English about economic policy under the Pinochet government. Arturo Valenzuela, ed., *Chile Under Military Rule* (the proceedings of a conference held at the Woodrow Wilson International Center for Scholars in Washington, D.C., in May 1980), includes useful articles for and against the Chicago policy written, respectively, by Rolf Luders (Chilean minister of finance and economy from August 1982 until February 1983) and Ricardo Ffrench-Davis. See also my "Rise and Fall of the Chicago Boys in Chile," *SAIS Review*, Summer 1983. In 1980, the World Bank published a useful, but now dated, study entitled *Chile, An Economy in Transition*, based on an independent evaluation by a team from the bank that developed its own statistics. The New York office of CORFO, the Chilean Development Corporation, publishes an English-language monthly, *Chile Economic Report*. Alejandro Foxley, *Latin American Experiments in Neoconservative Economics* (Berkeley and Los Angeles: University of California Press, 1983), is the English translation of *Experimentos neoliberales en América Latina* (available in *Colleción Estudios CIEPLAN*, no. 7 [March 1982]). Other useful sources (in Spanish) are *El Mercurio* (International Edition) and *Qué Pasa* (both pro-government, but now critical), *Hoy* (Christian Democratic), *Mensaje* (published by the Jesuits, very antigovernment), *Estudios CIEPLAN* (pro–Christian Democratic think tank, run by Alejandro Foxley), *Vector* (democratic socialist), and *Chile-America* (left-wing Christian, published in Rome). The best source for the current debate on economic policy is "Cuatro enfoques: Qué pasó con la economía Chilena?" *Estudios Públicos* (Santiago), no. 11 (Winter 1983): 5–135, with essays by Ricardo Ffrench-Davis, Juan Andrés Fontaine, Alvaro Garcia, and Thomas Wisecarver. Also very useful is Ernesto Tironi, "El model neoliberal Chileno y su implantación," *Documentos de Trabajo* (Santiago: Centro de Estudios de Desarrollo), no. 1 (December 1982). For two contrasting views on the effects of the Chicago program, see Fernando Dahse, *La mapa de la extrema riqueza* (Santiago: Aconcagua, 1979); and Joaquín A. Lavin, *El enriquecimiento de las personas en Chile* (Concepción: Ciencia y Technologia, 1980).

2   Argentina

The Frustration
of Ungovernability

Gary W. Wynia

Managing the Argentine economy is an unenviable task. Only 11 of the 36 ministers of economy from 1948 to 1983 have held the position for more than a year. The presidents they served did little better, averaging only 2.4 years in office. Of the fifteen presidents, only four were elected, and all four of these were overthrown by the military. These factors are hardly propitious for economic development.

The failure of Argentines to take full advantage of their abundant human and natural resources is well known, as is their persistent political turmoil. Their economic failures and political troubles are undeniably related, but their exact relation is less clear. It is tempting to portray the nation's economy as the innocent victim of its politics, as economists often do, but little enlightenment comes from such oversimplifications. The relationship between politics and economics is obviously reciprocal, making their distinction from one another and analysis of their causal connection more complicated than conventional wisdom would have it. Consequently, to comprehend Argentina's dismal economic fate and its causes, we must examine Argentines at work and search for the ways in which politics and other elements have affected public and private contributions to economic development.

Argentina in Perspective

Argentines take a perverse pleasure in their pessimism, always reminding each other how bad things are and how much worse they are bound to get. But their malaise needs to be put into perspective. True, every time the country seems headed for sustained economic growth, something happens, leaving Argentines to wonder if forces beyond their control have condemned them to languish in disappointment and frustration. But it is also true that most Argentines are far from desperate economically. Despite the nation's recent travails, it is still a country of 29 million talented people who have proved themselves adept at maintaining relative comfort amid persistent turmoil and uncertainty. Few Argentines know the kind of poverty common to most Brazilians, Peruvians, and Guatemalans.[1]

What Argentines suffer from today is less economic deprivation—though many of them are worse off than they were in the 1970s—than an inability to function as a cohesive community. Argentines are skilled at attending to individual and family interests, but have difficulty joining together to advance the common good. Rivalries among social classes, economic sectors, and political parties are intense, and pervasive distrust makes stalemate a way of life. One need only compare Argentines' attitudes toward each other and toward political authority with those of Brazilians or Mexicans to appreciate the greater depth of divisions within Argentine society. These divisions also serve as a reminder that greater national wealth and a larger middle class do not, by themselves, assure more social cohesion.

Two things have come to characterize public life in Argentina during the past half-century: the practice of veto politics, which makes governing so difficult, and the growth of the Argentine state and the importance of exclusive control over it to political survival.

Unlike the Institutional Revolutionary Party in Mexico, no single group or political party has monopolized public office in Argentina. Nor do two parties regularly exchange office as they do in Venezuela, Colombia, and Costa Rica. Not even the military, with all its power, has remained in control as long as in Brazil and Chile. Quite the contrary, in Argentina, nearly every partisan force has secured office, but none has been able to hold on to it very long. As one Argentine put it, "We have created a system that permits all sectors to alternate in power despite continuous interruptions of the formal political process. It is as if there is a tacit agreement that no government should be allowed to endure. In this way each sector can take its turn in power without ever having to share it."[2]

During World War II, the Argentine military evicted the upper-class conservatives who had governed the nation for most of its independent history, but before the armed forces could set their own course, an audacious labor movement led by Col. Juan Perón used the ballot box to fasten its grip on office and upset the old political order. A decade later, in 1955, the military sent Perón into exile, allowing the middle-class Radical Party, absent from the presidency since 1930, to return, first under Arturo Frondizi in 1958 and then Arturo Illía in 1963. The military took over in 1966, let the Peronists try again in 1973, and then stepped in once more in 1976.

How power came to be dispersed so widely and conflict to become so intense is the story of Argentina's modern tragedy, a tale of authority debilitated and never restored, even by the crudest and most autocratic methods. Culprits are easy to find, and every Argentine has a list, though predictably few of them match.

Traditionally, political authority was tightly held by the rural oligarchy that supervised the development of Argentina's export economy after 1860. When a native and immigrant middle class formed at the end of the nineteenth century, it was allowed to share in the spoils of government, but not to displace the nation's traditional rulers entirely. The emerging working class was treated less kindly, however, and its European-inspired anarchist and socialist organizers were harshly repressed, as they were in the rest of Latin America. Not until 1945 did the Argentine working class make its way into the political mainstream—but through the initiative of populist military politicians like Perón and not its own proletarian leadership. Perón's populism redefined the rules of Argentine politics. No longer would the few completely dominate the many. Instead, each would contend with the other in a pitched battle, on one side an oligarchy determined to seek revenge against a disrespectful working class and on the other, populist politicians who knew that their support within the working class made their permanent exclusion from politics impossible.

The posturing that began in the 1940s, dividing one set of rulers from another, prevails to this day. Most upper-class and some middle-class Argentines still consider Peronist rule unacceptable. The Peronists, on the other hand, believe that they represent the majority of the Argentine people and therefore are the nation's only legitimate rulers. Their exclusion is possible, they claim, only by the forcible denial of their rights to compete openly with all pretenders to political authority. Non-Peronist governments are, according to this way of thinking, un-Argentine and illegitimate. It reminds one of nineteenth-century Europe, where the battle was between those who thought political authority was derived from property and those who believed it came from head counts.[3]

Middle-class parties like the Radicals are caught in between. Distrusted by conservatives for their bourgeois nationalism and devotion to constitutional government even at the cost of permitting Peronist rule, the Radicals count around 30 percent of the electorate as their following, most of them urban but few of them from the working-class rank and file. Their rivalry with the Peronists and disdain for the latter's bullying ways have made alliances between the two parties against either the military or the oligarchy hard to achieve. Frondizi created a secret pact with the outlawed Peronists in order to secure his election to the presidency in 1958, but the alliance lasted only a few months. Illía, a firm believer in partisanship, never reached out to the Peronists, hoping instead to beat them at the polls in the 1965 congressional elections, only to be defeated by them.[4]

When Argentines went to the polls in 1983 for the first time in a decade, these rivalries still raged. The working class remained loyal to the Peronists, the Radicals had the support of most of the middle class, and the upper class could count only on small regional parties condemned to minority status. Unlike in Brazil, where in 1982 the military and local elites in the more traditional or backward states could form a political party that secured the votes of nearly half the electorate, the Argentines had nothing new to which to turn. Despite nearly two decades of efforts to change Argentines' political preferences, old loyalties remained.

Civilians do not struggle alone, of course. The Argentine armed forces have never hidden their partisanship. Making political judgments and acting on them is a way of life for them. They brought the conservatives back in 1930 and evicted them in 1943; they sent Perón away in 1955, Frondizi in 1962, Illía in 1966, and the Peronists again in 1976. Their interests do not always coincide with those of a single social class or economic sector. Nationalists and internationalists, labor and capital, have gained from military intervention at one time or another. As one student of Argentine history has noted,

> All political parties seek the help of the military in pursuit of their particular aims. Seldom is the military rejected because it is considered a threat to the political process or because it is viewed only as an instrument of the dominant classes. Rather the armed forces are seen as colleagues in a complex and at times byzantine game.[5]

In sum, officers and civilians have for decades joined together in a political process characterized by intense partisanship and deep distrust. Governments that operate under these conditions are more vulnerable than most to the attacks of opponents, making it almost impossible for any to complete its mission. Of course, authorities are not without some power of their own, especially in matters of day-to-day policy. As elsewhere, each government deals with merchants, industrialists, bankers, farmers, labor leaders, and multinational corporations as it makes and executes policies aimed at achieving its economic objectives. But its task is seldom routine since the aggrieved always have the option of trying to win the military to their side in an effort to intimidate or depose incumbents who threaten their interests.

If veto politics is the dominant feature of Argentine public life, the power of the Argentine state is not far behind in influence over the management of economic development and the conduct of political life.

Political patronage and state enterprise, the primary sources of the growth of Argentina's public sector, were not exclusively Peronist inventions. The Peronists simply carried to an extreme a process already under way. The Argentine state was never passive. The repression of rebellious regional elites in the mid-nineteenth century and later the opening of new territories through the armed expulsion of nomadic Indians fostered a strong military and bureaucracy. Economic matters were left primarily to the private sector, however; what Argentines could not provide for their own development, the British supplied for them, including their ports, railways, electric power, subways, and substantial capital. Demands for government intervention were frequent, however: tenant farmers called for restrictions on exploitative landlords, cattlemen for the regulation of foreign meat packers and shippers, and labor unions for guarantees of basic rights. Initially their pleas were ignored by an officialdom disdainful of anything that threatened the status quo. Only after the Radical Party dislodged the country's Conservative rulers in 1916 did the regulatory state begin to appear.

A party built on hundreds of neighborhood constituency organizations, the Radicals had debts to pay once in office. Theirs was a "clientelistic" regime, one that opened its doors to those unable to find a place within the agricultural or commercial bourgeoisie. They expanded public education, increased economic regulation, and gave the state control over the exploration and extraction of petroleum. Though not radical innovators by contemporary standards, they did accelerate the growth of the Argentine state.[6]

This tradition of patronage, public enterprise, and economic regulation from the Radicals was undiminished by the Conservatives, who returned in 1930 to revive an economy battered by world depression only to be forced by the Depression to increase state supervision of the banking system and the grain and meat trade and to create a government-subsidized packing and marketing corporation to compete with private firms. Moreover, the military added some of its own projects between its 1943 coup and Perón's election two and a half years later, sponsoring the creation of iron, steel, and munitions industries.[7] This was the beginning of a military involvement with public enterprise that grew rapidly thereafter, vesting the armed forces with a deep and enduring interest in state capitalism.[8]

Perón inherited the Radical tradition and gladly expanded on his predecessors' work. Public employment increased substantially, state enterprises multiplied with the nationalization of the railways and the utilities, social services grew, and regulation of the grain trade expanded, allowing the government to buy from farmers at fixed prices, sell at negotiated ones, and keep the difference to use on infrastructure projects, to subsidize domestic industry, and to line the pockets of Perón's closest colleagues. In the process, thousands of persons, many of them recent migrants to Buenos Aires from the interior, secured employment in government. But Perón went no further, preferring state-directed capitalism to any kind of socialism. The result was akin more to the American New Deal (carried to an extreme) than to Soviet socialism. Leaving most property in private hands, Perón took what he thought was the easy route to income redistribution. He seized profits rather than property. But he also left Argentines with an expectation that it was the state's responsibility to resolve their private conflicts by increasing public spending and investment, accepting huge deficits if necessary or leaving to another day the problem of finding more revenue. Moreover, he made Argentines more dependent on the state, not just for employment and the arbitration of disputes but also for the subsidization of industry by means of high tariffs and the purchase of goods and services from the nation's entrepreneurs.[9]

There is substantial disagreement today about how great a burden the Argentine state has become and what needs to be done about it, but few deny its high cost and gross inefficiencies. By the 1970s, most public utilities, nearly all natural resources, and 10 percent of manufacturing were state-owned. Included in the last category are firms that manufacture iron and steel, ships, petrochemicals, transportation equipment, explosives, and a variety of weapons, including light combat aircraft and personnel carriers. In 1972, the state owned 9 of the 50 largest firms (measured by sales), accounted for 40 percent of investment or 9 percent of the GNP, consumed 50 percent of imports, and owed 50 percent of the nation's foreign debt.[10]

Public enterprise is not necessarily harmful to economic development. Most Third World countries with development ambitions have no choice but to devote substantial public resources to their own advancement, borrowing on their future in the hope that their investments will pay rich dividends. Many of Argentina's several hundred state enterprises pay their own way. But some, like the debt-ridden national railways, cause an immense drain on the budget.[11] Moreover, public consumption has continued to rise in recent years. According to a World Bank study, it amounted to 24 percent of GDP in 1980, compared with 9 percent in 1960. This contrasts with Brazil (10 percent) and Mexico (12 percent), both noted for the rapid growth of their public sectors during the same period. And despite major efforts to reduce the rate of growth in the late 1970s, little has changed.[12]

Whether the Argentine public sector is regarded as an albatross depends, of course, on one's economic philosophy. Neoclassical economists argue that private initiative is stifled and economic growth retarded when so much economic power is concentrated in the hands of the state. Nothing less than a drastic reduction in the state sector through the sale of public enterprises to private investors and a massive dismissal of public employees will save the nation's economy, they insist. Most Argentines are less certain. Few blame the country's economic malaise entirely on the size of the public sector, and nearly all have something to lose by cutbacks in it.

Control over the Argentine state is coveted not only because of the wealth it puts at the disposal of a president, but also because of the fear of the misuse of the president's power. Such fears are not misplaced. Argentine presidents, especially those in uniform, have tried repeatedly to weaken their opponents. Working-class Peronists remember military presidents as their oppressors; the Radicals remember the Peronists' abuse of their authority. The result is an opposition that often seeks the removal of incumbents before being crushed by them and incumbents who are determined to deal harshly with anyone who threatens them. Each side reinforces the anxieties of the other, and the vicious circle of fear and repression continues.

Economics and Politics

Cyclical economic and political behavior in Argentina has been accompanied by a dispute over economic development policy. Everyone agrees that the nation has the natural resources to build a productive modern economy, but how to achieve that end is a matter of contention. Since World War II, Argentine economic strategists have been divided into two camps. One is noted for its nationalism and populism, a combination of values that yields policies aimed at protecting and, when necessary, subsidizing national industry while guaranteeing adequate social services for the urban working class. It was introduced into the country by Perón in 1945, and the Radicals incorporated many of the same objectives into their own platforms after 1955. As one might expect, the strategy received support from the labor movement, much of domestic industry, and public employees and was opposed by the landed elites and exporters who had directed public policy in pursuit of their own narrow interests before the war.

The "internationalist" strategy, a contemporary version of the prewar export strategy, calls for Argentina to live by the rules of the marketplace both internally and externally. Arguing that Argentina will prosper by using its comparative advantages in the world market and forcing its subsidized industries to modernize under the pressure of foreign competition, the internationalists' policy proposals include drastic reductions of tariffs, the sale of most state enterprises to the private sector, the elimination of price controls and interest rate subsidies, and the containment of social expenditures. Specific recommendations vary with current conditions, but the principle is always the same—reliance on private investors, both national and foreign, who are capable of surviving tough competition. Banks, large domestic industries, multinational firms, and the agricultural sector are among its strongest supporters, though how each fares under this strategy depends on the specifics of policy, none of which satisfies all of these sectors equally. The opposition to internationalism is led, not surprisingly, by labor and party leaders who resent its short-term regressive distribution of wealth and the denationalization of business.

Part of Argentina's economic instability derives from the fact that neither strategy ever dominates policy for long. Instead, control over policy has, like everything else, frequently shifted from one side to the other. As a result, in 1970 each blamed its opponents for its past failures and claimed that if given another chance, its policy could prove its value as the optimal road to the nation's development.

To make matters worse, Argentines entered the decade in political disarray. They did not have to be told that their behavior was self-destructive and that extraordinary measures were necessary to escape insecure governments incapable of completing their agenda. Nor was it hard to understand the poor prospects of any economic program. There was little reason for optimism in 1970. The only encouraging sign was an apparent recognition by politicians and military officers that the time had arrived to try something new. Party leaders spoke of new commitments to play by the rules if given the chance to govern again. Even the Peronists indicated their intention to involve all of the nation's economic sectors in the design and implementation of solutions to the country's economic malaise. Most Argentines doubted their sincerity, but once the ruling junta decided to hold elections in 1973, it had little choice but to let the still popular Peronists participate. The officers vainly hoped that non-Peronist parties would form a coalition large enough to win, but the Peronists won easily, electing stand-in Héctor Cámpora president in March 1973 so that he could authorize Perón's return and election six months later.[13]

The Peronists tried to begin anew but failed dismally. A government that was to usher in a new era of cooperation brought political chaos and economic disarray. The military resumed control in 1976, determined more than ever to set things right. Yet, even though they lasted longer than previous military regimes, they, too, met defeat.

The two governments, though quite different in ideology and method, shared a determination to deal with the country's economic woes by reforming its politics. Each tried to change the old rules, the Peronists using corporatist methods and the military autocratic ones. Their failure raises questions about the possibilities of political change. Was each government naive in assuming it could succeed, or were its particular efforts just badly conceived or misapplied? Were its economic policies undermined by politics or was it the victim of its own errors? And, finally, if democracy, corporatism, and authoritarianism cannot tame Argentina, what can? The way to begin to address such questions is to examine what the Peronists did between 1973 and 1976, and what the military junta did for seven years thereafter.

The *Pacto*: Politics Submerged

The Peronists had waited eighteen years for their chance to govern Argentina again. It had not been a patient wait, but one filled with protest and repression. When allowed to compete at the polls in 1962 and 1965 in congressional elections, the Peronists did quite well, securing pluralities both times, but the military tossed them out before they could take advantage of their triumphs. Their prospects would not have been much better in the 1970s had the military succeeded after its coup in 1966. General Juan Carlos Onganía and his colleagues had promised that they would be stern, never resting until the electorate had changed its ways. They interdicted political parties and labor unions and suspended political activity in order to allow a cadre of technocrats to proceed with the industrialization of the nation's troubled economy, unhindered by working-class aggression or the lobbying of farmers and merchants. The rebirth of the political process was to occur after the economy improved, but that never happened. Popular protests, centered in the interior city of Cordoba in May 1969, along with Onganía's unresponsiveness to the advice of his fellow officers, provoked them to remove him in 1970. With Onganía's departure came a reassessment of the military's political mission and a decision to let civilians have another try in 1973.[14]

The Argentina armed forces cope poorly with their political debacles. The Onganía experience was typical. Having battled with their fellow Argentines only to come up short, they retreated hastily after 1970. Imperious one day, they capitulated the next, demonstrating how precarious their authority was. Yet, though disconsolate about their performance, they did not accept their defeat as permanent. They stepped aside long enough to reorganize their internal command structures and wait until the next generation of service commanders could have a try at the nation's political reconstruction. While they waited, civilians were allowed to play their old games.

In 1973, many hoped that Perón would take advantage of his popularity among the working class to control it until something was done to straighten out the economy. Argentines wanted desperately to believe that he was returning with a new attitude, disposed to the reconciliation of all social classes and economic interests rather than the kind of partisan belligerency that had characterized his previous presidency. He gladly accommodated them at first, promising from Spain that he would have something for everyone when he returned.

What Peronism stood for at the time was as unclear as ever. One could find almost anything in its words and practices—democracy, authoritarianism, corporatism, or pluralism. No single label did it justice, for Peronism was not the offspring of some imported ideology with well-articulated values and well-developed logic but a hastily contrived product of political opportunism directed at the seizure of power in the name of the Argentine working class. It is an energetic and tenacious movement, a political community whose unity derives from the hope of triumph over hostile forces.

Ironically, it was one of Perón's less democratic habits that gave him the best chance for building a viable government on his return. Increased cooperation among diverse interests was needed, and corporatism had been one of Peronism's favorite ways of getting it. Perón had always preferred collusion to parliamentary politics. Because he had large parliamentary majorities when he governed the first time, it had been easy to concentrate power within the presidency, demanding that all who sought official favor deal directly with Perón and his staff. Inspired by the example of prewar European corporatism, Perón also tried to institutionalize collusion between the government and the private sector, using special advisory councils on which representatives of authorized business and labor organizations could participate in the formulation of economic policy. Real consultation seldom occurred, however, since Perón preferred to be unencumbered by even the weakest of constraints on his decisionmaking.[15] Nevertheless, a preference for institutionalized collaboration among economic sectors remained strong within the Peronist leadership and was easily resurrected in 1973 when the Argentines were ready to admit that unrestricted competitive politics had failed in their deeply divided society. Fortune had, it seems, turned a Peronist vice into a lifesaving virtue.

What the Peronists offered the country in 1973 was neither revolutionary nor very new to anyone familiar with politics in the more industrialized capitalist nations. Deliberate efforts to join workers and managers in the making of economic policy in order to avert disruptive responses to it are common in Europe.[16] Government councils that include representatives of business and labor often manage industrial, agricultural, and incomes policies. But making this kind of corporatism work in a nation like Argentina where private interests distrust each other so intensely required much more than in France or Scandinavia.

The Peronists knew that nothing could be accomplished economically until inflation was controlled. Progressive income redistribution remained their ultimate objective, but inflation came first. It was essential to convince organized labor that higher income and increased social services had to be postponed. Similarly, entrepreneurs had to commit themselves to meeting government objectives in exchange for a guarantee of labor cooperation. The method for doing both, the Peronists decided, was an agreement, the *Pacto*, among all economic sectors and interest groups to a program that explicitly delineated sectoral responsibilities.[17]

The social contract's appeal derived from the government's confidence that it could secure the cooperation of organized labor with anti-inflation measures—something no Argentine government had done since Perón managed it in 1952—and a belief that entrepreneurs had little choice but to cooperate with a program that promised to hold down wages. The contract was designed by advisers to the new government from the General Economic Confederation (CGE), a business interest group that included a majority of the nation's firms but not many of the largest domestic and foreign ones. The CGE had campaigned for over a decade for entrepreneurial and labor involvement in policymaking. Having failed to gain admittance under Radical Party governments in the 1960s, it had finally succeeded with the Peronists.[18] Moreover, José Gelbard, longtime president of the CGE, was made economics minister in the new government and given responsibility for making the social contract work.

The Peronist experiment, it turned out, was a colossal failure. Instead of harnessing the nation's political forces, the Peronists were consumed by them, especially those within their own movement. They were also victims of major errors in economic policy.

To begin with the latter, the Argentine economy enjoyed a good year in 1972. Export prices were up, improving the commercial balance, though at the price of increased inflationary pressures. But anticipation of a Peronist government for the first time in eighteen years touched off frantic speculation, accelerating the rise in prices. Gelbard met inflation with a wage and price freeze agreed upon by the signers of the social contract. Speculation quickly halted, as evidenced by a 25 percent drop in the black-market price of dollars. But the success was short-lived. By the end of the year, tensions created by the price freeze and the effects of the world petroleum crisis, including a rise in the

Table 2.1
Annual Growth Rates, 1973–1976
(percentage)

Year	Gross Domestic Product	Value Added by Manufacturing	Consumer Goods Price Increase
1973	6.1	6.4	63
1974	6.5	6.1	23
1975	−1.3	−2.8	183
1976	−0.2	−2.0	443

SOURCES: Inter-American Development Bank, *Economic and Social Progress in Latin America,* 1976, p. 8; 1977, p. 7; 1980–81, pp. 7, 12, 25.

cost of Argentine imports, provoked a new acceleration in prices and some shortages. But the government refrained from restricting monetary expansion and tightening fiscal policy at the moment such measures were needed. In 1974, it paid for its indecision when the incongruity between its price policy and its monetary and fiscal policies caused a ballooning of prices. In 1975, when the government belatedly dealt with the situation, it efforts were ineffective.[19]

But if its economic inconsistencies and mismanagement weakened its effort, it was the government's politics that brought its downfall. Had its economic policies been wiser and its politics the same, it still would have been forced out. As economist Guido DiTella has observed, "Political and economic forces are always related, but never to such a degree as they were during this period."[20]

The Peronists' primary problem was not the social contract, but their inability to satisfy the diverse membership of the broad coalition they had formed to restore them to power. Populist coalitions are large and amorphous, but their very diffuseness sooner or later causes problems. So it was with the Peronists, especially after Perón's death in mid-1974 deprived the movement of the one person who had the authority needed to hold off rebellions by warring factions. (See Tables 2.1–2.3.)

Rebellions began when Perón evicted Peronist Youth organizations from his regime during a May Day rally in 1974. Many leftists had joined the youth movement in the early 1970s in an effort to use Perón to achieve their radical agendas, and Perón welcomed their support while in exile. However, once he was in office, opposition to the Left among old-line Peronists and labor leaders caused Perón to denounce and evict them. But in isolating them from the coalition, he encouraged their joining the small but growing terrorist movements that later planted bombs under Peronist and non-Peronist alike.[21]

More devastating divisions arose when Perón's wife and successor, Isabel, was forced to choose between the Peronist right and the labor movement after members of the former insisted that she become more forceful with labor. Leading the plot was the contentious José López Rega, longtime personal secretary to Juan Perón and minister of social welfare in his government. Nothing was more central to sustaining the social contract than the loyalty of the labor movement to the Peronist government. Conversely, nothing would end it faster than labor's abandonment of its own government, but that is precisely what López Rega provoked when he found himself trapped between an economic policy that had failed to contain prices and working-class demands for huge wage increases at the time of the contract's renewal in mid-1975. Rather than try to make the regime's feeble corporatist machinery work, he declared war on uncooperative unions, igniting rank-and-file

Table 2.2

External Debt and Gross Reserves, 1972–1976
(U.S.$ millions)

Year	Public	Private	Total	Gross Reserves
1972	3,046	2,046	5,092	541
1973	3,316	1,670	4,986	1,462
1974	3,878	1,636	5,514	1,411
1975	4,941	3,144	8,085	620
1976	6,648	3,090	9,738	1,812

SOURCE: Consejo Técnico de Inversiones, *The Argentine Economy, 1982*, p. 133.

Table 2.3

Parallel Market Value of U.S. Dollar in Pesos, 1972–1976

1972	11.40
1973	11.10
1974	21.65
1975	130.00
1976	285.00

SOURCE: Consejo Técnico de Inversiones, *The Argentine Economy, 1982*, p. 129.

rebellions that did not end until he had fled into exile, leaving Isabel Perón to cope with the fiasco.

The lesson learned was a sad one. Corporatism requires strong leadership, constant care, and supervision. But the Peronists could only provide the first—and that only as long as Perón was there to lead them. Whether it was doomed to fail is a matter for conjecture, but undoubtedly its chances were slight. Leaders in a society that suffers from disruptive conflict cannot be blamed for turning to corporatism. Induced collaboration, under the tutelage of the state, holds a special appeal to those who have lost faith in liberalism. Working together always seems to make sense, but it succeeds only if all parties involved want to cooperate. That is seldom the case, however, since the distrust and selfishness that made corporatist solutions so appealing are often strong enough to assure that they do not work. Argentine entrepreneurs had signed the contract reluctantly, convinced that Perón could not make it work, and organized labor lost interest once it felt the bite of high inflation. Most critical, the Peronist leadership was never ready to make the effort required to orchestrate collaboration. Conspiracy, secrecy, and duplicity, not openness, consultation, and compromise, were its weapons. Rather than making a sincere effort to bring the nation together, it reinforced old divisions and created new ones. The Argentine armed forces could not have plotted a better scenario to induce their countrymen to welcome them back into office. In 1976, frightened by a rising tide of terrorism and record inflation, the Argentine middle and upper classes, along with many in the working class, resigned themselves to another authoritarian government, exchanging liberty for what they hoped would be security.

The *Proceso*: Politics Suspended

Argentine armed forces claimed vindication when they returned in March 1976. As the hard-liners among them predicted, constitutional government had again failed, making authoritarianism the winner by default. Having fulminated against the evils of democracy for years, they were delighted to be able to step in over few objections.

The military's attempt at authoritarian rule a decade before had served as a classroom for the members of the junta formed in 1976. Onganía tried to change Argentine politics in 1966, replacing its system of "black parliamentarism" with an autocracy led by a patriarch who arbitrated among class and sectoral disputes from on high. The arrangement was neither sophisticated nor complex; the junta merely terminated normal political activity and told Argentines to devote their energies to their work, their families, and to private recreations. Onganía hoped that this sobering experience would lead to a new set of political habits, but he did little to inculcate new political values. Instead, he devoted his attention to the nation's economy, its growth, and further industrialization, under the guidance of Minister of Economy Adelbert Krieger Vasena.[22]

Onganía and his advisers believed that Argentina would prosper once investor confidence was restored. The nation's political war had bred uncertainty, making it inhospitable to the investors it needed to finance the completion of its industrialization. Foreign investors in particular had to be assured that their investments were secure if Argentina was to attract technology and heavy industry. Accordingly, everyone was told to behave while Vasena convinced potential investors that the rules of the game in Argentina had changed. It would not be enough for Onganía to claim that he had cleaned things up so that constitutional government could be tried again; only by constantly assuring doubters that the suspension of conventional politics was indefinite could he hope to make his claim of real change credible.[23]

Onganía almost succeeded. In 1967 and 1968, foreign confidence in the Argentina economy grew rapidly, conditions improved, and Argentines conformed to the dictates of their uniformed patriarch. But the eventual revolt of the Argentines made it clear once again that even authoritarians could not subdue them. Led by students and workers and directed at an authoritarianism whose pedestrian values and regressive methods made life in universities and labor unions intolerable, the protest was more political than economic. And it accomplished much more than its organizers expected, for though put down, it succeeded in undermining Onganía's credibility and the junta's commitment to his project.

Onganía's demise might be considered evidence that the contumacious Argentines are unsubduable. But that was not the way his fellow officers saw it. If Onganía was a victim of anything, they reasoned, it was his own temerity in matters of political reform as well as his bad habit of ignoring the advice of his fellow officers. Argentines were subduable, but only if they were denied the means of protest and were forced to conform to a new political ethic by officers determined not to give up until the job was completed. Or so Gen. Jorge Videla and his colleagues believed when they set out to save Argentina with their *proceso* for putting the nation in order after deposing the Peronists in 1976.

Highest on the agenda was the liquidation of terrorists; the military's ruthless accomplishment of this goal over the next two years left 20,000 Argentines dead or missing. Simultaneously the armed forces suspended free political activity and attacked the Argentine economy. This time, however, they were much more ambitious than Onganía. Politics was set aside not just to restore investor confidence, but to allow the junta and its advisers the opportunity to transform the Argentine economy and, with it, much of society.

Inspired by the neoclassical market economics then popular among the Right in Latin America, they wanted to turn Argentina's heavily protected, state-dominated economy into a free-market one. Instead of looking to the state for help, Argentine producers and laborers henceforth would have to live by the rules of supply and demand. The populists had hoped that import-substitution industrialization would generate enough wealth to allow Argentines to live in peace with each other. But what it had actually created, the free-market ideologues told the Argentine people, was an undisciplined work force, a bloated government, and an indolent bourgeoisie. Had the Peronists not overreacted to depression and war by increasing the burden of the state and overprotecting domestic industry, Argentina would have participated in the worldwide economic expansion between 1950 and 1970. The time had come, Minister of Economy José Martínez de Hoz resolved, to convert Argentina from "an economy of speculation into an economy of production."[24] Once forced to compete at international prices, Argentine firms would either increase their efficiency and thrive or go under (which, according to the new ethic, was exactly what some heavily subsidized, risk-avoiding Argentine entrepreneurs deserved for their sins).

Had the plan worked, it would have changed Argentine politics for years to come. Its objective was nothing less than forcing Argentines to abandon their long-established practice of seeking the protection and tutelage of the state. In other words, liberal economics would, if it worked, destroy liberal politics, or at least the welfarist version of it developed in Argentina. When Argentines were forced to seek their welfare in the marketplace rather than the legislature, the presidential palace, or minister's chambers, then labor unions and economic-interest organizations would atrophy, losing their political purposes. What would follow was never made clear; but whatever it was, it would be a politics free of militant labor movements, contentious political parties, and a government that made half of the nation's investments.

There was always something naive about the whole scheme, causing many to question the seriousness of its authors. Critics could not be faulted for wondering if it was an elaborate hoax, created for the aggrandizement of the military and the upper class rather than for real political reform. Its dismal failure eight years later did little to disabuse them of such suspicions. Nevertheless, its initial appeal is not hard to understand. Frustrations built during years of veto politics provoked desperate searches for alternatives.

The liberalization of the Argentine economy, however, could not be achieved overnight. Moreover, there were even more pressing problems, such as the record 600 percent annual rate of inflation that the Peronists left behind. Consequently, from the outset Martínez de Hoz could not proceed swiftly with his plan, but had to implement it slowly, going through at least five phases in an attempt to deal with inflation and liberalization simultaneously.[25]

A rather orthodox stabilization program accompanied the announcement of the government's liberalization objectives in April 1976. The junta ended price controls and imposed wage controls, causing a sharp decline in real wages, increased taxes, and renegotiated the foreign debt after an agreement with the International Monetary Fund. Thanks to a bumper harvest, the trade balance improved; so by midyear did the rate of inflation, although it accelerated again at the end of the year. Despite its free-market protestations, the government resorted to a price truce among some 800 of the larger corporations in the second phase of its economic program, beginning in March 1977, in a desperate attempt to halt rising prices. Simultaneously it began a financial reform, freeing interest rates and liberalizing bank laws, which caused interest rates to rise. The third phase, which started in September 1977, involved a major attempt to deal with inflation by restricting the money supply, but high-interest rates deepened the recession and reinforced inflation by attracting an inflow of dollars. The government went after imported inflation next, and finally, starting in December 1978, it tried something new in foreign exchange policy, announcing monthly mini-devaluations and predetermined increases in wages and public-sector prices. Simultaneously it reduced tariffs, finally implementing one of the keystones of the liberalization scheme.

In 1980, Martínez de Hoz boasted that "we have done what an elective government with an election next year can't do—we have accepted short-term negative effects for long-term progress."[26] Indeed, it seemed that Argentines were responding to the new program. After declining by 0.2 percent in 1976, GDP grew by 6.8 percent in 1979 and manufacturing rose by 9.1 percent. Moreover, thanks to high interest rates that attracted a new capital inflow of $4.3 billion in 1979, Argentina's gross reserves increased from $1.8 billion in 1976 to $10.5 billion in 1979.[27] Equally impressive was the drop in inflation to 100 percent for the first time in four years. Clearly, progress was being made; foreign confidence in Martínez de Hoz and his plan was rising, as was the Argentine military's self-esteem.

But two years later everything had changed. Recession, capital flight, and a collapsing currency gripped Argentina. GDP fell by 6 percent in 1981 and manufacturing by 14 percent. The value of the Argentine peso, which was set at 2,000 to the dollar at the end of 1980, rose to nearly 70,000 two years later. And a foreign debt that was only $8 billion in 1975 skyrocketed to $37 billion by the end of 1982.[28]

One is tempted to blame Argentina's war with Great Britain over the Falkland Islands in 1982 for the nation's economic collapse, but it would be wrong to do so. The Argentine invasion of the islands was in part a political response to an already deteriorating economy rather than the cause of it. The explanation of the sudden collapse in 1981 remains in dispute among friends and foes of the liberalization effort, and no doubt will continue to be debated for some time. Friends absolve Martínez de Hoz, blaming instead the military and the way it handled the transition from Videla's presidency to Gen. Viola's in March 1981. Presidential changes, even military ones that are announced long in advance like this one, always cause worry in Argentina. The new president's refusal to allow Martínez de Hoz and his team to continue in office increased fears that the military's commitment to liberalization had weakened. As is their habit, Argentines took steps to protect themselves, which in turn helped undermine policy. Others, in contrast, placed the blame on liberalization itself, claiming that it was not feasible in a semi-industrialized country like Argentina. Too much had to be sacrificed by native entrepreneurs, and they in the end refused to cooperate with ideologues dedicated to the reorganization of the nation's industrial economy.

Wherever the fault lies, a few things are clear. First of all, an overvalued peso, high interest rates, and tariff reductions pushed Argentine industry into a crisis. Bankruptcies, which were on the rise, accelerated faster than expected in 1980 and involved some of the nation's largest firms. Among the casualties were major banks (a few of which had been created overnight to take advantage of Argentina's sudden attractiveness to speculators, only to collapse as fast as they had arisen). Fears that the government would soon lose control of the overvalued currency also caused capital flight in late 1980 and early 1981, and when Martínez de Hoz's departure was followed by the anticipated currency devaluations, even more people got rid of their pesos for fear that other devaluations would follow. When the impact of the 1981 world recession is added in, it is not hard to understand why conditions quickly deteriorated.

In addition, Martínez de Hoz's fiscal policy never lived up to its promise. He had proposed a drastic reduction in public consumption through budget cutting and the sale of public enterprises. But despite much fanfare, he actually accomplished very little. First of all, privatization was stymied by a lack of interest among businessmen in the purchase of the country's ailing public enterprises. Those sold were primarily small enterprises of lesser import. Second, although the government deficit, measured as a proportion of GDP, was reduced early in the term, it returned to nearly 4 percent at the end under pressure from the government's public works programs and defense spending in response to tensions with Chile.[29] The latter was crucial. Nothing handicapped Martínez de Hoz more than the military's resistance to budget cuts, or so he claimed after he left the government in 1981. The military, it seems, wanted it both ways: successful economic liberalization *and* a license to hold on to its public enterprises, expensive weapons, and personal privileges. But obviously the achievement of either demanded the sacrifice of the other.

Controlling the military budget is always difficult in Argentina, not just for civilians but also for officers who lead a military that is akin more to a feudal empire than to a rigid hierarchy. To stay on top, generals and admirals have to placate their colleagues, protecting their sinecures from civilian meddlers and giving them what they need to maintain the pretense of a serious military mission. It is a costly business that no one has been able to control, no matter how compelling the case for budget cutting. And Argentina's defeat in war only increased the military's determination to arm itself in the years ahead.

Table 2.4

Annual Growth Rates, 1976–1980
(percentage)

	Gross Domestic Product	Value Added by Manufacturing	Consumer Goods Price Increase
1976	−0.2	−2.0	443
1977	6.0	5.9	176
1978	−3.9	−10.8	175
1979	6.8	9.1	159
1980	1.1	−3.5	100

Source: Inter-American Development Bank, *Economic and Social Progress in Latin America, 1980–81* (Washington, D.C., 1983), pp. 7, 12, 25.

Table 2.5

External Debt and Gross Reserves, 1976–1981
(U.S.$ millions)

	External Debt			External Gross Reserves
	Public	Private	Total	
1976	6,648	3,090	9,738	1,812
1977	8,127	3,634	11,761	4,039
1978	9,453	4,210	13,663	6,037
1979	9,960	9,074	19,034	10,480
1980	14,459	12,703	27,162	7,684
1981	20,024	15,647	35,671	3,877

Source: Consejo Técnico de Inversiones, *The Argentine Economy, 1982*, p. 133.

Table 2.6

Parallel Market Value of U.S. Dollar in Pesos, 1976–1982

1976	285
1977	598
1978	1,016
1979	1,645
1980	2,030
1981	10,700
1982	69,000

SOURCE: Consejo Técnico de Inversiones, *The Argentine Economy, 1982*, p. 129.

One final tale of fiscal reform will suffice. In December 1981, the armed forces, disgruntled with President Roberto Viola's vacillations in the face of a rapidly deteriorating economy, replaced him with Army Chief of Staff Leopoldo Galtieri. Galtieri, in turn, selected civilian Roberto Alemann to serve as minister of economy. Alemann, a businessman of well-known integrity and neoclassical economic conviction, accepted on the condition that Galtieri would back a major budget-cutting effort, including reductions in military spending. Galtieri agreed, and, to everyone's surprise, the cuts began in early 1982. But then, before the celebrations got under way, Galtieri invaded the Falkland/Malvinas Islands on April 2, only to be ignominiously defeated by the British two months later. Alemann's fiscal policy fell with him.

Where to Go from Here

Argentines have paid a high price for their politics, but they seem attached to them. Although officials, given the political leeway they need to enforce unpopular measures, can accomplish something, their economic "miracles" are usually quite brief. Economic and political forces eventually defeat them. No matter how compelling in theory, each economic solution encounters realities its designers either ignored or could not control as planned. And regardless of how desirable the suspension of competitive politics seems to those in charge, one cannot hold back a people as urbane and assertive as the Argentines for long. Treating them like delinquents who do not know what is good for them does bring peace to the streets, but only temporarily.

Argentines are plagued by a very old problem; namely, determining the purpose of politics. More than Mexicans, Cubans, and Brazilians, they still argue over the fundaments of politics, trying to determine where individual interests end and social responsibilities begin. Each Argentine has an answer, but an agreement on one set of principles eludes them. What they need to decide now is not who is right, but how to get from a state of dissensus to one of consensus. Should it be done through the creation of an agreement on principles, as has been tried by constitutional governments in the past, or is it better to proceed slowly, building agreements and understandings incrementally? No doubt something of each is needed. Some agreement is necessary at the start, but consensus will have to be built gradually as trust grows. No single solution imposed on everyone by someone on high is enforceable. Instead, Argentines must develop an interest in political unity, and for that to happen they must discover that interest on their own.

What makes this kind of consensus building so elusive in Argentina is the national habit of hedging against failure. Argentines have experienced too many failures to place much faith in the next government's survival. Being rational, they know that if they rely heavily on any government or policy and it fails, they stand to lose a great deal, especially if they are among the last to jump from the sinking ship. So they hold back, even though in doing so they make the government's success all the more difficult. It is a habit that must be broken, but short of revolution—an unlikely prospect in Argentina as long as the military is in place—it can be ended only slowly, if at all. If this mindset does not change, there is little hope for anything but more replication of the past.

It is encouraging that those who campaigned for office in 1983 admitted that no party could rule the country without help from the others. Equally reassuring was their admission that if they were going to live within the confines of a mixed capitalist economy, as seems probable, they could not cavalierly violate its basic rules without inviting another disaster. Now they face the task of living by their words.

The results of the October 30, 1983, election offer new hope. To the surprise of many, Radical Raul Alfonsín defeated Peronist Italo Lúder by a 52 to 40 percent margin for the presidency. It marked the Peronists' first defeat ever in a free election. The importance of this result lies in its restructuring of the political contest in Argentina. For the first time, the Peronists have earned the role of the loyal opposition, and if they wish, they can change the Argentine game significantly. In the past, their defeats came only in contests from which they were excluded by the military, allowing them to act on the belief that their defeat had been illegitimate. The subsequent intense conflict between them and the Radical incumbents always ended in military intervention. Now they can make no such claim. Instead, they find themselves part of a government led by a legitimate victor, a government in which the Peronists control the Senate and the Radicals the House, a distribution of power that allows contributions to the resolution of the nation's problems from both sides. In fact, it requires it. Narrow partisanship by either side means self-defeat, and if their initial post-election statements are any indication, both sides are well aware of what will be required.

Argentine leaders also need the courage to take pride in the mundane and the essential, eschewing chicanery and petulance in favor of old-fashioned statesmanship. But Argentina needs the kind of leadership that understands that routine things have to be done well and without fanfare, and that much more must be turned into routine if the Argentine government is to become trustworthy.

The 1970s brought unprecedented violence and repression to Argentina and, with it, high hopes and great disappointments. It was a sobering experience for most Argentines, but what they have learned from it is not entirely clear. Maybe they now understand that the nation's political parties and armed forces are as much products of the public's wants as corrupters of it. One hopes that the Argentine upper class has learned that it cannot run the country as it wishes, that the middle class has discovered that its alienation does it and the nation more harm than good, and that the working class recognizes that if it is to live in a capitalist society, it cannot ignore the demands of those who supply its capital. If the nation's durable politicians are to succeed, they must be given room in which to do so. The constraints an elected president faces are abundant, and presidential decisions will always be criticized. But presidents will not become more efficient unless they are given a chance to learn how to do so.

Is this impossible for Argentines? It may be naive, but Argentine cries for peace, freedom, and civility raise hopes that they may try to do things differently.

Notes

1. In aggregate terms in 1979, Argentina's per capita GNP was $2,217, Brazil's $1,792, Peru's $848, and Guatemala's $1,002. Argentina had one hospital bed per 191 inhabitants, Brazil 255, Peru 536, and Guatemala 545. (Ruth Leger Sivard, *World Military and Social Expenditures, 1982* [Leesburg, Va.: WMSE Publications, 1982]).

2. Guido DiTella, *Perón-Perón, 1973–1976* (Buenos Aires: Editorial Sudamericana, 1983), p. 319.

3. This characterization draws on several sources, the most recent being the observations of French political scientist Alain Roquié in *Humor*, no. 101 (March 1983): 44–50.

4. Another alliance of sorts was organized in 1980 to pressure Argentina's military government to restore constitutional government. Called the *Concordancia* or *Multi-*

partidaria, it was created by five parties, the Peronists and Radicals being the largest, and lasted until elections were called in 1983.

5. Alain Roquié, "Hegemonía militar, estado y dominación social," in idem, ed., *Argentina, hoy* (Mexico City: Siglo XXI Editores, 1982), pp. 26–27.

6. On Radical Party governments during the 1920s, see Peter Smith, *Argentina and the Failure of Democracy: Conflict Among Political Elites, 1904–1955* (Madison: University of Wisconsin Press, 1974).

7. For an examination of the wartime military government, see Robert Potash, *The Army and Politics in Argentina, 1928–1945* (Stanford: Stanford University Press, 1969). See also Mark Falcoff and Ronald Dolkart, *Prelude to Perón* (Berkeley and Los Angeles: University of California Press, 1975); and Felix Luna, *El 45* (Buenos Aires: Editorial Sudamericana, 1971).

8. Alain Roquié, among others, makes the case for the military's deep vested interest in public enterprise convincingly in his monumental two-volume history of the Argentine armed forces, *Poder militar y sociedad política en la Argentina* (Buenos Aires: EMECE, 1982); see especially 2:418 ff.

9. On the Peronist program, see Gary W. Wynia, *Argentina in the Postwar Era* (Albuquerque: University of New Mexico Press, 1978), chap. 3.

10. Data published in the Argentine magazine *Mercado*, August 2, 1973, pp. 96–97.

11. Of the Treasury's outlays to cover public enterprise deficits in 1982, 70 percent (or 9.7 trillion pesos) went to the national railways (Consejo Técnico de Inversiones, *The Argentine Economy, 1982*, p. 114).

12. *Latin America Weekly Report*, July 1, 1981.

13. This curious plotting was necessary because the outgoing junta prohibited Perón's candidacy in the March elections. Accordingly, his friend Cámpora stood in for him and won. Perón returned triumphantly to Argentina in June, and Cámpora called new elections for September in which Perón received over 60 percent of the vote.

14. On the protests, see Daniel Villar, *El Cordobazo* (Buenos Aires: Centro Editor de América Latina, 1971); on the Onganía regime generally, the most complete study to date is Guillermo O'Donnell's *Estado Burocrático Autoritario* (Buenos Aires: Editorial Belgrano, 1982).

15. Wynia, *Argentina in the Postwar Era*, chap. 3.

16. The literature on European "neocorporatism" during the postwar years is abundant. On the concept and its development in Europe and Latin America, see Philippe Schmitter, "Still a Century of Corporatism," *Review of Politics* 36 (January 1974).

17. Gary W. Wynia, "Workers and Wages: Argentine Labor and the Incomes Policy Problem," in Frederick C. Turner and José Enrique Miguens, eds., *Juan Perón and the Reshaping of Argentina* (Pittsburgh, Pa.: University of Pittsburgh Press, 1983), pp. 46–53. See also Robert Ayers, "The 'Social Pact' as Anti-Inflationary Policy," *World Politics* 28 (1976): 478–80; for the document itself, consult *Review of the River Plate*, June 19, 1973.

18. The CGE was created during Perón's first government in the late 1940s and was sanctioned by him as the recognized spokesman for commerce and industry before his government. It was intervened and closed by the military in 1955 and then legalized once more by President Frondizi after his election in 1958. Afterwards it competed for attention with the more traditional industrial and agricultural societies and represented the interests of medium and small business. Its affinity for Peronism derives from its creation, nationalistic and protectionist sentiments, and desire for access to power.

19. Guido DiTella, "La Argentina Economica, 1943–82," *Criterio*, Christmas issue, 1982, pp. 746–63.

20. Ibid.

21. The Peronist Youth was just one part of the Peronist Left. Leading the calls for the radicalization of Peronism at the time were the Montoneros, a revolutionary group that had joined with the Peronists to support Perón's return in 1973. Once evicted, it was the Montoneros who organized the major terrorist attack on authorities in 1975 and 1976. When the Montoneros and the Peronist Youth tried to dominate the May Day rally, Perón was furious. According to one account, "he lost his self-control, abandoned his national unity speech, and unleashed an attack on the Peronist Left which amounted to a declaration of war. After just fifty seconds of praise for the quality of Argentine trade unionism, hearing slogans against the union leaders from the Left, Perón made his first reference to 'those stupid idiots who are shouting.' Perón continued, 'I was saying that through these [last] 21 years, the trade unions have remained intransigent, yet today some beardless wonders try to claim more credit than those who fought for 20 years.'" (Richard Gillespie, *Soldiers of Perón: Argentina's Montoneros* [London: Oxford University Press, 1982], pp. 149–51.)

22. Marcelo Cavarozzi, "Argentina at the Crossroads: Pathways and Obstacles to Democratization in the Present Political Conjuncture," Latin American Program Working Paper, no. 115 (Princeton, N.J.: Woodrow Wilson School, 1982), pp. 3. See also O'Donnell, *Estado burocrático autoritario.*

23. See Wynia, *Argentina in the Postwar Era*, chap. 7, for an elaboration on Onganía's motives. See also O'Donnell, *Estado burocrático autoritario.*

24. Quoted in Cavarozzi, "Argentina at the Crossroads," p. 4.

25. The phases are described in *Latin America Weekly Report*, March 6, 1982, p. 5.

26. Quoted in *Business Week*, July 21, 1980, p. 78.

27. Inter-American Development Bank, *Economic and Social Progress in Latin America, 1980 Report* (Washington, D.C., January 7, 1983), p. 7.

28. *Latin America Weekly Report*, January 7, 1983, p. 7.

29. Argentina and Chile both claim three islands in the Beagle Channel near Cape Horn. Access to Antarctica and the possibility of oil have motivated each to assert its claims during the past decade. An International Court of Justice Arbitration Award gave them to Chile in 1977, but Argentina refused to accept the decision. The rejection caused a strong Chilean reaction, touching off an arms race of sorts between the two countries. Conflict was averted by the intervention of the Vatican in 1980, but Argentina refused to accept the Holy See's proposal as well. An arms race with Chile may be over for the time being, but post-Falklands rearmaments will have the same effect as Argentines hastily buy weapons to replace those lost in that conflict and to increase the nation's military might even more.

3 Uruguay

Military Rule and Economic Failure

Martin Weinstein

Even when it comes to power by force, the ultimate test of any government, especially in a developing country, is its economic performance. The military took power in Uruguay in 1973 after a decade and a half of economic stagnation, high inflation, and social unrest. Massive repression eliminated the visible unrest and any fears about the resurgence of a revolutionary movement. Economic policy and performance soon became the regime's litmus test, its ultimate claim to legitimacy and justification for draconian rule.

For the first half of this century, Uruguay's small, highly urbanized population enjoyed the twin benefits of the joining of their livestock economy to the British imperial orbit and the redistributive effects of the welfare-oriented policies promoted by José Batlle y Ordóñez during the period prior to the Depression. Meat and wool exports paid for expansion of education and social security and health benefits. Even for three decades after his death in 1929, Batlle's legacy (*Batllismo*) remained the framework in which Uruguay's two traditional parties, the Blanco and the Colorado, vied for political power. The combination of a middle-class lifestyle, welfare-oriented government policies, and unquestioned civilian rule earned the country the justly deserved title of the Switzerland of South America.

The exhaustion of the import-substitution model by the mid-1950s brought a steady deterioration in economic performance. The economic crisis had no single cause, but government policy certainly contributed to it. The conversion of state enterprises (*entes autónomos*) from guardians of national sovereignty and motors of economic development, as envisaged by Batlle, into patronage machines of the Blanco and Colorado parties did not help productivity or decisionmaking. Montevideo virtually ignored the rural sector, the basis of virtually all of Uruguay's export revenue. The land tax system, which might have promoted greater efficiency, was nonprogressive and viewed as a vehicle for raising revenue for the urban sector. Even though the Blancos favored the agricultural sector, they continued the populist policies of the Colorados when they finally gained control of the collegial executive from 1959 to 1967. This was not surprising, given the overwhelming importance of Montevideo and its middle-class population. The economically important export and industrial interests behaved no better than the politicians. While the latter continued to seek votes and avoid hard decisions, the former sought to safeguard their position and wealth through financial speculation and capital flight.

During the 1960s, in the Western Hemisphere, only Haiti's growth rate was worse than Uruguay's. The resulting social and political tensions manifested themselves in the rise of an urban guerrilla movement (the Tupamaros) and increased unrest in the trade unions and at the university and secondary schools. First the police and then the military were called in to deal with the problems created by these economic and ideological tensions. The governments of Jorge Pacheco Areco (1968–1972) and Juan María Bordaberry (1972–1976) curtailed civil liberties and increasingly relied on the armed forces to maintain order. Finally, after an earlier, limited assumption of power, the military, with the acquiescence of President Bordaberry, seized total control on June 27, 1973.

The armed forces closed the Congress, destroyed the labor union movement, intervened in the university and secondary school systems, and banned leftist political parties, movements, and publications. In the mid-1970s, Uruguay had more political prisoners per capita than any other country in the world. The regime, having achieved totalitarian rule, determined that it would alter economic policy dramatically. The principal architect of its program was a monetarist technocrat, Alejandro Vegh Villegas, who was trained at Harvard and received his practical experience as an adviser to the military governments in Brazil and Argentina in the 1960s. Vegh served as minister of finance from 1974 to 1976 and was replaced by his deputy, Valentín Arismendi, who served until late 1982. Vegh wished to dismantle the protectionist structure of the Uruguayan economy, free the banking and financial communities from the restraints under which they operated, cut the budget, especially social spending, drastically reduce employment in the patronage-riddled bureaucracy, and sell off most of Uruguay's state-run corporations. He succeeded somewhat on the budget and monetary fronts and reduced some tariffs, but ran into opposition from some of the nationalist and populist military leaders when it came to mass reductions in government employment and divestiture of such state-run industries as oil refining. The basic thrust of the model was an attempt to reintegrate Uruguay into the world economy and reallocate domestic resources according to the efficiency of the marketplace.

Economic Performance

The fight against inflation was the highest priority for Vegh. Uruguay had suffered consumer price rises as high as 35 percent annually during the 1960s, and inflation approached 100 percent in 1972, the year before the coup. Vegh's strict monetary policy reduced it to the 40–67 percent level between 1975 and 1980. He managed this by strict control of the social service side of the budget and by a policy of depressed real wages. Ironically, Vegh might have had even more success on this front had he not been up against a voracious military. Almost half of central government expenditures in 1976 were destined for the armed forces and police. Since then, such expenditures have never been less than 40 percent of the budget.

The main thrust of development policy involved the liberalization of the economy—the removal or reduction of artificial and differential exchange rates, banking controls, price controls, and tariffs. The model included deregulation of finance and trade and a smaller role in the economy for the state, which accounted for 19 percent of the gross domestic product and 20 percent of the work force. In addition, inefficient domestic producers were to be allowed to succumb to import competition. Reduction of the country's dependence on traditional exports—wool, hides, and beef—became a primary government objective and one that met with some success in the late 1970s.

During this period, the government gradually reduced or eliminated price controls on beef and other food products, adding to the decline in purchasing power of the working class. It had lifted all price controls by March 1979 with the exception of selected foodstuffs, pharmaceuticals, and some medical and educational services. An overvalued peso kept internal inflation down as did tariff reductions. The main function of the latter, however, was to help make the economy more competitive internationally.

The regime's policy had its most significant impact on the industrial sector. The goal was clear: to force hitherto protected industries to become more efficient or go under and to stimulate the growth of export industries. The import-substitution industrialization model Uruguay had followed required high protective tariffs, especially in view of the small size of the domestic market. Vegh and his team regarded these industries as inefficient, high cost, and wasteful of resources. They implemented a phased reduction of tariffs and credit mechanisms such as artificial exchange rates (*recargos*) in order to let the strong survive and the weak die.

The government aggressively stimulated the growth of such industries as textiles, finished leather, and wool products that could compete in the international marketplace. Its principal mechanism was a system of tax credits (*reintegros*) for nontraditional exports. These credits grew in volume until they represented 13 percent of the value of total exports in 1975, and they produced the desired effect. The share of nontraditional exports in total trade rose from 25 percent in 1972–1973 to 64 percent in 1978 but dropped to 48 percent in 1980–1981. The ensuing worldwide recession lowered these percentages significantly. This category of exports, however, consists not of capital goods but of finished goods based on agricultural products (leather jackets and wool sweaters, for example). In 1977, some 95 percent of exports were therefore based, directly or indirectly, on the agricultural sector, which continues to suffer from low productivity. In addition, the 1981–1983 recession, coupled with protectionist measures against textiles and leather goods in the United States and Europe, wreaked havoc. These factors left Uruguayan industries, no longer the recipients of the tax rebates granted until the end of 1982, with high debts incurred during the expansionary climate of the 1975–1980 period.

Labor Under the Military

The military government has dealt severely with the traditional trade union movement. It declared the National Labor Convention (CNT) illegal in 1973 and banned all unions until 1981. During the last quarter of 1982, the government approved a collective bargaining law and associated legislation. At least on paper, some 180 unions were registered by the end of the year, but government-imposed restrictions prevented strikes and industry-wide organizations and limited their rights to engage in political activities. The leaders of the banned unions are prohibited from engaging in union activities. There are fewer than 30,000 union members in the private sector. Government workers are barely allowed to organize, although public employees were the largest component of the CNT, which at its peak in the late 1960s numbered some 250,000 members.

Unemployment rose dramatically in 1982 as the economic situation deteriorated, doubling to an annual average of about 11 percent and reaching almost 14 percent by December. On January 1, 1983, the government decreed

Table 3.1

Real Salary Index, Annual, 1968–1982

(1968=100)

Year	Country	Private Sector	Public Sector
1969	111	111	112
1970	110	111	109
1971	116	116	115
1972	96	98	94
1973	94	96	93
1974	93	96	91
1975	85	88	82
1976	80	81	79
1977	71	71	71
1978	68	68	68
1979	62	62	64
1980	62	58	67
1981	67	62	72
1982	67	62	72

SOURCE: República Oriental del Uruguay, Dirección General de Estadística y Censos, *Anuario Estadístico* (Montevideo, 1983).

a 15 percent pay boost; this was wiped out by the end of the month by a similar increase in the consumer price index.

The suppression of organized labor for almost a decade was a factor in the serious deterioration of purchasing power (see Table 3.1).

The principal labor organization in Uruguay is the General Confederation of Uruguayan Workers (CGTU). The CGTU has the support of the AFL-CIO's American Institute of Free Labor Development, the U.S. unions' labor education arm in Latin America. The CGTU is affiliated with the International Confederation of Free Trade Unions and the Inter-American Regional Labor Organization.

Other labor organizations in Uruguay are the Autonomous Confederation of Democratic Uruguayan Workers (CATUD), which split off from the CGTU, and the Uruguayan Labor Association (ASU), which is affiliated with the World Trade Union Federation and its Latin American subsidiary, and the Latin American Confederation of Labor, groups associated with the Christian Democratic movement. The recently formed National Commission for Labor Rights (CNDS) and the new Commission for Economic, Social, and Union Studies (CEESS) are trying to develop a following from, among others, such former affiliates of the CNT as the Uruguayan Bank Workers Association. The

CATUD and ASU together probably have fewer than 10,000 members. None of these organizations has official recognition. The government has provisionally accepted the CGTU, as evidenced by its inclusion in the official Uruguayan delegation to the annual conference of the International Labor Organization in Geneva.

Industrial and Exchange Rate Policy

Perhaps the most controversial aspect of Uruguayan economic policy has been the use of the foreign exchange rate. During 1974–1977, exchange rate policy played an active role in export development, with periodic adjustments compensating for domestic inflation. Since late 1978, reducing inflation has been the government's most important economic objective, and exchange rate policy has been fundamental to the stabilization program. In October 1978, the government began announcing a schedule of monthly devaluations of the Uruguayan peso against the U.S. dollar six to nine months in advance, with the understanding that the schedule would not be modified during the period covered. Under this policy, the peso has been maintained at a progressively overvalued rate, because the mini-devaluations have not compensated for the difference between international and domestic inflation.

The preannouncement of the exchange rate has been the cornerstone of the stabilization effort and part of the overall anti-inflation program. Reducing import barriers and eliminating capital controls have subjected the economy to greater international influences. "Increased foreign competition in the product market was perceived as a means of inhibiting domestic price increases, and greater availability of foreign capital was expected to reduce the real cost of credit to the private sector."[1] The progressively overvalued currency has facilitated such foreign competition, limiting the ability of domestic producers to raise prices as well as enabling cheaper imports. Furthermore, the government recognized that fiscal and monetary restraint was necessary for the viability of the anti-inflation program (the central government budget showed a surplus for 1979 and 1980, and only a slight deficit for 1981).

The stabilizing effects of preannouncing the exchange rate are most apparent in inducing a substantial reduction in the public's expectations concerning future inflation:

> This is a crucial element because, when inflation has been sustained at a high level for long periods of time, institutional developments, such as excessive inventory holdings, fully indexed wage settlements, and high mark-ups over original cost to reflect higher expected replacement costs, make achieving a

reduction in inflation more difficult. In this context, a clear signal from the economic policymakers that definitive measures are being taken to reduce the rate of inflation can, by itself, have a significant impact on inflationary pressures...The preannouncement of a gradual reduction in the rate of depreciation of the exchange rate may meet these conditions if it is taken as indicating a commitment on the part of the monetary authority to rates consistent with the announced policy.[2]

Significant success had been achieved in reducing inflation in Uruguay. The rise in the consumer price index, which was 86 percent in 1979, fell to 43 percent in 1980 and to 29 percent in 1981. But, as explained below, this policy proved disastrous in the face of world recession and the rising value of the dollar.

Since 1974, import liberalization has been designed to foster industrial efficiency and price competitiveness. According to the Ministry of Economy and Finance,

The current import policy is aimed at improving the allocation of productive resources via an approximation of domestic to international relative prices, so as to guide investment towards those sectors in which competition abroad is more likely to succeed. The import policy also included other objectives considered necessary for a sustained level of growth. These consisted in obtaining modern equipment and machinery for the technologically obsolete industrial sector, in securing a regular supply of inputs, and in curbing the rate of inflation.[3]

In 1975, the government eliminated quantitative restrictions on imports, the system of prior deposits for imports, and all foreign exchange controls. Import licensing, which had been used intermittently to reduce imports, remained only for statistical purposes. Most important, the government gradually reduced the maximum tariff rate from 300 percent in 1974 to 77 percent in 1981.

The principal legislation to encourage foreign investment, especially in industry, was promulgated in 1974. The Industrial Promotion Act of 1974, enacted to advance the establishment or expansion of industrial plants, grants benefits to projects declared to be in the national interest by the government. To qualify, a project has to support one or more of the following national objectives: (1) maximizing production and marketing efficiency based on adequate levels of size, technology, and quality; (2) increasing and diversifying exports of industrial goods that incorporate the highest possible value added to the raw materials; (3) locating new industries and expanding or reforming existing ones where this results in more advantageous use of raw material markets and available manpower; (4) encouraging selected technical research programs directed toward the economic use of heretofore unexploited national raw materials and toward the improvement of domestic products and the training of technicians and workers; and (5) stimulating the tourism sector by improving and expanding the nation's tourism infrastructure. Qualifying projects derive two major benefits under the Industrial Promotion Act. First, credit assistance is available through the Central Bank to purchase equipment, machinery, and domestic raw materials; to modernize or expand existing industries; and to finance accumulated tax debts arising from the inefficiency or unprofitability of an industry that is expected to be corrected under this law. Second, import surcharges, import tariffs, consular fees, port charges, and other taxes on equipment imported for the project may be waived.

The Foreign Investment Act guarantees foreign investors the right, through a contract signed with the government, to transfer capital and remit earnings on projects. For the purpose of this act, a foreign company is one whose capital originating abroad constitutes more than 50 percent of its total capital. The act guarantees (1) the right to remit abroad that portion of company profits corresponding to the contribution made by foreign capital and (2) the right to repatriate invested capital after three years, except in those cases where special contracts with the government covering specific terms or benefits fix longer repatriation terms. There is no personal income tax in Uruguay. Only net profits of industrial and commercial enterprises are subject to an income tax of 30 percent, paid on the income from activities in Uruguay. The tax is independent of the nationality and the residence of those taking part in the activities. There is also a value-added tax of 18 percent (12 percent for certain goods).

Regional Integration

An integral part of the Uruguayan government's international trade policy has been an attempt to increase trade with the countries of the Southern Cone.[4] In line with this policy and given the shortcomings of the Latin American Integration Association, Uruguay entered into bilateral trade agreements with Argentina and Brazil (the Uruguayan-Argentine Economic Cooperation Agreement is dated August 24, 1974, and the Trade Expansion Protocol June 12, 1975, under the Trade Cooperation and Friendship Treaty with Brazil). The objectives of the bilateral agreements are (1) to expand and diversify commercial trade, (2) to stimulate and coordinate investments, and (3) to foster regional integration through joint infrastructure projects.[5] The most effective instruments for achieving these objectives have been mutual tariff concessions on selected products and the creation of credit lines to finance Uruguayan imports of capital goods from these two countries. Through the initial and subsequent negotiations, Uruguay has obtained Argentine agreement to make 895 products duty free and Brazilian agreement to lower tariff levels below 4 percent for about 600 items. Among the most important Uruguayan exports benefiting from preferential access to the Argentine and Brazilian markets are paper products, chemicals, plastics, textiles, tires, ceramics, processed foods, and appliances.

Significant regional integration has been achieved (32 percent of total Uruguayan exports in 1980 went to Brazil and Argentina), and the Uruguayan and Argentine governments initiated negotiations in 1980 for the possible establishment of a full tariff union. The Uruguayan government's position was clear in a May 1980 speech by Minister of Economy Valentín Arismendi. Self-sustained economic growth based on exports was impossible under the present international economic situation for two reasons. First, the small domestic market of Uruguay simply did not provide the minimum internal market necessary for sustained export growth, and second, Uruguay was facing increased protectionism on the part of foreign countries (for example, the European Economic Community), a trend that will make it more difficult to develop export markets. In view of these developments, Arismendi claimed that Uruguay's only hope for self-sustained growth based on exports was to broaden the market for its products through an economic union with a larger country, in this case Argentina.[6]

Negotiations during 1980 focused on the legal and functional framework to be established rather than on a detailed discussion of commodity lists. Major points of contention at the technical level were definition of origin, export incentives, and some escape or safeguard clause. The country of origin question became important because the values of foreign components in Uruguayan manufactured products tend to be considerably higher than those in Argentine ones. The Uruguayan government requested the escape clause to win the support of worried businessmen. In fact, the Uruguayan government seemed much more interested in the integration negotiations than did the local business community. Businessmen in Uruguay are generally fearful of Argentine competition, believing the much larger Argentine capacity would overwhelm Uruguayan industrial and agricultural producers. The Uruguayan businessman, instead of viewing integration as an opportunity to expand his market, sees only the expected flood of products from Argentina. Although the government has tried to emphasize the opportunities offered, opposition is growing.

On March 16, 1981, Uruguayan economy minister Arismendi and Argentine minister of commerce Alejandro Estrada signed a joint declaration in which both countries agreed that the free-trade zone should enter into force as soon as possible. The declaration established a binational technical group, consisting of high officials designated by each government, to recommend specific provisions of a draft agreement setting up such a zone. However, since that time negotiations have been suspended because of economic and political turmoil in Argentina as well as increasing economic problems in Uruguay.

The Model Fails

In 1981, in the deepening worldwide recession, Uruguay found its export position deteriorating as external demand fell, the peso became increasingly overvalued, and protectionist measures increased in Europe, Latin America, and the United States. By the second half of 1981, Uruguay began to experience a severe recession. There were several reasons for this turn of events. Government policy was partly to blame as were international conditions beyond the control of Uruguay's generals and their technocrats.

One of the most serious internal causes of the recession was the very high real interest rates that banks could charge under the deregulation enacted in 1978. One result of these rates was a sharp drop in internal demand, especially for durable goods, a decline in capital investment, and a decrease in inventories since the cost of money made it unwise to accumulate stocks of goods. Domestic producers were also being damaged by a free-trade policy that increased the availability and reduced the cost of imported goods. Sales of such domestically produced items as tires, electric appliances, automobiles, and apparel were particularly hurt.

These trends continued throughout 1982. The only bright spot was the inflation front, where the combination of the recession and the overvalued peso helped reduce inflation from 83 percent in 1979 to 43 percent in 1980 to 29 percent in 1981 to 20 percent in 1982.

But 1982 also registered the worst economic performance since the military took power in 1973. Gross domestic product fell almost 10 percent, with manufacturing down 17 percent, construction down 15 percent, and commercial activity down 23 percent. Unemployment rose dramatically during the same period, reaching over 13 percent by the end of the year and growing to over 27 percent by March 1983. The trade deficit narrowed in 1982, but this was due to a sharp drop in imports owing to the severe recession in Uruguay rather than to an expansion of exports, which fell to $883 million from $1.2 billion the previous year.

The recession exacerbated Uruguay's debt burden, which grew rapidly after the quadrupling of oil prices by OPEC in 1974 required a massive infusion of capital for Uruguay to make up for huge balance of payments deficits. Western banks flush with petrodollars gladly extended loans to an Uruguay backing them with gold reserves. Additional dollars were attracted from Brazil and Argentina by allowing Uruguayan banks to pay high interest rates and by the lack of taxes on these accounts. Uruguay's foreign debt nearly quadrupled during this period from $515 million in 1976 to $2.26 billion by April 1981. The profile of those who held Uruguay's debt also changed significantly; increasing amounts were in the hands of private money-center banks and holders of Uruguayan bonds, while the shares held by international financial institutions and foreign governments declined. The debt stood at just over $3 billion by the end of 1981 and hit $4 billion by the end of 1982. On a per capita basis, Brazil's debt would have to be some $160 billion to equal the debt burden faced by Uruguay's citizens.

During 1982, the profile of the foreign debt changed as it expanded, with public debt increasing dramatically while private debt contracted by some 9 percent.

Argentine investment in real estate was the major source of foreign investment in 1980 and 1981. But as the political and especially the economic situation deteriorated in Argentina and its peso was devalued, such investment declined precipitously from $289 million in 1980 to $49 million in 1981 to only $10 million in 1982. The drying up of these investment funds coupled with the government's attempts to defend the overvalued peso led to a loss of some $570 million in reserves during the year.

On November 29, 1982, the Uruguayan government abandoned major components of its economic program. Reversing its three-year-old policy of using an overvalued peso to fight inflation, the peso was allowed to float freely like its Argentine and Chilean counterparts. The exchange rate promptly sank from 14 to 34 to the dollar. In addition, the government announced the following measures:

1. Wages were raised by 15 percent as of January 1, 1983, to be followed by the freeing of wage negotiations.

2. Export duties were eliminated.

3. The long-standing plan to reduce all tariffs to a uniform 35 percent was abandoned in favor of a five-tiered plan ranging from a minimum of 10 percent to a maximum of 55 percent. (The previous maximum had been 75 percent.)

The original government program had called for a reduction of tariffs to a maximum rate of 35 percent over a five-year period. The new program sets tariff levels by the degree of elaboration of the imported item, with the lowest rate for raw materials and the highest for finished goods.

Early in April 1983, the government announced that it had renegotiated $711 million (some 90 percent) of its short-term debt and had received another

$240 million in fresh loans. The government estimated that servicing the medium- and long-term debt during 1983 would take 25 percent of export earnings. Under the new agreement, Uruguay will pay 10 percent of this amount as previously scheduled and the remaining 90 percent over six years with a two-year grace period, at an interest rate of 2.25 percent above the Libor rate. The same banks also agreed to lend $240 million to the Central Bank on the same terms.

In addition, the regime negotiated a standby agreement with the International Monetary Fund for $410 million. Under this agreement, Uruguay pledged to hold inflation to 40 percent and reduce its current-accounts deficit from the more than 3 percent of GDP experienced in 1982 to 2 percent in 1983 and 0.75 percent in 1984. Since wages and pensions represent 70 percent of the budget, restrictions on spending in these areas can be expected if the regime has any hope of living up to the agreement.

The government's decision to devalue, in the face of massive reserve losses, in order to stimulate exports held the risk of rekindling inflation. To no one's surprise, inflation, given the devaluation, was 20 percent for the first two months of 1983, matching the total rate for all of 1982. The only reason the rate for all of 1983 might stay within the IMF target of 40 percent was that the recession showed no signs of abating.

Conclusion

The economic strategy employed by the regime sought a closer integration of Uruguay into the world economy both in terms of creating a more attractive investment climate and in letting the forces of the marketplace rationalize the use of resources in Uruguay. Aside from the stimulation of nontraditional exports through state subsidies and a now exhausted financial expansion based on a fleeting but fortuitous economic and political situation in Brazil and, especially, Argentina, the program has resulted in failure. There has been little direct foreign investment, few new jobs created in the export sector, an exponential increase in the foreign debt, and the dismantling of traditional industries producing for the local market. The timing of Uruguay's generals could not have been worse. They continued to open Uruguay's small and fragile economy to world market forces just as a severe recession was moving the industrialized countries back to various forms of protectionism.

Exchange rate policy was at the heart of the government's anti-inflation program. By keeping import prices low, it was felt, domestic producers would be forced to become more efficient and keep their prices down. The less efficient would not survive, but so be it. The Uruguayan government's decision to implement preannounced mini-devaluations starting in 1978 did help on the inflation front, but by 1981 the peso had effectively appreciated some 29 percent in value. The result was a less competitive export sector at the same time that a worldwide recession continued to deepen. The fight against inflation and the economic liberalization required belt tightening. Private consumption was reduced from 77 percent of GDP in 1973 to 63 percent in 1977, as real wages declined some 40 percent from 1971 to 1977. But the burden was not shared equally. During this same period, the employers' share of income went up 27 percent while labor's share declined by 34 percent.

The military government's priorities are also evident in the shift in government spending. During the early 1960s, education took 21 percent of the budget. By 1981, educational expenditures represented only 13.5 percent of budget outlays. Security expenditures rose from 14 percent of the budget to over 40 percent in recent years. Domestic policy is only half the story, however. Uruguay is extremely vulnerable to the international environment. This has been amply demonstrated at the global level, but even much closer to home, events over which it has no control can wreak havoc with policy. The Falklands war and devaluations in Brazil and Argentina are examples of events on Uruguay's borders that can turn the economy (for example, construction in Punta del Este) from boom to bust.

The Brazilian, Argentine, and Chilean economic debacles share much in common with Uruguay's. As in Uruguay, Chile's decision to fix the peso exchange rate to the dollar backfired as the value of the dollar rose in world markets, thus exacerbating the effect on exports produced by the worldwide recession. The dependent nature of all the Southern Cone economies has been painfully exhibited in recent years. The crushing debt burdens, harsh austerity measures required by the IMF, and the growing social and political unrest that accompanied them may be seen as a challenge to development models imposed on these societies by the military.

In Uruguay, however, the perceived threat to order and the free market that the crisis has provoked may lead to a hardening of the military's position on a return to civilian government. The three legalized parties—Blanco, Colorado, and the small Unión Cívica—demand general elections earlier than the military's November 1984 timetable, the lifting of all proscriptions on political leaders, and the full restoration of civil liberties. They are willing to accept the military's demand for the creation of a National Security Council, but argue that it should be established by future legislation rather than written into a new constitution. The military remained so insistent on its national security demands that the parties broke off negotiations in early July 1983. The government increased its repression in response, singling out a new group of student leaders and cracking down on an already heavily censored press. In mid-July, the military announced that while elections would still be held in

November 1984, it reserved the right to amend unilaterally the 1967 constitution.

If one looks at development in human terms, the regime has failed as miserably as it has in economic terms. Thousands of Uruguay's best professional, intellectual, and artistic minds are in exile. Now that a decade has passed, few really expect or intend to return. The university is a shambles, with little research of any technical merit or social relevance being conducted. Nearly a thousand political prisoners still languish in jail, and independent and leftist parties or trade unions remain illegal. The generals are still resisting the return of civilian government with the full restoration of civil liberties and a military under civilian control even as they hold out the promise of elections for the end of 1984.

The Uruguayan regime was successful at stifling political opposition, but it failed to provide substitute structures of participation and ultimately failed to revitalize the economy. The military's legacy to Uruguay has been eloquently captured by Juan Corradi in a superb essay on Argentina.

> The state withdraws from the public sphere to ensconce itself in the old *arcana dominationis* from whence it arbitrarily strikes in inappellable ways. To the underlying population, punishment arrives like the unfathomable act of a *deus absconditus*. They have to work out for themselves, like latter-day political Calvinists—the rules, the signs, that distinguish a "good" from a "bad" citizen. All they know is that their safety, their goods, their lives, are at stake. A subject in such straits becomes not only obedient, but potentially punitive of self and others. Fear then acquires a life of its own. It becomes its own object.[7]

The lack of success of the military's economic policies and its failure to achieve legitimacy or consensus would indicate that the plan to reinstitute a civilian government under military tutelage by March 1985 may have to be abandoned along with military rule—a final victim of the military's economic program, world economic conditions, and Uruguay's political culture.

Notes

1. Mario Blejer and Donald Mathieson, "The Preannouncement of Exchange Rate Changes as a Stabilization Instrument," *IMF Staff Papers* 28, no. 4 (December 1981): 761.

2. Ibid., pp. 763–64.

3. República Oriental del Uruguay, Ministry of Economy and Finance, "Economic Opening in Uruguay," *Uruguay Económico* 2, no. 2 (1981): 37.

4. This section benefited greatly from discussions with Mr. Mark Siegelman of the Office of International Trade Administration, U.S. Department of Commerce.

5. World Bank, *Uruguay: Economic Memorandum* (Washington, D.C., 1979), p. 33.

6. Valentín Arismendi, Speech to the American Association of Montevideo, May 22, 1980.

7. Juan Corradi, "The Mode of Destruction: Terror in Argentina," *Telos*, no. 54 (Winter 1983): 68.

Selected Bibliography

Baer, W., and M. Gillis, eds. *Export Diversification and the New Protectionism: The Experience of Latin America.* Urbana: University of Illinois, 1981.

Blejer, Mario, and Donald Mathieson. "The Preannouncement of Exchange Rate Changes as a Stabilization Instrument." *International Monetary Fund Staff Papers* 28, no. 4. Washington, D.C.: IMF, 1981.

Corradi, Juan. "The Mode of Destruction: Terror in Argentina." *Telos*, no. 54 (Winter 1983): 61–76.

Diaz-Alejandro, Carlos. "Southern Cone Stabilization Plans." In William Cline and Sidney Weintraub, eds., *Economic Stabilization in Developing Countries.* Washington, D.C.: Brookings Institution, 1981.

Economic Commission for Latin America. *Estudio Económico de América Latina: 1981–Uruguay.* New York: United Nations Economic and Social Council, 1982.

Finch, M. H. J. *A Political Economy of Uruguay Since 1870.* New York: St. Martin's Press, 1981.

Handleman, Howard, and Thomas G. Sanders, eds. *Military Governments and the Movement Toward Democracy in South America.* Bloomington: Indiana University Press, 1981.

Quarterly Economic Review of Uruguay, Paraguay. London: *Economist* Intelligence Unit, 1983. No. 1.

República Oriental del Uruguay, Dirección General de Estadística y Censos. *Anuario Estadístico.*

República Oriental del Uruguay, Ministry of Economy and Finance. "Economic Opening in Uruguay." *Uruguay Económico* 2, no. 2 (1981).

World Bank. *Uruguay: Economic Memorandum.* Washington, D.C., 1979 and 1982.

4   Brazil

Political Determinants
of Development

Werner Baer

Brazil's economic development since the early 1950s can be divided into three distinct periods—1950–1964, 1964–1973, and 1974–1983—differentiated by policy priorities and style of policymaking. A common denominator throughout these years was the process of industrialization and the growth of the state in allocating resources. Yet the way the state allowed the industrial sector to grow, the way it controlled and participated in the economy, and the way it handled sectoral, regional, and social imbalances differed considerably from period to period. This essay attempts to show how sociopolitical conditions in each period determined the economic policy structure.

Import–Substitution Industrialization, 1950–1964

During the 1950s, Brazil's government placed import-substitution industrialization (ISI) at the center of its economic development strategy.[1] The policy tools used to promote industry consisted of (1) protection of new industries through tariffs and exchange controls; (2) special incentives for foreign capital to establish production facilities in Brazil; (3) encouragement of maximum vertical integration of industrial enterprises, resulting in the appearance of many new domestic supplier firms; (4) the creation and/or expansion of state enterprises in basic industries (like steel) and public utilities

Table 4.1

Real Growth Rates

Year	Total	Industry	Agriculture
1950	6.5	11.3	1.5
1951	5.9	6.4	0.7
1952	3.7	5.0	9.1
1953	2.5	8.7	0.2
1954	10.1	8.7	7.9
1955	6.9	10.6	7.7
1956	3.2	6.9	−2.4
1957	8.1	5.7	9.3
1958	7.7	16.2	2.0
1959	5.6	11.9	5.3
1960	9.7	9.6	4.9
1961	10.3	10.6	7.6
1962	5.3	7.8	5.5
1963	1.5	0.2	1.0
1964	2.0	5.1	1.3

SOURCE: Fundação Getúlio Vargas, *Conjuntura Económica*, various issues.

to complement the growth of manufacturing enterprises; and (5) the establishment of the National Development Bank (BNDE) to provide long-term financing for state enterprises and, at a later stage, for the private sector.

Tables 4.1–4.3 show the positive impact of ISI policies in the 1950–1964 period. Industry was clearly the economy's leading sector, growing at an average yearly rate of 9.3 percent. Over the period, the structure of the economy changed to such an extent that by the early 1960s, industry's share of gross domestic product had surpassed that of agriculture. ·

The negative aspects of Brazil's ISI, which have been well documented in the literature,[2] include (1) neglect of agriculture, both in terms of the relative lack of investment and the absence of basic socioeconomic reforms; (2) neglect of exports, with no attempt to diversify them in accordance with the changing structure of the domestic economy and to eliminate the disincentives to exporting caused by an overvalued exchange rate; (3) inflationary pressures resulting from the rapid growth of government expenditures on ISI, the building of Brasília, the subsidization of price-controlled sectors, and the lag in the government's capacity to increase its revenues; (4) misallocation of resources due to extensive use of price controls in such areas as basic foodstuffs, public utilities, rents, and interest rates; (5) increased regional imbalances resulting from the location of most new industries in the advanced regions of the country; (6) proliferation of state enterprises, many of which practiced overemployment; and (7) the disappointing performance of industry as a generator of employment in a situation of high population growth and accelerating rural-urban migration.

Could these flaws in the ISI process have been avoided by wiser policies? Given the political milieu surrounding these events, it is doubtful that a substantially different path could have been followed.

The ISI decade of the 1950s was dominated by the presidencies of Getúlio Vargas and Juscelino Kubitschek,[3] who were elected in an open democratic system and depended on various socioeconomic groups to govern the country. The emerging system of populist politics was

> characterized by an emphasis on the urban electorate, with little, if any, tendency to institutionalize linkages between voter and government; concerned not about programmatic but pragmatic interests, the populist politician sought votes only to gain public office. Once successful, the populist used his position of influence not in the service of the electorate or the public good, but in the narrow, parochial sense of satisfying his clientele or political following. A populist politician represents clients who are able to deliver the popular vote needed for election. To maintain this arrangement, the politician must have access to payoffs: jobs, contracts, rewards, etc., which only the bureaucracy and central government can provide. In return, it is tacitly understood that he will not attempt to introduce real structural changes or to disturb the equilibrium of power between the central government's preeminence in policy-making and its clients nationally.[4]

Thomas Skidmore, in reviewing the Vargas years, feels that it "would be inaccurate to say that he placed top priority on a full-fledged industrialization

Table 4.2

Changes in the Sectoral Shares of Gross Domestic Product
(percentages; in current prices)

	1947	1953	1957	1960	1966
Agriculture	27.6	26.1	22.8	22.6	19.1
Industry	19.8	23.7	24.4	25.2	27.2
Other Sectors	52.6	50.2	52.8	52.2	53.7
Total:	100.0	100.0	100.0	100.00	100.0

SOURCE: Fundação Getúlio Vargas, *Conjuntura Econômica*, various issues.

Table 4.3

Measures of Inflation
(yearly percentage change)

Year	Cost of Living: Rio de Janeiro	Implicit GDP Deflator
1950		11.2
1951	10.8	12.0
1952	20.4	13.2
1953	17.6	15.3
1954	25.6	21.4
1955	18.9	16.8
1956	21.8	23.2
1957	13.4	13.2
1958	17.3	11.1
1959	51.9	29.1
1960	23.8	26.3
1961	42.9	33.3
1962	55.8	54.8
1963	80.2	78.0
1964	86.6	87.8

SOURCE: Fundação Getúlio Vargas, *Conjuntura Econômica*, various issues.

policy at the expense of all short-term goals. Neither Vargas's temperament, nor his political style, nor Brazilian political conditions would have permitted such a single-minded approach."[5] He dealt with short-run problems in a heterogeneous way since "on the external side he had to worry about the balance of payments and the need to adjust the ingredients so as to avoid chronic deficits. On the internal side he faced the problem of inflation, with its resulting social tensions, and the need to devise an investment strategy that would maximize the social as well as the economic benefits of further development."[6]

Vargas backed the Joint Brazil–United States Economic Development Commission's various recommendations, which, among other policies, implied the facilitation of foreign investment to achieve rapid industrialization. For political reasons, however, he also appealed to nationalistic, antiforeign groups by such steps as the founding of Petrobras, which gave the state a monopoly over oil exploration, and the enactment of stringent profit remittance laws. According to Skidmore, "Vargas' problem was to maintain the delicate balance between orthodoxy and nationalism in economic policy.

Attacks on foreign capital, for example, had to be balanced by exchange liberalization."[7]

The growing inflation under Vargas was also the result of political accommodation of the working classes, which received hefty wage increases, the costs of which producers were allowed to pass on.[8]

Kubitschek, even more than Vargas, stressed industrialization as the cornerstone of his economic program, but to win political support he followed a policy of "trying to find something for everyone while avoiding any direct conflict with his enemies."[9] The building of Brasília was designed, in part, to generate self-confidence among Brazilians and to divert attention from the many socioeconomic problems that Kubitschek was not in a position to resolve. He offered business groups credit and protection and appeased the landowning classes by continuing support for the coffee sector. "Kubitschek, like Vargas before him, never raised the land question in a way other than to suggest politically innocuous measures such as the expansion of rural credit, or the improvement of food distribution through the construction of new storage facilities."[10] The urban working class received additional generous wage settlements.

Kubitschek's politics of nonconfrontation increased inflationary pressures, and the politically inspired price controls (food, public utilities, interest rates) and subsidies led to both severe distortion in the allocation of resources and additional inflation.[11]

The overvaluation of the cruzeiro in those years resulted from the reluctance of policymakers to devalue the exchange rate in accordance with the inflation rate. The motivation for this reluctance was, in part, the fear of further inflationary pressures that devaluation brings and the desire to provide new industries with cheap imported inputs.

The fact that the overvaluation of the cruzeiro might discourage exports, especially of the nontraditional variety, was of little concern at the time since ISI was supposed to make the country less dependent on international trade. It gradually became clear, however, that ISI only changed the type of import dependence. While it decreased the importation of finished consumer goods, it also led to increased demand for imported inputs into the new industries, such as raw materials and special capital goods. The neglect of exports and the antiexport bias of exchange rate policies gradually placed Brazil in a dangerous balance of payments position.

In retrospect, however, one could make a case that the neglect of exports was politically unavoidable. ISI depended on foreign investment, and a major incentive to foreign capital was the large protected domestic market. Had the Brazilian government conditioned the establishment of foreign-owned firms on the massive exportation of Brazilian-produced goods, the multinationals might have refused to move into Brazil. Only after inducing foreign firms to invest massive funds in Brazilian production facilities did the government have the power to pressure them into exporting.

The neglect of regional balance is understandable from an economic point of view since it would have been extremely wasteful to enforce regional equity in the location of industries that depended on both economies of scale and external economies. This was politically acceptable for a while since in the 1950s governments did not attempt to accomplish basic structural reforms in a region like the Northeast and thus did not disturb traditional local powerholders. Only the severe drought in the late 1950s forced Kubitschek to found the Superintendancy for Development of the Northeast (SUDENE). The new agency presented a plan both for the transfer of resources to the region and for structural reforms, but it had little impact prior to 1964.[12]

ISI also involved a substantial growth of state participation in the economy. The state intervened through tariff and exchange controls, the fixing of selected prices, the establishment of public enterprises in key sectors complementary to private domestic and foreign industries, and the expansion of state banking (for example, the BNDE and state-owned commercial banks).[13] There was little political resistance to the economic growth of the state, as most politically influential economic groups benefited from it. The purists of the orthodox liberal economic school were relatively unimportant at the time.

Consolidation and Renewed Expansion, 1964–1973

The political turmoil of the early 1960s and the accompanying economic stagnation may have resulted, in part, from the many contradictions or imbalances arising from ISI.[14] Whether these problems could have been solved in an open democratic system has not been satisfactorily answered.[15]

The change of regime in 1964 resulted in a series of authoritarian governments whose economic policymakers felt that recovery from past excesses of ISI and future growth depended on controlling inflation, eliminating price distortions, modernizing capital markets (which would lead to increased savings), creating incentives to direct private investments into priority areas and sectors, attracting foreign capital (both private and official), diversifying exports, and efficiently increasing public investments in infrastructure and heavy-industry projects.

Among the principal policy actions taken were (1) strong stabilization measures, including restrictive fiscal and monetary actions; (2) drastic upward readjustments of controlled prices; (3) restrictive wage policies; (4) introduction of indexing to encourage savings and noninflationary financing of

Table 4.4
Real Growth Rate of Selected Sectors

Year	Total	Industry	Agriculture
1962–1967*	3.7	3.9	4.0
1968	11.2	13.3	4.4
1969	9.0	12.1	3.7
1970	8.8	10.3	1.0
1971	13.3	14.3	11.4
1972	11.7	13.3	4.1
1973	14.0	15.0	3.5
1974	9.8	9.9	8.5
1975	5.6	6.2	3.4

*Average yearly rates

SOURCE: Fundação Getúlio Vargas, *Conjuntura Económica*, various issues.

government deficits; (5) tax and credit incentives for investments in backward regions and such favored sectors as exports, capital markets, tourism, and reforestation; (6) the establishment of compulsory workers' social security funds, which were deposited in the government savings bank, the BNDE, and the newly established Housing Bank (BNH); (7) a considerable amount of autonomy for government enterprises in pricing, investment, and employment decisions; (8) a crawling peg system to keep the cruzeiro from becoming overvalued since inflation, though declining, continued; and (9) collaboration in planning with such international agencies as the U.S. Agency for International Development, the World Bank, and the Inter-American Development Bank, which led to the financing of large government projects.[16]

The positive impact of these actions was felt after a three-year lag, when Brazil underwent a spectacular growth period from 1968 to 1973: real GDP grew at an average yearly rate of 11.3 percent, and the industrial growth rate was 12.6 percent (see Tables 4.4–4.5); inflation was gradually reduced, reaching 13.7 percent in 1973;[17] and the savings rate increased from 17.5 percent in 1959 to over 21 percent in 1973. The rate of growth of exports averaged about 15 percent per year for the late 1960s and early 1970s, and by the mid-1970s a substantial proportion of exports consisted of nontraditional goods, over one-third being manufactured goods.

The negative aspect of this period was the inequitable distribution of the growth achieved. The 1970 census showed a substantial increase in the concentration of income since 1960 (see Table 4.6). Although considerable controversy emerged about the causes of the increased inequality, most writers

Table 4.5

Measures of Inflation

Year	Internal Prices	Cost of Living: Rio de Janeiro	Implicit GDP Deflator
1964	91.9	86.6	87.8
1965	34.5	45.5	55.4
1966	38.2	41.2	38.6
1967	25.0	24.1	28.8
1968	25.5	24.5	27.8
1969	20.1	24.3	20.3
1970	19.3	20.9	18.2
1971	19.5	20.2	17.3
1972	15.7	16.4	17.4
1973	15.5	13.7	20.5
1974	34.5	27.7	31.5

SOURCE: Fundação Getúlio Vargas, Conjuntura Económica, various issues.

attributed a large part of the blame to the policies followed by the post-1964 governments.[18] That is, the concentration was the result, in large measure, of the restrictive wage policies during the stabilization program of the second half of the 1960s (real minimum wages fell continuously in the second half of the 1960s), the emphasis on developing capital-intensive industries (for example, the petrochemical sector), and the tax incentive programs, which benefited the higher-income groups.

An ironic twist in this period, dominated by a regime ideologically committed to strengthening the market economy, was the rapid expansion of the state sector. In order to raise efficiency, state firms were given a high degree of independence to set prices, to determine their own investment programs (which included expansion into new fields of activities, thus turning firms like Petrobras and Companhia Vale do Rio Doce into conglomerates), and to pursue independent employment policies. In the financial sector, state institutions also grew very rapidly due to deposits of new social security funds. In most sectors the growth of the state in the economy acted as a complement to other ownership sectors by providing basic inputs and finance and was thus not seen at the time as being detrimental to private property. Only in the mid-1970s did the economic expansion of the state become a political issue.[19]

The economic policies of this period were also a function of the prevailing political situation, i.e., an authoritarian, often quite repressive, regime. Skidmore, in reviewing this period, asks: "Did the authoritarian system make possible options that had been ruled out for a democratic, representative government of divided and sharply defined constitutional powers? There is much evidence that it did. . . By 1964 it was doubtful if any democratically elected president could carry out the stabilization program that was essential if Brazil was to resume growth within the capitalist system. It was either stabilization under an authoritarian government or social revolution under a government of the Left."[20]

Not only was an authoritarian regime necessary to enforce stabilization measures, but also to act as an umbrella for those managing state enterprises according to efficiency rules, with little regard to the equity consequences of their actions, such as higher utility prices or unemployment. Protection from open debate or popular pressures on the formulation of economic policies also enabled the government to pass legislative decrees favorable to foreign investors, such as the repeal of strict profit remittance laws or export incentives to foreign firms. The drastic modernization of the tax system, which increased the number of individual income taxpayers from 470,000 in 1967 to more than 4 million in 1969, was made easier to administer under decree rule since "under an elected government these new taxpayers could have been expected to lobby effectively to undermine such a dramatic change in tax policy."[21] Similarly, the ability of the government to rule by decree facilitated the widespread use of tax incentives for favored regions and sectors.

Growth Under External Shocks and Domestic Political Opening, 1974–1983

General Ernesto Geisel assumed the presidency in March 1974, a few months after the first oil price shock. He was committed to a gradual political

Table 4.6
Changes in Income Distribution

	PERCENTAGE	
Group	*1960*	*1970*
Lowest 40 Percent	11.2	9.0
Next 40 Percent	34.3	27.8
Next 15 Percent	27.0	27.0
Top 5 Percent	27.4	36.3
Total	100.0	100.0

SOURCE: Calculated from Fundação Instituto Brasiliero de Geographia e Estatística, *Censo Demográfico, 1970.*

opening and to policies to ameliorate the extremely uneven distribution of income. The latter had been the subject of an increasing amount of domestic and international criticism.[22] These sociopolitical goals would obviously be more easily achieved in a rapidly expanding economy where no specific group would be asked to make sacrifices in absolute terms for the sake of redistribution. In addition, it was important to Geisel, as the successor of President Emílio Médici, under whose government Brazil experienced its unprecedented boom, to preside over a continually expanding economy, thus avoiding invidious comparisons that might undermine his political authority.

Given these circumstances, the refusal of the Brazilian government to adjust the economy to the petroleum price revolution of 1973–1974 is understandable. In fact, every effort was made to maintain high growth rates, and the Second National Development Plan envisioned large investments and rates of growth for most sectors, including basic industries, economic and social infrastructure, and mining.[23] The plan and subsequent government policies contained no attempts to make choices in the light of scarce resources.

Even though Brazil had achieved high savings rates and made great strides in amplifying and diversifying exports, the drastic rise of its import bill (from U.S. $6.2 billion in 1973 to $12.6 billion in 1974) could be paid only by massive foreign borrowing. This was made easy by the huge supply of Eurodollars, which resulted from the accumulation of petrodollars in the international banking system and the decline in demand for funds by the recession-bound economies of Europe and the United States.

Besides maintaining high growth rates, the Geisel administration was also committed to raising real wages. A rise in the standard of living of the average Brazilian was thought to be important for the gradual political opening of the country. As Tables 4.8–4.9 show, real wages rose throughout most of the 1970s.

For many industrial enterprises, the rising cost of labor was accompanied after 1974 by the increasing costs of fuel and related inputs. Since the government did not want to adopt a confrontational stance by explicitly allocating shares of the national product, it allowed firms to raise their prices more or less in accordance with increased costs of production. A large part of Brazil's economy was price-controlled in the 1970s through such agencies as the Interministerial Council for Prices (CIP), which was fairly lenient in allowing cost increases to be passed on through price adjustments.

Thus the ambition of the government to keep investment and growth at high levels in all major sectors and to raise the standard of living of workers and its unwillingness to force the productive sector to absorb increased costs led to a competitive fight for shares of the GNP through a wage and price spiral. The

Table 4.7
Real Growth and Rates of Inflation, 1972–1982
(percentages)

		Inflation Measures			
Year	GDP	Industry	Agriculture	General Price	Consumer Price
1972	11.7	13.4	4.1	16.8	14.0
1973	14.0	16.0	3.6	16.2	13.7
1974	9.5	9.1	8.2	33.8	33.8
1975	5.6	5.6	5.2	30.1	31.2
1976	9.7	12.5	2.9	48.2	44.8
1977	5.4	3.9	11.8	38.6	43.1
1978	4.8	7.4	−2.6	40.5	38.7
1979	6.8	6.6	5.0	76.8	76.0
1980	7.9	7.9	6.3	110.2	86.3
1981	−1.9	−5.4	6.8	95.2	100.6
1982	1.0	1.0	−2.5	99.7	101.8

SOURCE: Fundação Getúlio Vargas, *Conjuntura Econômica*, various issues.

monetary base to accommodate the growing inflation was provided by a complex financial system that had developed since the mid-1960s.[24]

Throughout the 1970s, high growth rates (see Table 4.7), though not as high as in the 1968–1973 boom years, assured real gains for most sectors and social groups. These rates were sustained by the avoidance of a real transfer of resources abroad. Through the device of foreign borrowing, this meant that for many years Brazil transferred to future generations the payment of the real price of the petroleum price revolution.

Although economic growth was sustained until 1980, the rate of inflation increased, reaching the 100 percent level at the end of the decade (see Table 4.7), and the country's foreign indebtedness jumped from $12.6 billion in 1973 to $43.3 billion in 1978 and close to $90 billion in mid-1983. The large debt and the high interest rates of the late 1970s and early 1980s increased the debt-servicing burden to such an extent that by 1981, interest and amortization amounted to over 65 percent of export receipts.

The justification for this tremendous increase in Brazil's indebtedness was that investment resources were being applied to projects that would result in either further import substitution or the expansion of the country's export capacity. The latter was estimated in the light of optimistic views about the

Table 4.8
Real Minimum Wages
(1965 cruzeiros)

Year	Rio de Janeiro	Sao Paulo
1965 (December)	52.93	50.71
1967	53.14	50.75
1968	52.88	50.04
1969	51.23	49.13
1970	50.84	50.20
1971	51.87	50.17
1972	54.20	50.88
1973	55.34	51.83
1974	49.93	47.06
1975	53.81	51.47
1976	53.56	53.74
1977	53.92	54.86
1978	55.03	55.30
1979	58.80	62.18
1980	62.29	66.43
1981	63.98	71.72
1982	62.64	72.81

SOURCE: Banco do Brasil, *Boletim.*

future of Brazil's export markets, which had expanded very rapidly since the late 1960s.

In 1979, when Geisel's successor as president, João Baptista Figueiredo, took office, it was becoming evident that growth could not continue with an increasing debt and rising rates of inflation. To make matters worse, international pressures had forced the government to commit itself to the gradual removal of fiscal and credit subsidies to exports. Given the need to continue the rapid expansion of exports, however, this made it necessary for the government to increase the rate of devaluation of the cruzeiro. The government had allowed the cruzeiro to become overvalued (the rate of devaluation lagged behind the difference between the rate of inflation in Brazil and that of its trading partners). Because of the export-incentive program, the overvaluation had not hurt exports in the past. The removal of tax incentives and subsidized credit for exporters, however, called for an increased devaluation as a compensating measure. The problem was that the greater devaluation would augment inflationary pressures and would substantially increase financial burdens of firms with foreign debts.

Although a slowdown seemed a logical means of decreasing the growth of imports and dampening inflation, Figueiredo's commitment to a political opening leading to direct elections for all offices except the presidency made this a difficult choice. The policies of his economic ministers wavered for two years, and it was only in 1981–1982 that economic expansion was brought to a dramatic halt.

The world recession substantially reduced Brazil's export expansion and forced the government to renegotiate its debt with the International Monetary Fund and other creditors. The government instituted measures—such as a drastic reduction of government investment, high real interest rates, substantial devaluation of the cruzeiro—that were designed to solve the balance of payments and debt-servicing problems but forced austerity on the population.

In evaluating the economic policy actions of the Geisel and early Figueiredo periods in political terms, it is clear that the gradual de-authoritarianization of Brazil explains much of what happened. The political opening was perceived as requiring a good economic performance in terms of growth and the avoidance of a confrontation in the fight for shares among various socioeconomic groups or between the government and specific economic sectors. The resulting inflation was tolerable, as most savings were

Table 4.9
Growth of Average Wages

Year	Money Wages[a]	Real Wages[a]	Real Average Industrial Wages[b]
1973	23.6	8.2	10.0
1974	30.1	3.4	−3.2
1975	41.8	12.9	10.1
1976	49.8	6.9	2.1
1977	43.1	6.5	7.0
1978	−5.0	−43.7	11.9
1979	51.8	−7.0	−17.4
1980	114.3	28.0	5.7
1981	132.6	31.4	15.1
1982	122.9	32.2	—

[a] Associação Brasileira de Industria de Base wages.

[b] Eduardo M. Modiano, "A dinámica de salarios e preços na economia brasileira, 1966/81," *Pesquisa e Planejamento Económica*, April 1983, p. 65; real wages obtained by subtracting cost of living increases from money wage index supplied in article.

Source: Calculated from Fundação Getúlio Vargas, *Conjuntura Económica*, various issues; real wages=money wage index minus cost of living index.

protected by an indexing system. The increased foreign indebtedness was also tolerable as long as the export-incentive system made possible an over-valuation of the cruzeiro, which protected economic groups with large foreign debts.

Remarkably, the decline in growth and the increasing unemployment that began in 1981 did not interfere with the political opening and the November 1982 congressional and gubernatorial elections. In 1983, however, uncertainties increased as the recession continued and the country continuously renegotiated its debt. It is too early as of the date of this writing to ascertain whether the April 1983 riots in Sao Paulo represented an isolated incident or the prelude to increasing sociopolitical tensions as the stagnation continued.[25] It is also not clear whether the austerity measures begun in 1981 can be continued in an open political system.

Brazil's Extended Public Sector

Throughout this period the growth of the state sector continued. In the second half of the 1970s, there was a considerable amount of debate over the dangers of too much *estatização*, and a vocal group of domestic private sector critics conducted a campaign for the privatization of state enterprises. The Brazilian government reacted to these pressures by stating its intention to sell a large number of state enterprises to private interests. By 1983, however, the number of state firms sold was small, consisting mainly of bankrupt enterprises taken over by BNDE and gradually brought back to financial and operational health by technicians of the development bank.

The present importance of the state in the Brazilian economy is not the result of a carefully conceived scheme. It is the outcome of a number of circumstances that, in most cases, increasingly forced the government to intervene or participate in the country's economic system. These circumstances include reactions to international economic crises; the desire to control the activities of foreign capital, especially in the public utility and natural resource sectors; and the ambition to rapidly industrialize a backward economy.[26]

The presence of the state in Brazil's economy makes itself felt through different, but interrelated, institutional channels. These include the fiscal system, the central bank, the government (federal and state), commercial and development banks, the *autarquias* (federal and state sectoral production-control entities), productive enterprises, and the price control system. Regulation of prices in one form or another has pervaded the Brazilian economy since the early part of the century. Certain sectors, including foreign trade, also have production controls. Many key agricultural products, public utility rates, and a great number of manufactured products are regulated by state entities. In straight fiscal terms, government expenditures amounted to 21 percent of GDP in the early 1980s. This multifaceted intervention of the state in the economy is not monolithic. It has often been characterized, in fact, by a lack of coordination and communication among the various entities involved.

Since the early part of the century, the state (central regime and individual states) has grown as both a commercial and as an investment banker. In 1981 the Banco do Brasil (60 percent owned by the federal government and 40 percent by the public) accounted for almost 37 percent of the loans held by the 50 largest banks; all government banks accounted for 58 percent. The federal and state governments constitute the most powerful investment bankers in the Brazilian economy. Through the BNDE, the Bank of the Northeast, the BNH, and various development banks of individual states, they provide more than 70 percent of the loans devoted to investment. In sum, the state controls the financial "commanding heights."

In the directly productive sector, a 1981 survey of the 8,068 largest firms revealed that the share of net assets of state enterprises was almost 50 percent, of private Brazilian firms 40.2 percent, and of multinationals 10.4 percent. The share of sales of state firms was 25.5 percent, of private Brazilian firms 52.2 percent, and of multinationals 22.3 percent. Finally, state enterprises accounted for 18.4 percent of employment, private firms for 67.5 percent, and multinationals for 14.1 percent.

State investments are highly concentrated in certain basic industries. In mining the state is dominant, with 66 percent of assets. An idea of the sectoral distribution of sales can be obtained from Table 4.10. Multinationals and domestic private firms outweigh state enterprises in most manufacturing and in agriculture, although the state is strongly represented in metal products and chemicals. In steel, state firms account for two-thirds of sales. The state petroleum company, Petrobras, dominates petroleum exploration and refining and has steadily increased its share of gasoline distribution. Through subsidiaries, some of the giant state firms increasingly participate in joint ventures with multinationals. The state has developed an aviation industry. EMBRAER, a public firm run by the air force, produces small passenger and fighter planes. By the early 1980s, all public utilities were government enterprises.

The dynamism of many state firms has been characterized not only by expansion within their respective fields, but also by growth in areas that are complementary to their initial specialization. Petrobras and the state mining firm Companhia Vale do Rio Doce have expanded into, among other activities, fertilizers, fishing, bauxite mining and aluminum production, and cellulose.

Table 4.10
Share of Domestic, Foreign, and State Firms
in Total Sales, 1981
(percentages)

	Domestic	Foreign	State	Total
Domestic Dominated				
Housing Construction	100.0			100.0
Sales of Motor Vehicles	100.0			100.0
Communications	97.8		2.2	100.0
Clothing	95.1	4.9		100.0
Wood and Wood Products	91.9	8.1		100.0
Agriculture	95.0		5.0	100.0
Retail Sales	91.2	8.8		100.0
Heavy Construction	88.7	6.0	5.3	100.0
Supermarkets	81.3	4.7	14.0	100.0
Food	68.5	31.5		100.0
Paper and Cellulose	76.5	23.5		100.0
Nonmetallic Minerals	56.7	43.3		100.0
Metal Products	66.5	33.5		100.0
Foreign Dominated				
Wholesale Commerce	44.7	45.2	10.1	100.0
Machinery	40.5	55.3	4.2	100.0
Electrical Machinery	44.1	55.9		100.0
Automotive Parts	44.0	56.0		100.0
Textiles	45.5	54.5		100.0
Transportation Products	27.6	62.5	9.9	100.0
Beverage and Tobacco	31.0	69.0		100.0
Hygienic and Cleaning Goods	28.7	71.3		100.0
Plastics and Rubber Products	25.4	72.1	2.5	100.0
Communication, Office Products	16.9	76.2	6.9	100.0
Petroleum Distribution	10.8	59.2	30.0	100.0
Pharmaceuticals	19.5	80.5		100.0
Automobile Assembly	2.0	98.0		100.0
State Dominated				
Public Utilities			100.0	100.0
Chemicals and Petrochemicals	7.8	11.0	81.2	100.0
Mining	28.3	9.6	62.1	100.0
Steel	26.6	10.5	62.9	100.0
Transport Services	43.9		56.1	100.0

SOURCE: "Os Melhores e Maiores," *Exame*, September 1982.

The government also controls most savings. Its own savings and government-administered forced savings through various types of social security funds amounted to 70 percent of total savings in the early 1980s.[27] Thus a substantial amount of private investment is financed from public resources, like the development bank. Little private capital is raised through the issue of new shares, and the most actively traded stocks are those of government-dominated firms. Therefore, financing expansion of private domestic firms depends on retained internal funds, foreign financing, or domestic funds from government financial institutions.[28]

The ad hoc nature of the growth of state involvement in Brazil's economy accounts, in part, for the lack of an analytical framework that explains the nature and functioning of its state capitalist economy. What sort of resource allocation paradigm would be adequate for a society in which private property is prevalent and multinationals are an important part of the economy, but the state is both an important regulator and a direct agent? Although there exists little theory to guide the construction of an adequate paradigm, a consideration of alternative hypotheses about the control of resource allocation may provide a starting point.

First, one could claim that despite the large role of the state, market forces in the broadest sense determine the allocation of resources and the direction of development. State enterprises respond to market signals much as do private enterprises. State planning serves the purpose of mobilizing and channeling savings to potential bottleneck industries. In this view, the state is no more than an adjunct to market forces despite its preponderance.

The weakness of this theory is that it ignores the many politically set prices and the politically motivated allocation of investment funds. The minimum wage, for example, is a political price and has important income distribution ramifications. Government intervention in many markets— products, technology, finance, imports—through incentives, restrictions, and price controls is another example. In other words, public policy and its underlying politics need to be more adequately incorporated into this analysis.

Another perspective is that state policy serves the interests of foreign and national industrialists and is largely controlled by them. These groups, it is claimed, need public planning to ensure the vitality of the private sector. With the government providing needed infrastructure, private firms are free to produce, shape consumption, and make a profit. Government-set prices guarantee that the market functions to the benefit of the private producers.

Although this approach links political to economic analysis, it does not account for the aggressive expansion of state enterprises at the expense of the private sector. In the regulatory area, the power of public bureaucracies over the private sector has increased substantially. The *estatização* debate in the 1970s is evidence of the tension between the public and private sectors.

Still another hypothesis is that technocrats and military entrepreneurs have assumed dominance of the allocation of resources. The very system of free enterprise that the military and technocrats sought to save with government intervention has now bred new sources of independent economic and political power: public enterprise and its bureaucracy. They form an independent group relatively free from the influence of the private sector and try to allocate resources to expand their own power and wealth.

This hypothesis may be generalizing from a trend that has yet to mature. It assumes the formation of a new class and may ignore the degree of decentralization in the federal enterprises and bureaucracies; in reality the technocrats hardly work as a group. More important, even if state entrepreneurs and bureaucrats occupy positions of widespread power, it is not clear that their interests as a group are fundamentally different from those of private producers.

Power struggles are certain to exist within the government sector, especially between central planners and the executives of government enterprises. Although Brazil's public enterprises are subordinate to specific ministries (or to holding companies that, in turn, are subordinate to ministries), they do not necessarily follow commands issued from above. The managers of public firms are obviously much more conversant with the industry (the technical aspects, the market structure) than most of the personnel in a ministry and are thus often in a position to influence the ministry rather than the other way around.

Disciplining an insubordinate firm could have dire consequences for a ministry since a demoralized state firm could become ineffective or rebel in ways that are difficult to control. Older public firms have over the years developed political contacts that they use to bring a ministry into line.[29]

Recently one type of insubordination has placed the central government in a dilemma. Public enterprises spending beyond their approved budgets have openly challenged the state to stop them—that is, to run the risk of having a state entity renege on its financial obligations and thus jeopardize the credit of all state enterprises and the government.

Brazil also faces the problem of controlling abuses by public enterprises of their monopoly positions. Public enterprises having a monopoly in the manufacture and sale of a crucial product may, for example, engage in various games with their customers, such as delaying deliveries unless special commissions are paid on the side. On another level, there is always the temptation for directors of public enterprises that purchase millions of dollars worth of equipment to award contracts to domestic and multinational enterprises that pay the largest commissions.

The position and functioning of a state enterprise is also affected by the prevailing political regime. A closed authoritarian regime, like the one that prevailed until recently in Brazil, may offer more opportunities for state firms to pursue efficiency goals. For instance, there may be less pressure on state firms to charge subsidized prices for favored groups or to locate new facilities in backward areas.

The basic problem, however, is that over time the absence of account-ability to groups outside the power structure can lead to abuses of power, both in terms of decisions on pricing and investment and in terms of corruption.

A more open system forces the management of a public enterprise to account for its behavior, which is regularly scrutinized by opposition groups. There is also more pressure on public firms to attend to the needs of various socioeconomic groups. But an open system can also lead to abuses, such as forcing investments whose political returns outweigh their economic returns, leading to overemployment and investing in or developing subsidiary activities in economically weak sectors.

When the Brazilian government tried to reduce the rate of growth of the economy in the early 1980s, it had difficulty controlling the activities of state enterprises. The most important had developed their own political power base and for a long time were able to maintain their investment activities and their purchases of foreign equipment against the wishes of the central economic policymakers. The latter, however, also acted in contradictory ways. In 1981 and 1982, in a desperate effort to avoid a balance of payments crisis, they goaded state enterprises with the best international credit standing to borrow more abroad than was necessary for their activities in order to bring more foreign exchange into Brazil. It was difficult for many state firms to respect government orders to refrain from investment projects when they were being asked to borrow abroad for investment purposes.

The government created a new agency—the Secretariat for the Control of State Enterprises (SEST)—in 1979 in order to systematize control and coordination of public firms. By 1983, it had seemingly begun to achieve effective control over the activities of state enterprises. However, it became clear that it was impossible to curtail the state sector drastically by selling public enterprises to the private sector since few private firms had the necessary capital. Also, the complementarity of the state, domestic private, and multinational sectors was such that a reduction in the level of activities of state firms severely affected the private sector. Many private firms depended on state enterprises to market their products and provide inputs.[30]

Conclusions

The relation between the prevailing political regime and the economic policies that successive Brazilian governments have followed is close. Over the entire period covered, there was a general consensus that industrialization was a cornerstone of the country's growth and development. In the 1950–1964 period, the constellation of interest groups that had to be appeased in the open democratic system explains what economists would judge on technical grounds to have been basic policy inconsistencies. It is doubtful, however, that an avoidance of the "mistakes" that resulted in unbalanced growth among sectors, in inflation, in balance of payments problems due to an overvalued exchange rate, and in the neglect of export promotion could have made the governments of Vargas and Kubitschek politically viable.

The measures taken to redress some of the inconsistencies of the 1950–1964 period—the stabilization program, the use of tax incentives, the freedom given to state enterprises, the indexing system, and the forced savings program—seemed to require an authoritarian regime in order to restrain the socioeconomic groups whose interests were being sacrificed.

Similarly, the gradual political reopening in the 1974–1983 period helps explain the government's willingness to increase the country's foreign indebtedness and to tolerate the resurgence of inflation in order to maintain a rate of growth high enough to minimize the impact of the increasingly liberated and vocal interest groups. The crisis of the early 1980s, which has forced Brazil to adopt severe austerity measures, bringing the rate of growth down to very low levels and creating high unemployment, has so far taken place in an atmosphere of continued political opening. It remains to be seen if an open democratic system can tolerate the austerity measures being forced on the government by the international economic crisis and thus break with past experience.

Notes

1. Werner Baer, *The Brazilian Economy: Growth and Development*, 2nd ed. (New York: Praeger, 1983), chap. 4.

2. Ibid.; Joel Bergsman, *Brazil: Industrialization and Trade Policies* (New York: Oxford University Press, 1970); and Donald E. Syvrud, *Foundations of Brazilian Economic Growth* (Stanford: Hoover Institution Press, 1974), chap. 2.

3. For a summary of the period, see Thomas Skidmore, *Politics in Brazil, 1930–1964* (New York: Oxford University Press, 1967), chaps. 3–5.

4. Riordan Roett, *Brazil: Politics in a Patrimonial Society*, rev. ed. (New York: Praeger, 1978), pp. 38–39.

5. Skidmore, *Politics in Brazil*, p. 93.

6. Ibid.

7. Ibid., p. 100.

8. Ibid., p. 134.

9. Ibid., p. 167.

10. Ibid., p. 168.

11. Werner Baer, "The Inflation Controversy in Latin America," *Latin American Research Review*, Spring 1967, pp. 4–6.

12. Baer, *The Brazilian Economy*, chap. 11.

13. Ibid., chap. 9.

14. Skidmore, *Politics in Brazil*, chap. 8.

15. For an interesting interpretation of the 1964 change of regime, see Gustavo Gomes, "The Roots of State Intervention in Brazil" (Ph.D. diss., University of Illinois, 1983).

16. For details, see Baer, *The Brazilian Economy*, chap. 5.

17. There has been some controversy concerning the low point that inflation reached in 1973 because of the way in which the statistical data were treated. Some critics have claimed that the inflation rate never fell below 20 percent.

18. Ricardo Tolipan and Arthur Carolos Tinelli, eds., *A Controvérsia Sobre Distribuição de Renda e Desenvolvimento* (Rio de Janeiro: Zahar Editores, 1975), especially articles by Fishlow and Hoffman; see also Edmar L. Bacha, "Issues and Evidence on Recent Brazilian Economic Growth," *World Development*, January–February 1977, pp. 47–67.

19. Baer, *The Brazilian Economy*, chap. 9.

20. Thomas Skidmore, "Politics and Economic Policy Making in Authoritarian Brazil, 1967–71," in Alfred Stepan, ed., *Authoritarian Brazil: Origins, Policies, and Future* (New Haven, Conn.: Yale University Press, 1973), p. 19.

21. Ibid., p. 22.

22. Tolipan and Tinelli, *A Controvérsia*.

23. Republica Federative do Brasil, *Projeto do II Plano Nacional de Desenvolvimento, PND (1975–1979)* (Brasília, 1974).

24. Baer, *The Brazilian Economy*, chap. 10.

25. For details, see *Veja*, April 13, 1983.

26. For a detailed description of the growth of the state in the Brazilian economy, see Baer, *The Brazilian Economy*, chap. 9; and Peter Evans, *Dependent Development: The Alliance of Multinational, State and Local Capital in Brazil* (Princeton, N.J.: Princeton University Press, 1979).

27. Baer, *The Brazilian Economy*, pp. 216–17.

28. For a detailed analysis of the functioning of Brazil's private sector, see Annival V. Villela and Werner Baer, *O Setor Privado Nacional: Problemas e Políticas Para Seu Fortalecimento*, Coleção Relatório de Pesquisa, no. 46 (Rio de Janeiro: IPEA/INPES, 1980).

29. Fernando Antonio Roquette Reis, "A Administração Federal Direta e as Empresas Publicas: Analise de Suas Relações, Recommendações e Alternativas para Seu Aprimoramento," in *A Empresa Pública no Brasil: Uma Abordagem Multidisciplinar* (Brasília: IPEA, 1980).

30. Baer, *The Brazilian Economy*, chap. 9.

5   Peru

Military and Civilian Political Economy

David Scott Palmer

Peru is one of the many Latin American countries to experience extended periods of both democratic and authoritarian rule since the early 1960s. Between 1963 and 1983, Peru had civilian governments for more than eight years and military governments for almost twelve. Both types of regimes pursued policies—successfully and unsuccessfully—designed to stimulate economic growth and economic development. Both were constrained by international and domestic factors largely beyond their control, and both committed errors in policymaking that had adverse effects on growth and development.

Yet before concluding that there is little difference between authoritarian and democratic policymaking in terms of economic change in Peru or that military and civilian regimes alike are largely prisoners of forces beyond their control, we should analyze the major policy initiatives of the period. Few specialists on Peru would disagree that the country in the 1980s had changed greatly since the 1960s, and most would conclude that government policies accounted for a large portion of the observable differences.

A closer examination of the period reveals a growing willingness by civilian and military regimes alike to use government policy instruments to try to accomplish national development objectives. Also observable is the fact that a government's ability to accomplish its objectives is much affected by the actions of its predecessors—for better or for worse. Furthermore, the economic consequences of policies often differed from the political consequences. In other words, we must distinguish between the political and economic effects of policies to understand what has happened in and to Peru since the 1960s.

After examining the basic constraints on both types of governments in recent years, this paper analyzes the most significant policy initiatives in terms of their implications for economic growth and development of the civilian government of Fernando Belaúnde Terry (1963–1968), of the Revolutionary Government of the Armed Forces (GRFA) of (1968–1980) in both of its phases, and of the second democratically elected administration of Belaúnde (1980–). Finally the paper assesses the effects of these policies on the political economy of Peru, with special reference to the differences between democratic and authoritarian regimes.

Constraints on Public Policy in Peru

The constraints on decisionmaking and implementation of decisions are both numerous and complex. They include factors near and remote, domestic and international, temporary and permanent, institutional and personal. Both decisionmakers and the policy process are constrained by multiple factors that operate like a funnel to narrow options and choices as the policymaking process moves toward, and then through, the funnel on its way to becoming policy output. That output in turn affects the surrounding environment, which then has an impact on some of the constraints, thereby affecting future policy initiatives.

In Peru, one of the most permanent and important constraints is that of geography.[1] Much of the terrain is rugged mountains; most of the rest is heavily forested jungle. This makes communication networks difficult, expensive to build and maintain, and often hazardous. Geography also limits the quantity and quality of arable land to perhaps as little as 10 percent of the land area, one of the lowest percentages in Latin America.[2] Furthermore, prevailing wind and ocean current patterns make for very erratic rainfall over most of the country except the jungle areas. The cold Humboldt Current off the Peruvian coast is rich with marine life and contributes to the maintenance of guano deposits on the coastal islands. But the cold current also keeps virtually the entire coastal plain of Peru rainless. Most coastal agriculture is therefore limited to river valleys and dependent on expensive irrigation systems. In turn, highland agriculture is precariously balanced between limited soil and erratic rainfall.

The large Indian population is also an important constraint. It constitutes about 35 percent of the population today (compared with over 50 percent historically). Because its members speak Quechua or Aymará, dress in traditional garb, and practice traditional subsistence occupations like farming and weaving, the Indian population participates only at the margins of the national society and economy. If indeed it is true that the Indian filter serves to slow social mobilization and decrease concomitant new demands on the national government, it is also the case that the substantial Indian sector does not consume the products of the national, modern economy.[3] Because the Indian population tends to be concentrated in the sierra of the south-central and southern parts of Peru and has a different language, lifestyle, and dress, one can still speak of the country as a dual society.[4]

This highlights another basic constraint: Peru is an intermediate-sized country with an intermediate-sized population, many of whom do not consume the products of the modern sector. Its resources, both human and material, are relatively small, and it has not had the capacity historically to deal on an equal basis with large countries or large corporations. Its scope for independent action to cope either with domestic or international issues is limited.

Another enduring element is that of geology. Peru boasts significant deposits of many mineral resources, including gold, silver, lead, copper, mercury, tungsten, molybdenum, iron, and oil. At the time of the Conquest, Spain's decision to make Lima the capital of a viceroyalty, with the concentration of the imperial bureaucracy that this required, was due principally to the large deposits of precious metals. The carryover into the post-independence era of the impedimenta of almost 300 years of Spanish colonial rule as a core region of the empire constricted Peru's ability to evolve liberal democratic institutions.[5]

The large and diverse mineral deposits also served to attract substantial foreign investment in the last decades of the nineteenth century and throughout most of the twentieth. Although this investment created new patterns of dependency and an infrastructure of enclave economies, the ripple effects on employment, unionization, tax revenues, and the expansion of public services, as well as on the domestic bourgeoisie, were considerable.[6] These resources and their exploitation by foreign interests also contributed to the War of the Pacific (1879–1883), by which Peru lost to Chile the nitrate-rich department of Tarapacá, mortgaged its economic future to English interests to pay off war debts, and undermined an incipient civilian political order.[7]

The substantial mineral resources, then, affected the evolution of both the economy and the polity of Peru. A minerals-based export economy was subject to changing prices on the international market, to foreign investment and foreign technology, and to the external pressures, both public and private, to which these subjected the host-country government. The political system was affected more generally by the authoritarian practices inherited from Spain and their tension with the core elements of the imported liberal model.

The patterns of political instability and of alternation between authoritarian and democratic governments became well established in the post–War of the Pacific period and continue to the present. Except between 1895 and 1914, Peru has not experienced extended periods of civilian democratic rule. Since 1914, only one elected president has turned power over to an elected successor (Manuel Prado, 1939–1945, to José Bustamante y Rivero, 1945–1948). With the military as a political alternative that has established its legitimacy through regular coups, all civilian governments are limited in their actions by what they feel the military will tolerate. The alternation of civilian and military governments since early in this century also makes impossible the establishment of a predictable political order with its accompanying sense of economic stability. As a result, institutions are more fragile and more tentative, and individuals often more concerned about increasing their personal choices in the face of uncertainty, even at the expense of the collectivity.

The failure of the political system to become more stable and more institutionalized since 1930 is explained not only by the Great Depression, which cut government revenues by almost two-thirds between 1929 and 1933,[8] but also by the arrival on the political stage of Peru in 1931 of a new political party, the Alianza Popular Revolucionaria Americana (APRA). The appearance of APRA marked the beginning of a reformist political organization with the capacity to move Peru from a conservative or liberal orientation to a radical (in the European sense of middle class) one.[9] Although a latecomer as a radical party in Latin America (comparable parties had been formed in Chile in the 1870s and in Argentina in the 1890s), it was the first well-organized grass-roots political movement Peru had ever known, with energetic leadership and a comprehensive nationalistic ideology to go with it.[10] Partly due to its inflammatory rhetoric, but more because of an early deadly confrontation with the military (memories of the Trujillo massacre of 1932 were kept burning), APRA never achieved the presidency of Peru.[11] Through at least 1962, and possibly even in 1968, the military intervened whenever it appeared that APRA might be in a position to take power.

In the confrontation between the institutionalized military and institutionalized APRA is written much of the modern political history of Peru. Politics and policies alike were conditioned over an entire generation by the presence of APRA, whether the government was civilian or military.

Partly due to the failure of any reformist party to come to power before the 1960s and partly because of the high concentration of power and wealth in Peru, the size and scope of government remained small.[12] Only about

6 percent of the labor force was employed by the government up to that time, and in most years public investment was less than 2 percent of GNP. A private institution collected taxes until 1964, and most public utilities remained in private hands until the 1970s. The private sector was heavily represented on the boards of directors of some public institutions, such as the Central Bank and the industrial and agricultural banks. A tradition of highly talented career public servants did not exist.[13]

As a result, when suddenly called on by the reformist administrations of Belaúnde and the military to assume a large number of new responsibilities, the government bureaucracy was ill-equipped to perform them. One of the prices, then, of the delayed arrival of reformers onto the center of Peru's political stage, civilian or military, was the gap between the strong reformist impulse of the leadership and the limited capacity of a government from a different era.[14]

The First Belaúnde Government, 1963–1968

Given the overwhelming attention to the period of military rule between 1968 and 1980, it is easy to overlook the often ground-breaking efforts of the preceding moderately progressive government. In fact, as one of its members has suggested, a number of the Belaúnde government's most important measures enabled the succeeding military government to move forward more easily and more quickly with its own reform agenda.[15] This is particularly true of the agrarian reform law of 1964, the tax reforms of 1967 and 1968, preliminary negotiations with several foreign copper companies over major new investments in Peru, the rapid expansion of education in the 1960s, and the successful refinancing of the public foreign debt. Furthermore, the rough-and-tumble politics of a civilian government with opposing executive and legislative branches and the spectacular collapse of the administration's legitimacy over its handling of the long-festering International Petroleum Company (IPC) nationalization together gave the incoming military government considerable political freedom in which to operate. In addition, the period illustrates the proposition that the economic forces operating in and on Peru were manageable, but the political forces were not.

While Peru's first comprehensive agrarian reform law came nowhere near accomplishing its ambitious goals—less than one-fifth of a projected 100,000 farm families had benefited by 1968—it served as the starting point for the military's 1969 agrarian reform decree and continued to be used into the early 1970s.[16] By building on the legal and institutional mechanisms established under the earlier law, including the Land Reform Institute, the military was able, almost from its first weeks in office, to pursue its commitment to give land to the tiller.

The major tax reforms were decreed under threat of economic chaos and possible coup late in the Belaúnde administration, during a special 60-day grant of extraordinary powers to the executive by the Congress. They had the effect, however, of giving the incoming military government substantial new sources of revenue, more progressive in nature and more dependent on direct taxes.[17] The reforms included such measures as the elimination of bearer shares, which allowed the tracing of dividend income; higher tax rates on personal income; a profits tax on interest paid abroad; the introduction of a central government tax on real estate; a gasoline tax; and increased excise taxes. For the first time in some years, growing budget deficits could begin to be financed domestically rather than by foreign borrowing. Such external borrowing had become the principal mechanism of the Belaúnde administration to pay its bills because of the unwillingness of the opposition-controlled Congress to pass funding measures to pay for the reforms that were being undertaken.

This is a clear example of the interplay of democratic political forces that served to thwart the consolidation of civilian government in Peru in the 1960s. In particular, the APRA party perceived that its chances for electoral victory in the presidential and congressional vote scheduled for 1969 depended on its ability to embarrass the Acción Popular (AP) administration of President Belaúnde and to limit its successes. By adopting a blatantly populist "No new taxes" slogan, APRA leaders felt they had found a key to the presidential palace that had eluded them for so long. Economic interests opposed to the taxes, who used their control of major newspapers to trumpet their own opposition, encouraged them in this course of civic irresponsibility. Only too late did APRA appreciate that its antiadministration approach discredited civilian government itself. In facilitating a military takeover, the APRA leaders sealed their own political fate. The 1968 coup was followed by numerous measures hostile to APRA interests, ensuring that the first generation of APRA leaders would never reach the presidency for which they had been struggling since 1931.

The unraveling of the historic agreement to nationalize the IPC in the weeks before the military takeover also illustrates the degree to which political considerations overrode an admittedly controversial compromise by the civilian government of a long-standing economic as well as political problem.[18] The basic issue was whether the foreign-owned and -operated producer and refiner of most of Peru's oil owned the subsoil rights, as it claimed, or whether it merely leased them from the government of Peru. The legal case was complex, and the IPC was certainly an exception to the general legal principle going back to Spanish colonial times that the crown (or state) owns all subsoil rights. The private company had defended its position successfully for over fifty years and had enlisted the support of the U.S. government to help protect its interests. The IPC case represents an example of how forces outside the direct control of the government of Peru can constrain its range of independent action. Indeed, much of the tension between Peru and the United States during the Belaúnde administration, resulting in relatively scant economic assistance to Peru during the height of the Alliance for Progress, is traceable to this relationship.[19]

However, the agreement between the government of Peru and the IPC might well have stood up had a key participant from the Peruvian side not decided to make his opposition public in September 1968. Carlos Loret de Mola, head of the Peruvian government oil agency, falsely accused the Belaúnde administration of deceiving the Peruvian people by keeping secret an oil-purchase arrangement between the government company and the IPC that was unfavorable to Peru. The only explanation for Loret de Mola's action was his desire to launch his own candidacy for the presidency within the AP.[20] What he succeeded in doing was administering the coup de grace to an already weakened civilian administration and ensure the long-rumored military takeover.[21]

The various positive steps that the civilian government had made toward addressing the major issues of the day—agrarian reform, expansion of social and educational services, the need for regional development corporations, a domestic peace corps, a new tax structure, and even the resolution of a long-standing problem of a foreign corporation's rights within national territorial boundaries—did not succeed in institutionalizing civilian government. Short-term partisan and personal interests undermined the progress that was made. A military government, with many of the same policy goals but with a very different approach, stepped into the breach. Its eventual arrival at the same end as its civilian predecessor, for at least some of the same reasons, gives us insights into the differences between democratic and authoritarian regimes—and the similarities as well.

The Military Governments, 1968–1980

As a long-term institutionalized and reformist military government, the Revolutionary Government of the Armed Forces (GRFA) was a new phenomenon in Peruvian politics. Never before in the history of Peru was the military establishment in power for so long. Never before did it try to accomplish so much. The GRFA originated in the manifest deficiencies of the ostensibly reformist Belaúnde administration, in the perception that national honor had been sullied in the IPC affair, and in the growing economic difficulties of 1967–1968.

The coup also arose from changes within the military establishment itself from the 1950s onward.[22] The military had become more coherent and more fully developed as an institution through a combination of intensive study, most notably in the Centro de Altos Estudios Militares (CAEM), and concrete experiences. These included civic action programs, the brief antiguerrilla combat of 1965, and the 1967 disagreement with the United States over the Peruvian Air Force's efforts to purchase jet fighter planes. This combination also contributed to the military establishment's expanded definition of national security, which slowly came to encompass national political and economic development and not simply the more traditional goals of boundary maintenance and defense.

The military came to power with a fairly clear reformist developmental ideology. While its members were far from united on procedures, the military as an institution had come to believe that political and economic reform was necessary to protect and enhance Peru's national security. Many of its members were also persuaded that between 1963 and 1968 civilian government had demonstrated its incapacity to implement its reformist promises. In their mind, the political parties had forfeited their claims to legitimacy. Given this perception of the limitations of traditional democratic civilian government, the military establishment believed that a new political structure must be built, beginning at the grass roots, and that this structure would have to be closely linked to the workplace. Hence, much of the military's energy during its first phase in power (1968–1975) was devoted to building what it came to call a "fully participatory democratic system."[23]

The military's second major objective within this expanded definition of national security in terms of national development was to eliminate dependency. This was to be accomplished through a more assertive foreign policy, more active industrialization, strong support of an Andean common market, more diversified economic growth, and much tighter restrictions on foreign investments. The public sector would expand as necessary.[24]

The approach to be followed was a series of decrees from above to avoid the limiting compromises or the immobility of civilian politics. Through them the old politics would gradually wither away, to be replaced by a new communitarian system of economic and political democracy. The economic model to be followed was quintessentially reformist. At all levels it was based on the assumption of a continuing expansion of the resource pie and an improved distribution of the increases to benefit the less wealthy. The distribution of the existing pie was to remain the same. What would change was the elites' basis of wealth, from agricultural to industrial, through a series of incentives for redirecting investment. Foreign investment would continue to be encouraged, but within a new set of controls. Government was to expand to control central parts of the economy, but the domestic private sector was envisioned as an equal partner in stimulating growth.

Most students of the Peruvian experiment conclude that the GRFA failed to accomplish either of its major political and economic objectives in spite of its multiple policy initiatives. Many argue further that Peru was much worse off when the officers left power than when they took over.[25] A number of indicators seem to bear this out. Peru's public foreign debt increased from $801 million in 1968 to $7.98 billion by the end of 1979. Economic growth in the postwar period up to 1966 averaged 5.4 percent a year; from 1975 to 1980, it averaged only 1.7 percent. Inflation in 1968 was 19 percent; in 1979, 67 percent. The exchange rate for the Peruvian sol went from 44 to the U.S. dollar in October 1968 to 250 in December 1979. In 1968 there were 364 major strikes involving 108,000 workers; in 1979, 577 strikes affected almost 517,000 workers.[26] Open unemployment in the Lima metropolitan area was 5.9 percent in 1969 and over 8 percent in 1980.[27]

Contrary to original expectations, the private sector did not provide the bulk of new investment, leaving the government to take up the slack. Already installed industrial capacity was not effectively stimulated, and incentives for importing capital goods were often counterproductive to expanding employment and real economic development.[28] The agricultural and industrial cooperatives, whatever their political effects, served as disincentives to expanding employment by worker and employer alike. The employment stability law, virtually assuring worker tenure after three months' employment, dissuaded employers from increasing their work force. Nationalization of foreign enterprises, mostly in the mining sector, gave the government greater control over the "commanding heights" of the economy but at the considerable cost of lost tax revenues and the various, if mixed, benefits of new foreign investment. Massive foreign loans to finance the shortfall and maintain the rhythm of reforms were often relatively short-term. When growth did not match repayment schedules, the refinancing required and the fiscal restraints imposed from outside sharply increased Peru's external dependency. This was exactly the opposite of the military's economic goal. Other than the rapid expansion of the government, which itself had both positive and negative elements, the economic objectives of the Peruvian revolution clearly failed to materialize.

Some of this failure can be attributed to bad luck. A disastrous earthquake in 1970 killed over 50,000 persons and required a massive reorientation of resources. A shift in the El Niño current in 1972–1973 contributed to the virtual disappearance of the anchovy, at that time the single most important foreign exchange earner for Peru. Exports of fish meal dropped by over $189 million between 1970 and 1973, and a vibrant industry employing upwards of 100,000 collapsed and was taken over by the government out of sheer humanitarian necessity.[29] The promising discoveries of exploitable deposits of oil in the northern jungle in 1971 and 1972 were followed by several years of mostly dry holes. Hence, Peru did not become, as originally projected, a net oil exporter by 1975. This would have been in time both to reap the benefits of OPEC-induced price increases and to begin to pay back the short-term foreign debts. When Peru finally reached this export goal in 1979, the economic crisis had destroyed the viability of the Peruvian economic model. Furthermore, the serious (and ultimately fatal) illness of President Juan Velasco Alvarado in 1973 both undermined the unity of the armed forces at a critical juncture and contributed to increasingly erratic policy.[30]

By the time Gen. Francisco Morales Bermúdez took over in August 1975, the economic damage had been done. It was left to his government to try to salvage what it could of the reforms and of the waning prestige of the armed forces. Most of its efforts, however, were dedicated necessarily to the economic crisis and the obligatory refinancing of the debt. In the process of grudging accession to the International Monetary Fund's formula of fiscal retrenchment, wages declined, unemployment increased, and devaluation-induced inflation accelerated.[31] Even so, herculean efforts by Minister of Finance Javier Silva Ruete, combined with sharp improvements in world prices for Peru's products, permitted some economic stabilization and at least a temporary easing of the massive debt repayment problem by 1979. Nevertheless, the situation was sufficiently bleak by 1977 that the military government agreed that the only cure was to return to civilian rule. After a constitutional convention in 1978 and the drafting of a new constitution by 1979, national presidential elections were held and civilians once again took over in July 1980.[32]

In spite of the serious economic problems, the military regime pursued a much more aggressive Third World policy and worked through the Andean Pact to tighten foreign investment regulations. Diplomatic relations to various new Third World and socialist countries were expanded, with some trade and economic and military assistance benefits. Peru's terms of trade actually improved in most years of the military rule. Yet Peru's dependence increased sharply during the *docenio* of military government, largely due to growing foreign indebtedness.

Although the GRFA failed to accomplish most of its economic objectives, its reformist efforts were more successful. Under the 1969 agrarian reform law, about 8.5 million hectares (1 hectare = 2.5 acres) were allocated to 375,000 farm families over a ten-year period, mostly in agricultural cooperatives.[33] Under the industrial law and its modifications between 1970 and 1972, some 3,900 industrial cooperatives, involving approximately 260,000 workers, were established to enable profit-sharing and worker participation in management and ownership.[34] The National Agrarian Confederation, operated under official sponsorship between 1973 and 1978, included at one point 1,644 local agricultural units (mostly peasant communities or agricultural cooperatives), with a membership of up to 1.4 million or more.[35] Both union confederations and unions proliferated during the docenio. The number of recognized unions increased from 2,436 in 1969 to 4,589 in 1978, with a total membership of almost half of Peru's wage earners, or close to a million workers.[36] The government itself expanded markedly, if not always efficiently, developing certain technical expertise in the process and catching up to a certain degree in size with the state sectors of many other Latin American countries. Public employment increased from 165,000 in 1964 to over 480,000 in 1977.[37]

The military's stated goal of a "fully participatory social democracy" was certainly not reached. The key organization set up in 1971 to facilitate this process was the Sistema Nacional de Apoyo a la Mobilización Social (SINAMOS). Even though it received a substantial budget and had a large staff, conflicting signals over its mission and overblown and unrealistic expectations led to substantial popular opposition and its eventual abandonment by 1978.[38] Many of the reforms, particularly in the industrial community, were watered down because of strong management pressure during the Morales Bermúdez administration or remained practically stillborn, as with the social property law.[39]

Even though the military's reform objectives for citizen participation were not reached, however, neither was the status quo retained. Substantial segments of the country's population became incorporated into one or another of the various local participation units fostered or facilitated by the military, even though their activities often countered the regime-support goals of the military government. In fact, this was one of the curious paradoxes of the GRFA in the participation area. It never mobilized substantial mass support, nor did it gain the confidence of even those modern elite sectors that many reforms were designed to benefit.[40]

The elections of 1978 and 1980 demonstrated quite dramatically one of the most important consequences of the military government in terms of citizen incorporation into the political system. In the 1978 elections for a constituent assembly, fully 36.3 percent of the total vote went to seven parties of the Left. In 1980, Marxist party participation increased; even though the total Marxist presidential vote declined from the 1978 levels, each of the five loosely coalesced groups received sufficient votes to elect one or more of its candidates to the Senate or the Chamber of Deputies—a total of nineteen in all.[41] Furthermore, union membership expanded dramatically, mostly to locals affiliated with the confederation dominated by the pro-Moscow communist party, the Confederación General de Trabajadores del Peru (CGTP).

What happened, then, as a consequence of the incorporation of large numbers of people into the system during the years of military government was the creation of a viable Marxist-oriented left for the first time in Peruvian history. Furthermore, and perhaps more significantly, these political organizations were prepared to participate in the electoral system as it opened up again for the return to civilian rule. In other words, the military docenio helped to create and legitimize a radical left that it could not co-opt, but that nevertheless was willing to play by the rules of the political game. In this fashion, the military government unintentionally helped to channel a new generation of political activists to work within the system rather than against it. Thus they made an important contribution to the possibility of future political growth and stability in Peru in accordance with their expanded national security goals.

The Second Belaúnde Government, 1980–

Civilian government returned to Peru in July 1980 under reasonably auspicious circumstances.[42] The victory of former president Fernando Belaúnde Terry by the unexpectedly solid margin of 45.6 percent of the vote gave his incoming administration a clear popular mandate. With a congressional majority as well, in coalition with the small but influential Partido Popular Cristiano (PPC), a major weakness of Belaúnde's earlier government was avoided. The widely perceived failure of the military's twelve years in power gave the civilian politicians substantial negative legitimacy. The military's own recognition of its need to return to the barracks and stay there in order to regroup and rebuild provided an added margin of security for civilian rule. Since the military had successfully renegotiated the large foreign debt and had begun the process of fiscal retrenchment at a time of rising world prices for Peru's products, a difficult but more stable economic situation greeted the incoming civilians than would have been the case a few years earlier. The international prestige of leading members of the new government's economic team assured good relations between Peru and the world financial community. Although serious problems remained, among them inflation, depressed wages, and a much expanded government with continuing obligations and responsibilities, the prognosis for the new civilian regime was quite optimistic.

The severe world recession that commenced a few months after Belaúnde assumed office lowered world prices and sharply escalated interest rates. In 1982, for example, agricultural prices declined by 60 percent in international trading and mineral prices by 30 percent. Even oil prices steadied and then declined for the first time in a decade, leaving Peru, a modest oil exporter, unable to reap new foreign exchange benefits in that area.

Then in late 1982 and continuing throughout 1983, the El Niño current arrived again. This periodic flow of warmer ocean currents by the Peruvian coast simultaneously reduced nutrients for fish and caused heavy rainfall along the normally desert north coast as well as drought in the southern sierra areas. Fish for consumption, canning, and fish meal virtually disappeared. Cotton-, sugarcane-, and rice-growing areas in the coastal valleys were heavily damaged, as were many irrigation systems. Roads and railroad beds were washed away, interrupting farm-to-market transportation as well as the shipment of minerals for export. Thousands of rural families in the southern sierra were forced to the brink of starvation by the crop failure resulting from the 1983 drought. The government estimated that above and beyond the human suffering, at least $600 million in foreign exchange earnings were lost because of El Niño in 1983 alone.

A third unexpected negative development was the emergence in 1980 of a radical guerrilla movement called Shining Path (Sendero Luminoso). Sendero began its antiestablishment activities with such symbolic acts as hanging dogs from lampposts and exploding small bombs late at night at the doors of public buildings. Within a few months, however, its actions became much more violent and much larger in scale and had spread from the organization's original stronghold in the south-central highland of Ayacucho to Lima and other parts of Peru. By mid-1983, close to a thousand fatalities could be attributed to Senderista or anti-Senderista activities, along with acts of sabotage, particularly to electrical systems and to private companies, of $100 to $150 million. The belated but strong military response beginning in December 1982 diverted substantial government resources (probably close to $200 million), as did the need to repair damages caused by sabotage. The government's apparent inability to deal with the problem quickly and decisively, as it had with the Movement of the Revolutionary Left uprising in 1965, was one of the factors contributing to the dramatic loss of public confidence in the Belaúnde administration (from over 70 percent public approval in 1980 polls to less than 20 percent by early 1983).

Other elements in the slippage of the government's popularity included persisting and increasing inflation (from 59 percent in 1980 to 73 percent in both 1981 and 1982), the removal of most subsidies for basic foodstuffs and gasoline, wage settlements that in general kept both white- and blue-collar incomes below their 1974 peaks, and the inability of the Belaúnde administration to restore and maintain economic growth (the 1980 figure of 3.6 percent was followed in 1981 by a 4.4 percent growth rate, but the rate declined to 0.2 percent in 1982 and was estimated to be at least –6.0 percent for 1983).

Although government expenditures declined somewhat (by $300 million in 1982 and $700 million in 1983), the public sector deficit remained unacceptably high, equaling 8.8 percent of GNP in 1982. Sharply reduced tariffs (from an average of over 100 percent in 1980 to 40 percent by the end of 1982), designed to reduce inflation and to make domestic industry more efficient, caused many local enterprises to teeter on the edge of bankruptcy or fail by mid-1983.

One factor behind the remarkable survival of civilian government under these adverse circumstances has been the good relations between the major figures of Peru's economic team and the international banking community. Both finance ministers of the Belaúnde administration, Manuel Ulloa and Carlos Rodríguez Pastor, worked in that community before joining the government. This meant that the required refinancing as well as substantial new loan arrangements could be worked out in a climate of greater confidence, thus avoiding what otherwise might have been the early economic collapse of the government.

Another factor is that the military has no desire to return to political power after its lengthy and bruising experience. The armed forces appear to have a new appreciation of the problems of governing, with or without a legislature, and seem on the whole to have made their peace with the major political parties, including their historic nemesis, APRA. In addition, they now have an intermediate-crisis response step that avoids many of the problems associated with a full-fledged coup. The Social Mobilization Law, passed during the military's last weeks in office, enables the armed forces to exercise authority in local or regional emergency situations when the president so authorizes. Furthermore, the present civilian government has accommodated military needs, including special funds for emergency activities (as in Ayacucho), for military purchases (including a special $400 million allotment in 1982), and for police salaries—raised for the first time in 1982 to parity with army pay scales.

Another positive factor is that the Marxist Left, with the exception of Sendero and a few tiny splinter groups, sees possibilities under civilian rule for expanding its organizational base in parties and unions as well as its electoral strength. The Marxists elected a number of representatives to Congress, and they emerged from the 1980 municipal elections as the second electoral force in Peru, with well over 20 percent of local council seats. The CGTP and other Marxist unions together comprise close to 80 percent of organized workers. Their growing strength makes their leaders optimistic that continued civilian rule can only work to their advantage, as it did in the November 1983 municipal elections and may do in the March 1985 presidential and congressional races. At this juncture, then, the Left frowns on either guerrilla initiatives or military moves that might jeopardize its improving position under civilian rule.

The brutal methods of the Senderistas since March 1982, following a massive raid and jailbreak in Ayacucho, have alienated both their fellow Marxists and the bulk of the population. Sendero has not concerned itself with public relations, particularly among the bourgeoisie, and its support is limited to its Ayacucho heartland and some extremist elements in the universities. Its presence has forced the military to concentrate on a major security problem rather than on regaining political power and has heightened popular acquiescence in the civilian status quo, if not support for the Belaúnde government itself.

Finally, the APRA party was apparently revitalized during 1982, when the party elected a new generation of progressive leaders headed by Alán García. With the possible restoration, after fifteen years, of APRA to its historic place on the democratic left, Marxists could have some serious competition for votes. Furthermore, APRA's revitalization, combined with the apparent end of the military veto, could make the party a serious and viable contender for the presidency in 1985. Since the AP has no one of the Belaúnde's stature to succeed him, APRA's regeneration may provide the Peruvian political system with a real democratic alternative.

Such a possibility diminishes the likelihood of a military disruption before the elections. In addition, the 1985 presidential elections are the first in which there must be a runoff election between the top two contenders if no candidate gets 50 percent of the vote, and there is thus little possibility of an indecisive outcome that might invite a military response. Thus the civilian administration of Belaúnde seems likely to be only the second elected government in Peru since 1914 to be able to hand power over to an elected successor, even though his administration has been unable to solve the major economic problems of the country. In the short run, the linkage between economic problems and political chaos is complex and indirect. But if the civilian government that succeeds Belaúnde also confronts a combination of bad luck and a bad economy, political turmoil, military takeover, and repression cannot be far away.

Conclusions

Both military and civilian governments have contributed to the substantial political and economic changes in Peru since the 1960s. Yet neither has been able to accomplish through the policy process what it intended. This was due in part to such basic constraints on the system itself as the resource structure and geography. It was also in part the result of external constraints, such as the often negative role of the United States; declines in world market prices in 1966–1968, 1976–1978, and 1981–1983; and the strictures of the IMF after 1978. Both civilian and military governments were guilty of errors of commission, such as the mishandling of the IPC and the devaluation problems under Belaúnde or the simultaneous pursuit of industrialization, rapid state expansion, nationalization, and worker-participation enterprises under the military. Both types of governments were limited also by misfortune. The first Belaúnde government faced an opposition Congress and APRA intransigence, and the second had to cope with the worst world recession since the 1930s and natural disasters. The military had to cope with the failure to find oil, Velasco's illness, the earthquake, and El Niño. Under these circumstances, it is quite remarkable that much was accomplished, and not at all surprising that serious problems remain.

At the same time, the military and civilian governments differed in important ways. The pace of economic and political reforms was much more rapid under military than civilian governments. This was not only because a reformist approach and a tentative beginning had already been established under the preceding civilian government, but also because the military had a more coherent strategy based on national security goals and the advantage of being able to work through decree laws rather than through Congress. The military also carried out its initiatives with much more nationalistic fervor, often with strong anti-U.S. overtones and with a Third World perspective.

The reformist initiatives of the first military government substantially changed the size of government, the nature of workplace organization, and the number of people incorporated into unions and production and industrial cooperatives. It was limited by the wide-ranging nature of the reforms themselves, which exceeded the capacity of available resources and discouraged private sector initiative. It was also limited by the internal contradictions of some of the reforms themselves. The new worker-participation organizations often improved the economic situation of members but discouraged employment expansion and productive private investment. Nationalizations and new programs expanded government power but limited possibilities for new foreign or domestic private initiatives. The lack of tax reforms limited domestic resource extraction.

These limitations, in turn, had multiple effects. They led the military governments to seek sizable loans from abroad to continue the pace and intensity of the reforms. They also contributed to the end of the economic growth necessary to continued income redistribution. By a somewhat different route, then, the military leaders confronted the same obstacles to further expansion of reforms as the civilian government had several years before— growing external dependency and the limitations on further expansion and deepening of reforms that this implied. Whereas under civilian rule the democratic process itself constrained reforms, under military rule the reforms themselves ultimately prevented the GRFA from accomplishing its goals of eliminating dependency.

In the final analysis, excesses of authoritarian policymaking were primarily responsible for the continuing and even growing problems of the political economy of Peru. One can argue, however, that the reforms of that authoritarian period were both necessary and overdue for the future political and economic well-being of the country. Excesses were committed and problems remain, particularly in the short term, but an expanded and more competent government is now available to deal with economic issues in the future. Also, the new national bourgeoisie may soon be in a position to contribute more actively to further economic growth.

Even though many of the economic consequences of the major reforms were negative, their political consequences were not. They helped bring into the system a much expanded spectrum of the population on terms that are largely system-supporting rather than system-corroding. In particular, the Left in Peru was much strengthened and legitimized and assumed political responsibility inside rather than outside that system. Government was expanded, and its purview broadened to levels found in most other Latin American countries. If the present delicate balance among political forces, including the military, can be maintained under civilian auspices for another ten years, the resulting advances in political stability and political institutionalization will form the final and most positive legacy of the reformist years.

Notes

1. See, for example, Preston James, *Latin America* (New York: Odyssey Press, 1959), pp. 169–201.

2. Comité Interamericano de Desarrollo Agrícola, *Peru: Tenencia de la tierra y desarrollo socioeconómico del sector agrícola* (Washington, D.C.: Organization of American States, 1965).

3. David Chaplin, "Peru's Postponed Revolution," *World Politics* 19 (1968): 393–420.

4. Instituto Nacional de Planificación, *Informe sobre la situación económica y social del Peru, 1963–64* (Lima, 1964).

5. David Scott Palmer, "The Politics of Authoritarianism in Spanish America," in James M. Malloy, ed., *Authoritarianism and Corporatism in Latin America* (Pittsburgh, Pa.: Pittsburgh University Press, 1977), pp. 379–84.

6. David G. Becker, *The New Bourgeoisie and the Limits of Dependency: Mining, Class, and Power in "Revolutionary" Peru* (Princeton, N.J.: Princeton University Press, 1983).

7. Henry E. Dobyns and Paul L. Doughty, *Peru: A Cultural History* (New York: Oxford University Press, 1976).

8. David Scott Palmer, *Peru: The Authoritarian Tradition* (New York: Praeger, 1980), Table 5.1, p. 69.

9. Peter F. Klaren, *Modernization, Dislocation, and Aprismo: Origins of the Peruvian Aprista Party, 1870–1932* (Austin: University of Texas Press, 1973).

10. Steve Stein, *Populism in Peru: The Emergence of the Masses and the Politics of Social Control* (Madison: University of Wisconsin Press, 1980), pp. 129–87.

11. David P. Werlich, *Peru: A Short History* (Carbondale: Southern Illinois University Press, 1978), pp. 197–98.

12. Rosemary Thorp and Geoffrey Bertram, *Peru, 1890–1977: Growth and Policy in an Open Economy* (New York: Columbia University Press, 1978), esp. pp. 182–229.

13. Pedro-Pablo Kuczynski, *Peruvian Democracy Under Economic Stress: An Account of the Belaúnde Administration, 1963–1968* (Princeton, N.J.: Princeton University Press, 1977), pp. 13–17.

14. See discussion in E. V. K. Fitzgerald, *The Political Economy of Peru, 1956–1978: Economic Development and the Restructuring of Capital* (Cambridge, Eng.: Cambridge University Press, 1979); and in Thorp and Bertram, *Peru, 1890–1977*.

15. See Kuczynski, *Peruvian Democracy Under Economic Stress*; as well as several articles in Abraham F. Lowenthal, ed., *The Peruvian Experiment: Continuity and Change Under Military Rule* (Princeton, N.J.: Princeton University Press, 1975).

16. Colin Harding, "Land Reform and Social Conflict in Peru," in Lowenthal, *The Peruvian Experiment*, esp. pp. 236–41.

17. Kuczynski, *Peruvian Democracy Under Economic Stress*, pp. 230–43.

18. Richard Goodwin, "Letter from Peru," *New Yorker*, May 17, 1969.

19. Kuczynski, *Peruvian Democracy Under Economic Stress*, Table 21, p. 125.

20. For two quite different versions, see ibid., pp. 106–21; and Augusto Zimmermann, *Historia secreta del petróleo* (Lima: Editorial Gráfica Labor, 1968).

21. Jane S. Jaquette, *The Politics of Development in Peru*, Latin American Studies Program Dissertation Series no. 33 (Ithaca, N.Y.: Cornell University, 1971), p. 197.

22. Alfred Stepan, *The State and Society: Peru in Comparative Perspective* (Princeton, N.J.: Princeton University Press, 1978), esp. pp. 117–57.

23. David Scott Palmer, *"Revolution from Above": Military Government and Popular Participation in Peru, 1968–1972*, Latin American Studies Program Dissertation Series no. 47 (Ithaca, N.Y.: Cornell University, 1973); Evelyne Huber Stephens, *The Politics of Workers' Participation: The Peruvian Approach in Comparative Perspective* (New York: Academic Press, 1980); and Henry A. Dietz and David Scott Palmer, "Citizen Participation Under Innovative Military Corporatism in Peru," in John A. Booth and Mitchell A. Seligson, eds., *Political Participation in Latin America*, vol. 1, *Citizen and State* (New York: Holmes & Meier, 1978), pp. 172–88.

24. This retrospective summary of the military's goals makes them sound much more coherent than they actually were at the time. The Plan Inca, purportedly the

military's plan of government from the outset of military rule in 1968, was released only in 1974 and is also much too complete and cogent a statement of the military's goals.

25. Daniel M. Schydlowsky and Juan Wicht, "The Anatomy of an Economic Failure," in Cynthia McClintock and Abraham F. Lowenthal, eds., *The Peruvian Experiment Reconsidered* (Princeton, N.J.: Princeton University Press, 1983), pp. 94–143. See also John Sheahan, "The Economics of the Peruvian Experiment in Comparative Perspective," in ibid., pp. 387–414. Much of the following economic critique relies on these analyses.

26. David Scott Palmer, "The Post-revolutionary Political Economy of Peru," in Stephen M. Gorman, ed., *Post-revolutionary Peru: The Politics of Transformation* (Boulder, Colo.: Westview Press, 1982), pp. 217–18.

27. Inter-American Development Bank, *Economic and Social Progress in Latin America, 1973 Report* and *1980–81 Report* (Washington, D.C.: Inter-American Development Bank, 1974 and 1981).

28. Roberto Abusada-Salah, "Políticas de industrialización en el Perú, 1970–1976," *Economia* (Lima: Universidad Católica), 1 (1978).

29. Sheahan, "Economics of the Peruvian Experiment," p. 398.

30. See Guillermo Thorndike, *No, mi general* (Lima: Mosca Azul, 1976).

31. Schydlowsky and Wicht, "Anatomy of an Economic Failure," argue that the IMF formula for Peru was wrong because it misdiagnosed the country's economic problems.

32. Sandra L. Woy-Hazelton, "The Return of Partisan Politics in Peru," in Stephen M. Gorman, ed, *Post-revolutionary Peru*, pp. 33–72. For a discussion of the disengagement process, see David Scott Palmer, "Reformist Military Rule in Peru, 1968–1980," in Robert Wesson, ed., *New Military Politics in Latin America* (New York: Praeger, 1982), pp. 141–43.

33. Cynthia McClintock, "Post-revolutionary Agrarian Politics in Peru," in Gorman, *Post-revolutionary Peru*, p. 141.

34. Martin J. Scurrah and Guadelupe Esteves, "The Condition of Organized Labor," in Gorman, *Post-revolutionary Peru*, pp. 123–26.

35. Cynthia McClintock, *Peasant Cooperatives and Political Change in Peru* (Princeton, N.J.: Princeton University Press, 1981), pp. 262–69. The membership estimates are mine and are based on an average population of 835 per community, from sources cited in Palmer, *"Revolution from Above,"* p. 144.

36. Scurrah and Esteves, "The Condition of Organized Labor," Table 4.2, p. 108.

37. Fitzgerald, *Political Economy of Peru*; and idem, "State Capitalism in Peru: A Model of Economic Development and Its Limitations," in McClintock and Lowenthal, *Peruvian Experiment Reconsidered*, pp. 65–93.

38. Cynthia McClintock, "Velasco, Officers, and Citizens: The Politics of Stealth," in McClintock and Lowenthal, *Peruvian Experiment Reconsidered*, pp. 275–308; and Sandra Woy-Hazelton, "The Infrastructure of Participation in Peru: SINAMOS," in Booth and Seligson, *Political Participation in Latin America*, pp. 189–208.

39. Peter S. Cleaves and Martin J. Scurrah, *Agriculture, Bureaucracy, and Military Government in Peru* (Ithaca, N.Y.: Cornell University Press, 1980).

40. Cynthia McClintock hypothesizes that the reform strategy itself was to blame. By keeping various sectors off balance through both the timing and the substance of reforms, friends were discouraged and foes made even more implacable ("Velasco, Officers, and Citizens," esp. pp. 306–8).

41. Jack W. Hopkins, ed., *Latin America and Caribbean Contemporary Record*, vol. 1, *1981–82* (New York: Holmes & Meier, 1983); and sources cited therein.

42. No comprehensive analysis has yet been undertaken of the second Belaúnde administration. But see the review articles on Peru in ibid., and vol. 2, *1982–83*. See also the articles on Peru in the *Yearbook on International Communist Affairs* (Stanford: Hoover Institution Press, 1982 and 1983).

6 Mexico

Party-Led Development

William Glade

The Road to Development

It was in the eighteen years spanning the administrations of Lázaro Cárdenas, Avila Camacho, and Miguel Alemán Valdés (1934–1952) that the mise-en-scène of contemporary Mexican development fell into place. By the end of that interval, the dramatis personae in this remarkable production had all been introduced. Setting the stage had been an arduous, costly, and at times even sanguinary process. But much was accomplished in the 1930s, and thanks partly to exigencies stemming from international conditions in that decade and the next, nearly all the major institutional furnishings of the drama had been assembled by the time Adolfo Ruiz Cortines (1952–1958) assumed the presidency.

The end of the Cárdenas administration in 1940 has appealed to a number of observers as a critical date; in their view, whatever reformist proclivities there may have been in the post-revolutionary period were pretty much spent after this folk hero left the presidency. By that time, far-reaching changes had indeed taken place.

Thanks are owed to the Fund for Multinational Management Education and to the Council of the Americas for permission to use parts of a study prepared by the author for a seminar sponsored by them in spring 1983.

The church, shorn of its wealth and political influence, had been placed under the firm control of the state when Cárdenas halted the last fanatical wave of persecution of 1931–1936. The military, for its part, had never been a particularly cohesive force in the Mexican political arena, though it had often been a decidedly disturbing one. Through a mixture of co-optation and internal rivalry, it, too, was tamed and subjected to the authority of civil government. In 1938 the last armed rebellion by an old-style chieftain was put down. Also dismissed from the political arena by 1940 were the former economic overlords of Mexico. A landed oligarchy born during the colonial age, which grew to its full powers after the liberal reforms of the 1850s opened the door to vast land grabbing, was subdued, or at least cowed, by the revolutionary violence of the 1910s and 1920s. During the 1930s, the land-owners were largely eradicated as a significant political force by massive redistributions of land. Foreign capital, intimidated since the 1917 constitution announced the end of the privileges it had enjoyed during the long rule of Porfirio Díaz, was decisively brought to heel in the 1930s by the nationalizations of railways and the petroleum industry, as well as by the agrarian reform. Having already been weakened from the physical destruction wrought by revolutionary strife, its power was additionally undermined by the financial and organizational wreckage brought on in the advanced economies by the Great Depression.

Protracted economic devastation, then, severed the links between economic power and political influence, helping to pave the way for a regime in which control of the political machinery itself was paramount in the country's economic and social order. The political process per se became preponderant and laid the basis for the directive economic role of the state.

The emergence of this policy autonomy was also fostered by various reforms and the strengthening of new constituencies. Under Cárdenas, for example, the system of state-sponsored education expanded considerably. The official message of secular salvation was preached to a citizenry that was more than ever favorably disposed to the government because of improved access to the structure of opportunity.[1] Labor unions and peasant organizations had, by the end of the same administration, been accorded full legitimacy—on a leash from the state, to be sure, since their welfare depended on the implementation of new legislation. Before the decade closed, both had been brought under the aegis of a newly expanded and reorganized ruling political party.[2] When it was established in 1929, the National Revolutionary Party (PRN) was essentially a vehicle for mobilizing the power of the political machine of Plutarco Calles. In 1938, Cárdenas reorganized the party into a less personalistic and more group-based structure called the Mexican Revolutionary Party (PRM).

In addition to these changes, the political trajectory through Cárdenas established the strong alliance between the state and the intelligentsia, which, though it never developed the inner cohesion of an interest group, has nevertheless functioned as one of the major props of and influences on the regime. Just as state patronage enlisted the services of prominent artists to build an official mythology and help legitimate the system by adroit manipulation of symbolic expression, so also ways were found—support of higher education, the establishment of government-backed publishing houses, the distribution of sinecures and other favors, and a tacit if broadly permissive regulation of the developing media industries—to mobilize a sizable portion of the available intellectual resources on behalf of the state apparatus and the task of restructuring society and the economy. With the intelligentsia and its scarce talents and skills employed in support of official aims, the state was better able to define policy options, to build consensus, and to propound its vision of the present and the future, not to mention its self-serving interpretation of the past.

These trends in the reshaping of social forces gave the government a relatively unimpeded scope for formulating and implementing its own interpretation of the national design set forth, in general terms, in the 1917 constitution. Solidly ensconced in the machinery of state and dealing with a fragmented and only weakly organized society, save for associations operating essentially under the tutelage of the state, the political and bureaucratic elite enjoyed ample policy space for devising new approaches as well as for defining the objectives of public policy. The chief constraints were those set by resource availabilities. All things considered, this comparatively unhampered expression of what one could call a bureaucratic or political preference function constitutes a convincing historical example of the relative autonomy of the state that political economist Michael Kalecki described as an intermediate regime and Marx referred to as Bonapartism.

In sum, by the time Avila Camacho was elected in 1940, an extensive program of social, political, and economic reforms had been implemented. Compared with conditions under the *Porfiriato*, much progress had been made in totally reorganizing the Mexican system. Thereafter, according to one school of thought, revolutionary zeal began to flag as a new bourgeoisie came into its own, industrial development supplanted agrarian reform at the top of the national agenda, and consumption replaced collectivization as a central concern in social processes.

Although such a periodization is undeniably useful, it can be argued that this way of dividing the play into acts overlooks important continuities between the Cárdenas and subsequent administrations. In several respects, it is entirely plausible to take 1934 as the inception of an extended period of developmental evolution.[3] By then, overt violence had mostly subsided, the Calles puppet show was over,[4] and the worst of revolutionary factionalism was past. The governing party was assuming a political configuration that with only slight modifications—around the time it was rechristened the Institutional Revolutionary Party (PRI) in 1946—would carry it through to the present. Under Cárdenas and his successors, the tutelary relationship that would support but subordinate officially sanctioned proletarian interest organizations to the state was settling into a regular pattern. The Confederación Nacional Campesina was set up in 1935; the Confederación de Trabajadores Mexicanos, in the following year. Both represented a confirmation of old ties and their consolidation as part of the institutionalized basis of the regime.

Just as significant is the buildup in the 1930s of two new sets of domestic interests and their smooth induction into the political process: the bureaucracy of the mushrooming public and parastatal sectors and the industrialists and other business groups.

The first of these was the product of a burst of institution building on the part of the government that has extended from Cárdenas to today and established the public and parastatal sectors as the driving force in the economy. The actual policies and institutions that fortified what might be called a state bourgeoisie are examined below. Suffice it to note at this point that this articulate group, lodged strategically close to the sources of power, was incorporated into the official party in 1943 as the major segment of the Confederación Nacional de Organizaciones Populares, following up an idea proposed by Cárdenas. With it and the impetus given education and official patronage of the arts and letters, the government acquired additional means for mobilizing backing from a middle class that was mostly urban but, thanks to the agrarian reform, partly rural as well. Nurtured also by the resumption of domestic economic growth from 1932 on, this segment of society was all the more inclined to applaud the national project emanating from the state and to reaffirm the new gospel that artists, writers, and mandarins of the media proclaimed.

The other new actor in the political drama first appeared in a modest role during the national economic recovery of the 1930s, although as an interest group it was barely visible in policy circles prior to the 1940s. By Alemán's time, as Sanford Mosk notes, the business-industrial interest had plainly joined the chorus of voices to which the state paid heed,[5] though by no means can it be assumed that this new group, either then or later, overpowered the other contending interests.[6] On the contrary, the new industrialists and other business interests rising out of the program of state capitalism were only too aware of the multiple forms of their dependence on government help and of contradictions between their preferred goals and the practical accommodations with which they have had to live. The major groups—the Confederation of National Chambers of Commerce, the Confederation of Industrial Chambers, and an independent-minded subsidiary of the latter, the National

Chamber of Manufacturing Industries—have operated under the terms of legislation laid down in the 1930s and perform officially endorsed representational and consultative functions. The National Employers' Confederation, the Mexican Bankers Association, and the Mexican Association of Insurance Institutions also have special status as officially recognized peak organizations, although, unlike the others, they are set up as private associations.

Over the years, a good many Mexicanists have come to believe that an *haute bourgeoisie* composed of the large financial and industrial interests seized the reins of power in Mexico sometime after Cárdenas. Taken as evidence for this perspective is the pronounced policy shift from the late 1950s away from investment in agriculture and the winding-down of land redistribution. It is true that by means both direct and indirect, ranging from the provision of loan and equity capital to tax inducements and protection from foreign competition, Mexican authorities have pushed manufacturing development aggressively, following, like many other Latin American countries, an accumulation model based on import-substitution industrialization. But any conclusion that this was pressed on an otherwise indifferent or unwilling state by the industrial fraction of the bourgeoisie is, to say the least, simplistic. Industrialization, with or without private capital, had by the mid-1940s entered the belief system of the day as a self-evident good.[7] The private sector's efforts were welcome, but the state, too, forged ahead in this drive, encouraged by a labor movement eager for new jobs.

Business associations supported most of the pro-industrial policies, to be sure, but in an age in which population was burgeoning and rapid urbanization was getting under way, the state hardly needed such prompting to press ahead with its industrial policy, even though the apparent urgency of the task diverted resources from agriculture from the late 1950s onwards.

Although capitalist interests were, in the case of some major associations, formally subject to state oversight, they nevertheless have displayed considerable independence of action and were never brought under the discipline of the party.[8] Capital flight and resistance to tax reform, as during the Luís Echeverría period (1970–1976), gave the business sector ways of exerting pressure on government, though in the case of capital flight, the cumulative effects of tens of thousands of savers responding rationally to drastically misaligned exchange rates has far more explanatory power than do political aims. Some business groups, emboldened perhaps by the rise of giant financial-industrial conglomerates by the 1970s, have been outspoken in their criticism of the state's orchestration of economic processes, but other segments of the business community have tended to be more ambivalent, or at least circumspect. The vast regulatory and fiscal panoply of public authority, with its capacity to bestow favors on suppliers of the state as well as on users of its products and services, has given the government the upper hand.

Undermining the contention that the state had capitulated to the bourgeoisie is the number of important measures antithetical to the interests of the supposed new ruling class and its foreign allies. The introduction of a compulsory profit-sharing scheme was one such, as were the growing regulation of foreign capital and technology transfers and the government's leftist foreign policy. The extraordinary swelling of the parastatal sector, the refusal of the governing elite to divest the state's major holdings despite importuning from the business associations, and the failure of Mexico to join the General Agreement on Trade and Tariffs (GATT) in the 1970s must be reckoned other major defeats for this group. The sweeping 1982 nationalization of Mexican commercial banks and their equity shares in industry, along with the constitutional proclamation in 1983 of the state's amplified role in the economy, reveals fairly straightforwardly that the pivotal institutions in the Mexican system remain those of the public and parastatal sectors.

While it might be supposed that rapid industrialization would have narrowed the policy space of government in yet another respect, namely through strengthening the influence of organized labor, this does not appear to have happened. One possible explanation for the comparative docility of labor is the buying-off of union leaders through official favors; another, the countervailing power of employers. Whatever the explanatory weight of such factors, the movement's parts took on, with the growing complexity of the industrial structure, an increasingly variegated character with a corresponding fractioning of interest. The steady expansion of the economy served additionally as general security for organized labor against the unemployment and underemployment problems that have plagued other segments of the work force. What is more, the sustained growth of the economy over many years induced no little upward mobility, through skills advancement, higher real wages, and more fringe benefits. Thus, the unionized work force was shielded from the adverse income-distribution trends in the economy as a whole. This seems to have helped considerably to dampen labor militancy. No doubt awareness of these critical relations between circumstances and labor attitudes accounts for the evident nervousness in governing circles during the terms of both Echeverría and José López Portillo (1976–1982), when the aggregate growth rate dipped.

In short, a reasonable interpretation of the dynamics of policymaking by the mid-1950s, the end of the formative period, is that government was still only loosely constrained by the policy preferences of the different interest groups, although all the major ones had entered the picture by that time.[9] This included the foreign investors who were returning to Mexico in a rising wave, but with a sphere of operations that had shifted increasingly into manufacturing. Industrial policy had acquired new prominence, with the political-bureaucratic alliance harnessing national objectives to changing conditions in the world economy. Conditions were more orderly than in earlier times, but the dispersion of political forces still allowed public authorities room for policy maneuvering in erecting the system of state capitalism.[10] In spite of subsequent challenges to this scheme of affairs, a continuing latitude for state guidance was maintained by the distinctive, virtually sui generis, political style the regime evolved (see below). But just as a preliminary survey of the political matrix is necessary for understanding the economic dynamics of an intermediary regime, so also a review of the economic trends and circumstances is essential for interpreting the dynamics and issues that have propelled the system forward.

The Mexican Miracle Play

The drop in the gross domestic product in 1982 was all the more unsettling because of Mexico's nonpareil performance among the developing nations of the world. Not since 1932 had aggregate output fallen. The year 1933 can therefore be taken as the point of departure for a half-century of uninterrupted material expansion and an economic counterpart to the formative social and political transformations that tied the Cárdenas period to its two successors. Just as the three consecutive administrations set the policy stage for practically all that followed, by the same token the growth of those years, pausing for a slight tremor in 1953 after Ruiz Cortines took office,[11] fed into the cumulative economic success that went on to change a nation once almost entirely dependent on primary production and exporting into one of the three leading manufacturing powers of Latin America.

The pace of growth, though consistently positive, was uneven in the early years of this long wave, owing to the impact of such exogenous variables as the world depression and drought on the down side to the stimulation of World War II and the Korean war on the up side. Even so, for much of those five decades, the year-to-year variability in growth rate was moderate while the rate itself held astonishingly high. Averaging 6.7 percent annually during the 1940s, the growth rate hovered around 6.1 percent for the next decade or so and averaged 7.5 percent for the 1962–1970 period.[12] After the post–World War II adjustments and those of the Korean episode had been digested, the rate of increase in the price level before the 1970s was decidedly modest for an industrializing Latin American country.[13] Not without reason was the policy design for this achievement, particularly in the 1959–1970 interval, known as *crecimiento estabilizador* ("stabilizing growth").

This enviable record is important for understanding Mexico's problems since the early 1970s. Decade after decade, experience led Mexicans to expect that each year's GDP would invariably top that of the year before. No recent administration has wanted, therefore, to be the first to fail to keep the economy moving ahead. When, for instance, the growth rate dropped early in Echeverría's term, the government reacted by accelerating spending so much that the prolonged period of price stability ended. The same psychology may well have led the López Portillo administration to delay bringing the growth rate down to keep it more in line with nonborrowed resource availabilities.

Mexicans were also unfamiliar with anything like the policy gyrations to which they were introduced in the Echeverría presidency, and most had never experienced an unstable growth of the sort the economy exhibited during his term and the next. Further, prior to the 1976 devaluation, which was several years overdue, not since 1954 had the peso been devalued against the dollar. When from 1973 through 1981, double-digit inflation fluctuated in the teens and twenties (some claim higher), this provided, along with the unsettling 1976 devaluation, a quite unaccustomed set of monetary conditions for Mexicans—even before the rate of inflation leaped, in 1982, to just over 98 percent. Owing to the recency of the transition to a high-inflation economy, neither business firms nor households have yet become used to the kind of inflationary environment (and exchange rate instability) with which their counterparts in Brazil, Argentina, and Chile have long had to cope.

Before these troubles, there was reason for the Mexican policy community to feel even smugger than the statistics might suggest. They had, after all, begun their long march amid much adversity. Few human resources, scant capital, and an abundance of infrastructural and organizational devastation as an aftermath of civil war—such was the unpromising scene when things got under way. There were no ready historical precedents for what Mexico was trying to do, examples that might have been studied as a source of instruction or emulation. Neither was there any suitable body of development theory at hand. Not until more than a decade later did economists begin to adapt neoclassical, Keynesian, or other doctrines to the special problems of countries such as Mexico. There were also no development agencies and banks to which to turn, no technical assistance teams on call—just a tattered capitalism and a collapsed world economy that had cast a pall of doubt on the efficacy of the kind of economic analysis practiced up to then.

There had been intermittent discussion and occasional legislation to promote industry in the 1920s and 1930s, but in those years manufacturing was almost of necessity secondary to agriculture. Doubtless political and ideological factors entered into the government's decision to tackle first the rehabilitation of the rural sector; yet there were compelling economic reasons as well. Agricultural production had suffered greatly from the protracted disinvestment brought on by years of fighting and insecurity. Pending development of alternative arrangements for crop financing, production management, and marketing, the breakdown of traditional agricultural institutions centered on the hacienda was another blow. During the 1930s, bad weather contributed further damage. How to deal with rural unrest, with its unsettling effects on the urban business and political climate, was another matter to be resolved.

Notwithstanding all the other problems with which it had to contend, the Cárdenas government moved resolutely to bring a new order out of rural chaos and to take up the practical question of how to provision the population—an issue that could hardly be skirted at a time when the foreign markets for primary exports were in disarray. It was evident that if Mexico was to eat better as part of its struggle against poverty, it would have to produce nearly all of the increase desired.

Huge expanses of land were seized and redistributed, and public investments were pumped into such rural infrastructure as roads, schools, irrigation systems, and, by the end of the decade, rural electrification. The vindication of these policies came sooner than might have been expected: there was a significant recuperation of agricultural output by the early 1940s. During the three administrations after Cárdenas, the emphasis was less on additional land redistribution than on consolidation of existing gains and the complementary investments needed to boost productivity. In some areas, so much advance was registered that an important export agricultural sector arose. Despite this temporary de-emphasis of land reform, each post-Cárdenas government distributed more land than had any pre-Cárdenas government. During the presidencies of Adolfo López Mateos (1958–1964) and Gustavo Díaz Ordaz (1964–1970), land redistribution was stepped up again to a very high level, surpassing in the latter term even the amount the Cárdenas administration had redistributed.

The externalities of agrarian restructuring began to show up in the 1940s and thereafter, at a time when foreign suppliers of manufactures were cut off by wartime conditions and when there was a growing unsatisfied demand in the United States for consumer goods and other manufactured items. At home, the agrarian reform had brought the rural population out from behind the institutional walls of the hacienda and into the embryonic national market, or at least into proximity thereto. The revival of farm production, the spreading of communications and transport networks, the beginnings of rural schools and human capital formation in agriculture—in conjunction with a postreform environment of greater social, geographical, and occupational mobility, and corresponding new incentives and aspirations—gave a notable impetus to expansion of the home market for consumer goods, which, if they were to be supplied at all, had to be produced locally. Thereby began, perhaps initially more a product of the conditions then prevailing than of conscious design, the mid-century industrial revolution in Mexico. In short order, however, the attraction of manufacturing development proved so irresistible that an accumulation model based on import-substitution industrialization became the centerpiece of the national project.

During 1940–1952, the engagement of Mexico with the world economy changed significantly. The multiple economic impacts of World War II not only gave a significant impulse to the embryonic industrial development of the previous two decades, but also ensured that national policy would increasingly aim at incorporating the external sector much more fully into domestic growth.

Three decades of sustained rapid industrialization accomplished much. By the 1970s, the country had become a leading manufacturing power of Latin America, with a broad range of industrial production. The versatility of Mexico's production capacity was strengthened by at least three circumstances. In the first place, Mexico's industrial policy had not, with conspicuous exceptions such as the iron and steel industry, pressed strongly for a deepening of the industrial structure. Consequently, Mexican industry, unlike, say, its Argentine counterpart, was able to establish itself on the basis of imports of cheap and efficient capital equipment rather than on protected local sources of higher-cost and lower-quality machinery. Also favorable to the cost structure in manufacturing production was the fact that many Mexican industries grew up under comparatively moderate de facto protection, thanks to the over-valued peso in the decade or so before the 1976 devaluation and to the permeability of Mexico's northern frontier, over which undocumented workers heading north pass undocumented goods heading south. Both circumstances have operated to mitigate the effects of protectionism and to force cost cutting on national producers, accelerating the buildup, through learning by doing, of human resources at both managerial and skilled labor levels. Low labor and transport costs in relation to the country's main export market, the United States, were a third factor in structuring Mexico's comparative advantages—in agriculture and minerals as well as in industry, not to mention the striking growth of the tourist industry and the reliance on migrant workers as foreign exchange earners from the 1940s onward.

Most of the effort and capital used in this transformation of the economy were Mexican, but Mexico also drew heavily on foreign sources. The agrarian reform and modernization together with continuing public investments in infrastructure and the increasing integration of regional economies brought into being a particularly dynamic national market, one that extended even beyond the rapidly growing cities. In due course, the evident new stability of the reform-minded regime looked as appealing as the much different Porfirian stability had looked in its day. New technologies and marketing and managerial skills poured in as part of the large-scale influx of foreign investment capital, their spread throughout the local economy facilitated by the investments in education and communication. A regulated welcome awaited foreign companies, to "compatibilize," as Mexicans put it, foreign capital with national interests. But the stability of the investment climate, the growth of internal demand, and the relatively high quality of the government's economic management all operated to make the country a singularly attractive place for expansion by many of the world's leading manufacturers. In retrospect, it seems indisputable that it was the very extensiveness of the control powers held by the state as well as its commanding position in key sectors of the economy that provided the policy space needed for allowing foreign enterprise to enter in such volume and variety.[14]

Any review of the sources of growth, however, would be incomplete if it omitted the extraordinary success of Mexico in building new institutions. For example, fiscal incentives, loans at concessionary rates, and protection and inducements of varied sorts (such as the 1936 Law of Industry Saturation, import quotas, and rising domestic sourcing requirements for manufacturing components) were employed to bring into being a modern industrial sector and to update portions of the agricultural sector. The evolving production system counted also on a steadily improving distribution system and a widening range of business services. Of particular importance was an increasingly sophisticated system of financial intermediaries for encouraging and channeling domestic savings into capital formation, a development that has attracted much scholarly attention over the years.[15] Nowhere, though, was organizational development more evident than in the public and parastatal sectors.[16]

One of the first components of this new structure was the state banking system centered on the Bank of Mexico, which was established in 1925. The following year saw creation of the National Agricultural Credit Bank. In the 1930s and 1940s came several additions: National Urban Mortgage and Public Works Bank (1933), National Ejidal Credit Bank (1935), National Warehouses (1936), National Foreign Trade Bank (1937), National Workers' and Industrial Development Bank (1939), National Bank for Cooperative Development (1941), and a series of others, including special investment trust funds to cater to particular industries and other groupings.[17] Still other parastatal financial institutions were launched in subsequent years, and with the acquisition of the Somex Bank in the 1970s, the state returned to the business of commercial banking that the Bank of Mexico had performed at its outset. Of all the state's financial ventures, however, none was more important than Nacional Financiera, which from 1934 on spearheaded the country's industrial development drive.[18]

Year after year Nacional Financiera's able staff guided state investments into a growing array of industrial ventures: cement, chemicals, iron and steel, electricity, wood and paper, agricultural processing, machinery, vehicles and engines, textiles, railway cars, and so on, giving the parastatal sector considerable leverage over the nation's manufacturing sector and a beachhead in mining. Additional leverage has been supplied by the Federal Electricity Commission, an agency established in 1933 primarily as a regulatory body but with a growing involvement in production after the end of that decade; in 1960, the entire public service electric power industry was nationalized.[19] Railway tariffs and the pricing policies of the state oil company, Petróleos Mexicanos (Pemex), have been employed as further instruments of industrial policy.

Meanwhile, the state trading company, once aimed chiefly at stabilizing crop markets, expanded and diversified until, in the early 1970s, it was operating production enterprises and a nationwide chain of retail stores.[20] Still other entities were added to the state's portfolio as time went on; during the Echeverría period, their proliferation caused much alarm in some business circles.

A vast network of politically determined prices, a large state bourgeoisie, and a patronage system linked with state management of the economy alongside that built on public administration and the distribution of electoral offices were three other relevant facets of this progressive elaboration of the machinery of state. Not only did the parastatal sector ramify into almost all the main branches of the economy even prior to the banking nationalization of 1982, but it also equipped the state with an unusually broad repertoire of instruments for working toward its various political and economic ends. (That, in the process, this also created multiple leakages from the federal treasury to cover the operating deficits and capital budgets of state enterprises is of further significance for the present situation.)

With the recent banking nationalization—and the concomitant acquisition of the banks' shareholdings in major industrial firms—the profile of intervention rose, but it is important for perspective to recognize that the original basis of the system was essentially re-established. During the 1960s and 1970s, Mexico's successful industrial revolution and the rise of a vigorous and efficient financial system based on large banking chains began to evoke shades of Rudolf Hilferding's *Finanzkapital*, for it brought on stage formidable new private-sector actors who, with their foreign partners, seemed capable of challenging the primacy of the state and the domination of the PRI. The political class and the intelligentsia were especially discomforted, and the allegation was widely made that business groups had gained control of Mexico. To the extent that political ends were sought and realized through the bank nationalization—namely, redressing the balance of political forces by quashing the power of the new Mexican *zaibatsus*—to that extent it restored systemic equilibrium to its customary locus. Thus, far from constituting a radical departure in policy, the measure was, in this sense, profoundly conservative. The historical hegemony of the party/government bureaucracy was reasserted, and government regained its traditional freedom to adopt an independent economic policy.

Style in the Mexican Political Theater

Some incline toward the view that the revolutionary process has built a shared civil culture, one with democratic, or at least democratizing, tendencies and relatively broad participation, albeit not necessarily in forms most familiar to the Anglo-American world.[21] This perspective normally highlights the responsiveness of the policy process to varied interests, remarks its inclusionary character and populist garb, and looks to the stable yet fluid consensus that has for decades served as the fulcrum of Mexican politics.[22] An alternative reading of the historical script sees the revolutionary process as leading, through authoritarian controls, to the triumph of a bourgeoisie that, as the morality play progresses, sheds its disguise of reformism and stands starkly revealed in the embrace of foreign capitalists.[23] "Associated dependent capitalist development" is the title nowadays bestowed on the work by those of this persuasion, most of whom share the vision, if not the technique, of Rivera and Siqueiros.

Clientelism and corporatism have not operated as mutually exclusive alternatives.[24] To some extent, the former has functioned as a preferred mode of interaction within the governing apparatus, where patronage has been raised to a high art (or perhaps a sport of Olympic quality). Indeed, it would not be much amiss to conceptualize the government-party apparatus as an immense patronage system, one amplified further by the parastatal sector's growth. As seen externally, the complex amalgam of party functionaries and state bureaucracy has often opted for corporatist types of relationships. But there are elements of corporatism within the party structure and more than a touch of clientelism in relations between the politico-administrative class and its assorted constituencies, that is, between government agencies or parastatal enterprises and their suppliers and customers. A habit of looking for exact real-world counterparts of ideal types is very misleading. Further, all along, and certainly much before the term was coined to deal with South American regimes, the political dynamics of Mexico were shaded as well by a tinge of bureaucratic authoritarianism. To add to the complexity, Mexico also exhibits, at least at a formal level, the multiple parties and some of the nonexclusionary interest organizations that are normally associated with liberal pluralism.

As all this suggests, one of the hallmarks of the Mexican system— perhaps ever since the aboriginals took on Spanish ways and the Spanish missionaries provided a new saint for each of the ancient deities—has been its capacity for improvisation and pragmatic adaptation, notwithstanding the thematic continuity that runs through the liturgical language of revolutionary political discourse. The complex overlay of organizations and differently structured processes resulting from this improvisation has, moreover, multiplied opportunities for distributing roles that are administrative and, even if only nominally, of leadership dimensions. Thus, insofar as the Mexican political regime may be construed as a nationwide patronage structure geared primarily to the distribution of status, it has helped to stabilize the system by muting, though not obliterating, differences based on class, region, and interest lines.

Four characteristics of the PRI as a political party have much to do with the durability of the institution, a durability a number of other Latin American parties have tried unsuccessfully to emulate. First, it is multiclass and aspires to national coverage. Within its organizational ambit lie innumerable rewards for loyalty and aids to career advancement, folded in a generally relaxed party discipline and loose organizational structure that, in turn, is to a considerable extent enveloped by the apparatus of government. Compared, say, with the suffocating clutch of the communist party in the Soviet bloc, the disciplinary mantle of the PRI falls lightly indeed over the Mexican body politic, but it is nonetheless effective. As a mechanism for spotting potential leaders and for inducting them into the system, it has operated rather like an additional ministry, one for political affairs, dutifully beckoning to the up-and-coming to associate with its mission, or at least with its patronage structures. This is especially true during electoral campaigns when the party springs vigorously into action.

Closely related to the remarkable absorptive capacity of the PRI in the recruitment of cadres is its ability to function as an information-gathering system, monitoring the political horizon to identify and appropriate the concerns of various groups—including the political opposition—and bring those that show constituency-building promise into the program of government. Some claim the system is primarily unscrupulous, for thievery and corruption have sometimes risen to such prominence that the quest for personal enrichment on the playing fields of the public sector seems almost a major motivation for political activism and the source of what passes for political commitment. Cynical observers have on occasion even referred to the system as a kleptocracy. However, in campaign after campaign the PRI has proved as adept as the magpie in spotting attractive platform baubles and making their glitter part of its own nest. Very few notions appear to be unambiguously beyond its reach.

There is a third element that smoothes the path of the party/government bureaucracy and effectively buttresses the PRI's near-monopoly of cherished political symbols. This is the institutionalized renewal that has been built into the allocation of political posts from the local level up to the very highest in the land. Every six years there is a massive turnover of both elective and appointive posts, with changes in the latter sometimes and changes in municipal posts always taking place more frequently.[25] Reappointments to a position are not unknown, but they are used sparingly so as not to impair the self-renovating dimension of a bureaucratic-political elite that is, at the same time, self-perpetuating. On each rotation, many names move within the structure and only a few leave it altogether, so that over the years the government-party machine has managed to build up considerable experience, through learning-by-doing, in handling the larger affairs of society, even though this custom has tended to forfeit the development of more specialized managerial skills. Micro-level efficiency has, in effect, been sacrificed for macro-level stability. (This cumulation of governing experience, together with the relative solidarity of the ruling group, contrasts significantly with the inexperience and tendency toward factionalism of the political opposition.)

A hopeful sign of what this turnover may portend is already evident in some of the economic agencies; namely, a progressive upgrading of the public and parastatal sectors' technical capability as they incorporate new entrants with improved university training through study abroad or in the better national institutions. The evidence is not yet available on another point, but it looks possible—again in key economic organizations—that a younger generation of technocrats, coming from more comfortable family backgrounds than the politician-bureaucrats they are replacing, may bring to their work more of a public service orientation than the self-aggrandizing outlook sometimes displayed by public functionaries heretofore.

Of considerable importance are two other effects of the periodic turnover. On the one hand, the circulation of individuals through the system has, while building informal lateral linkages throughout the structure for the exchange of information and other purposes, managed to confirm popular perceptions that the system is not closed. It has also kindled widespread expectations that opportunity might yet swim into view. Considering the historical expansion of the public-sector opportunity structure, such expectations have, for many, been sound. Thus, the practice has actually aided in recruitment and commitment since rewards are periodically redistributed and the opportunities are thereby maximized for players to enter the game and at least stay in motion—if not progress upwards. On the other hand, while cliques (camarillas) play an important short-term role within the system as springboards for individual advancement, it also seems to be the case that the individual portfolios of loyalties shift in response to changing situational opportunities. The longer-run effect of recurrent job shuffling is thus to keep the configuration of cliques fluid and to lessen the chances of their hardening into factionalism.

The cohesiveness of a governing apparatus that has operated with such durability and versatility might at first glance seem hard to explain, especially given the high rate of turnover in office and the laxity of overt party discipline (though not of informal monitoring and control). Much depends on the context of secular expansion and on the axis around which the whole pyramidal system revolves: the office of the chief executive. An office in which exceptionally broad administrative and legislative powers are concentrated, the Mexican presidency has been aptly described as a limited-term monarchy, one that governs, if not with the full authority of absolutism, then certainly with fewer institutional encumbrances than constrain most elected heads of state.[26] Much of the Iberian tradition of bureaucratic patrimonialism carries over into this role and its superordinate relation to the complex of formal government hierarchy and the PRI that constitutes the chief political organizing instrument. By and large, it appears to be the strong sense of institutional self-preservation and the exigencies of organizational maintenance that set the practical limits on the exercise of presidential power. Basic legitimacy, we may postulate, derives not only from the continuity of presidential power with the Iberic political tradition but also from the skill of the incumbent in managing all the balancing that is needed to keep the complicated structure intact.

All these aspects of political and administrative circulation have a great deal to do with the system's ability to deliver an atmosphere of certainty and incremental, rather than disjunctive, policy changes. The connection between them and the secular expansion of the public and parastatal sectors should, moreover, be obvious. Yet there may be risks in store for the system much beyond the perils of the current IMF stabilization program and the adjustments required to bring the external debt back into line with resource realities.

Towards a Social Balance Sheet

The optimism that inheres in the Mexican system, together with the distributions of benefits of various sorts through myriad government programs and a pervasive network of politically determined prices for the many parastatally produced goods and services, brings into focus the central importance of the government's reform agenda (both the deeds and the promises) and the system's reliance on a long-term expansion of the parastatal sector. While it is easy to criticize the microeconomic inefficiencies and the "distortions" in resource allocation induced by subsidies, protectionism, and an array of other interventionary measures, and while it is now fashionable to decry politically determined prices as "artificial," such judgments must themselves be subject to two criticisms—besides the obvious objection that the market being a social artifact, market prices are no less artificial than those fixed by custom or administrative action.

In the first place, departures from market equilibrium positions produced by the kind of institutional order that prevailed up to the Revolution or, for that matter, during the two decades or so of civic upheaval after 1910, can hardly be faulted as being "suboptimal." The Revolution and its governments represent an incontrovertible societal assessment—a revealed preference, as it were—that the old order, and the distribution of power, wealth, and income it gave rise to, had come to lack fundamental acceptability. Any given set of market prices has, after all, only as much legitimacy as the underlying institutional relationships it reflects and projects, and in the Mexican case it is precisely these that public policy was consciously directed to changing.

At the same time, public authorities have usually recognized the provisional usefulness of prices as scarcity indicators despite their other shortcomings. Consequently, notwithstanding inspired criticism from the Left that the Revolution has been sold out, the government never attempted, for all its reiteration of "socialist" ideals, to impose what in any case would have been unworkable; namely, a centrally planned economy in which all or even most prices were administratively determined. In two crucial policy areas, the government, until quite recently, anchored the price structure in real scarcity relationships. By keeping the economy relatively open through exchange and trade policies, public authority could avoid the worst excesses of an insulated price system save for periods in which the exchange rate got out of line and produced the predictable economic mischief. Second, in dealing with the monetary measuring rod itself, the stance of the government was, until the 1970s, moderately conservative; direct intervention and selective credit allocations were used to pursue public policy objectives instead of the cruder, and far more inflationary, fiscal-monetary packages that were customary in so much of Latin America.

The second objection to the pure-market critique comes also from the historical record. The price structure and allocation patterns generated as government carried out the institutional business of the Revolution define a social preference function that has shifted a massive volume of resources from less productive to more productive uses and fostered an impressive amount of capital formation. They have also yielded a regime continuity and a modulated evolution of policy that have spared the country, from the 1930s on, the political travails and disruptive policy shifts that afflict social processes and depress capital formation and aggregate productivity in most of Latin America. Offsetting micro-level inefficiency, in other words, has been a macro-level efficiency great enough to sustain the striking growth record of the past fifty years—without, one might add, the harshly repressive measures some hemispheric governments have had to invoke to try to enforce their chosen versions of economic tidiness.

In analyzing the policy environment and investment climate of Mexico since its half-century upswing in aggregate growth began, there is simply no meaningful way to dissociate economic variables from political and social ones. Given the nature of the Revolutionary phenomenon, the relationship among these different types of variables has been intimate and interactive, with the public and parastatal sectors serving as the means for overturning and reformulating extensive sets of social relations and expectations.

What the Mexican experience seems to establish is that a less-developed country embarking on a period of rapid development must design policies that produce change as much as growth. What is more, the changes entailed extend much beyond the three sorts ordinarily acknowledged, that is, changes in production functions, changes in the composition of inputs, and changes in the composition of goods-and-services output. Besides the goods and services conventionally reckoned as products in the national accounts, any system also produces social relations from which derive the nonincome components of welfare, that is, a relational output. Social recognition and status structures, perceptions of life chances and security, the amount of associational rights and voice in decisional processes, the quality of working conditions, the social acceptability of income distribution—such factors as these make up the category of relational output, which, like the flow of goods and services, requires resource inputs for its provision.[27] Further, as a type of collective or public good, relational output can be both prized in its own right (as consumption) and valued for its part in the production process (as investment). Within limits, as history shows, trade-offs can be effected among all three categories of valued output.

Viewed in this light, the *Porfiriato* was a period in which the strong negative value assigned the regime's relational output ultimately outweighed gains registered in the aggregate production of goods and services. Correspondingly, during much of the Revolutionary period, losses in the production of goods and services were, at least to some extent, offset by improved relational output. From the early 1930s, the system apparently succeeded, for an extended interval, in registering increases in all three components of output: agrarian reform, changes in labor's status, and the expansion of the state sector and rapid industrialization (with the new employment opportunities created thereby in derivative tertiary activity) all tended to boost fairly strongly the welfare gains associated with relational output. These nonincome welfare components, especially in their expectational aspects, may even for a while have offset, at least partially, adverse trends in real income as defined by goods and services alone, which several observers remarked by the end of the 1950s. All along, the language of politics, with its heavy use of revolutionary symbols, was played up in an attempt to mold both expectations and assessments of actuality in respect of relational output.

By the end of the 1960s, however, diminishing returns had set in, and earlier revolutionary reforms were wearing thin, no longer so readily capitalizable into political (and environmentally stabilizing) credit. The growing concentration of economic power and wealth, glaring inequality in the distribution of income, and significant regional disparities in standards of living and economic vitality were all, in a sense, contradictions born of economic success but contradictions that nevertheless eroded the value of the system's relational output. Concurrently, the employment-generating capacity of industrial growth and expansion in the tertiary sector was being overtaken by demographics, thanks to advances in health and nutrition. Meanwhile, a shift in policy emphasis that began around the late 1950s, from capital formation in the rural sector to urban-industrial investment—involving a massive provision of urban infrastructure, housing, and plant and equipment—started in time to weaken the balance of payments by shrinking the agricultural surplus, the excess of agricultural exports over agricultural imports. The erosion of sectoral strength was gradual and at the time not particularly disconcerting. Moreover, like many of the other problems, the lag in agricultural output was to some extent a function of systemic success, namely, the rise in demand brought on by population growth and higher per capita incomes.

At this point, though, another policy error came into play, the stabilized exchange rate that Mexicans took as emblematic of their vaunted policy success in the development field. Modest as it was in comparison with other major Latin American countries, inflation gradually ran into the fixed exchange rate policy set after the devaluation of the mid-1950s, so that by the end of the 1960s, the peso was becoming progressively more overvalued. As could have been foreseen, consumer imports were encouraged to the detriment of local producers, and investment in import-competing lines was discouraged. Foreign travel by Mexicans was in effect subsidized at the same time that the tourist industry in Mexico lost its competitive edge. Mexico's border trade, a traditional source of foreign exchange earnings, began slowly to shift in favor of the U.S. side of the frontier. The expansion of nontraditional exports of manufactures was hampered, although in testimony to the efficiency attained in that sector, their growth, in the late 1960s and early 1970s, nevertheless averaged about 15 percent annually. Of special detriment was the fact that capital export began to look more attractive as savers sought to protect the real value of their assets.

Political unrest was, therefore, coupled with economic dislocation as Echeverría took office. Although it was plain that demography and exchange rate policy, as well as the sectoral distribution of investment, had much to do with the difficulties, the malaise of the times provoked a mounting concern that the first wave of import-substitution industrialization had crested and begun to subside, leaving the country in a grave structural predicament.

Under Echeverría, the severe adverse economic tendencies came to a head. Exchange rate maladjustment grew progressively worse, as it was not until 1976 that a corrective devaluation was finally made. Balance of payments problems were exacerbated by other policies of the administration. Reacting to the slowdown of 1971 on the advice from those in government who were more nationalist and statist in orientation, the president replaced the "stabilizing growth" strategy with a populist "shared growth" (*desarrollo compartido*) approach, demonstrating (it was intended) the president's power to steer the nation in a new course if he were so minded. A spate of new development programs ensued, but they were in some cases ill-conceived and in most instances poorly coordinated, although they did expand the opportunity to recruit more public functionaries and rejuvenate the bureaucracy.

The practical effect of this new orientation was mainly that the government went overboard on public spending and, reverting to a policy bent of long standing (a kind of institutional perseveration, as it were), plunged ahead with the creation of a multitude of new agencies and public enterprises. From 12.6 percent of GDP in 1971, the state's participation in the economy rose to 17.8 percent in 1975. While below the government's share in several other countries (where, in most instances, military expenditures inflate public budgets), this was a rapid enough spurt to provoke alarm in some quarters and to strain the real resources of the economy. Not surprisingly, aggregate growth quickly recovered, but under conditions that raised the inflation rate to over 22 percent in 1974.

Such an unfortunate outcome of stimulative policies came partly from the populist stance, which made it difficult for government to revise the deficit-generating pricing policies of many parastatal firms. Partly, though, the problem stemmed from the inability to increase tax revenues substantially through fiscal reform.[28] Both circumstances revealed that, at least temporarily, there had been some reduction of the autonomy of the state in relation to civil society. As a result, the step-up in spending led to a rise in the public sector borrowing requirement, from 0.9 percent of GDP in 1971 to 4.9 percent in 1975 and 4.7 percent the following year. This, in turn, both drained funds from the domestic money markets and occasioned a rise in foreign borrowing. For this reason, the public sector was the largest client for new foreign loans, but a few years later, exchange rate policy encouraged private firms to add to the external indebtedness as well—while compounding their difficulties when the inevitable devaluation was eventually made. From 1970 to 1975, foreign indebtedness more than quadrupled.

For several reasons, there was a steady deterioration in the ability to finance enough imports to maintain the desired growth rate. Dollarization and capital exports grew, while Mexico's external position worsened also on account of the critical situation in rain-fed agriculture and a rapidly dwindling agricultural surplus. Mexican travel abroad rose, as did sundry consumption imports, while service exports (mainly tourism) weakened and the recession of 1974–1975 abroad undermined merchandise exports. On top of everything else, the president embarked on a flamboyant foreign policy that underscored the reservations foreign investors were beginning to have about the prospects for Mexico. At one point he even provoked a costly boycott of the Mexican tourist industry.

There were episodic attempts to bring about administrative and fiscal reform, and the government at last reversed its traditional natalist stance. Following years of neglect, the government began anew to devise "integrated" programs for agricultural rehabilitation. Yet these and other measures ultimately proved unavailing, and as the administration moved through its last year in office, the general loss of confidence in its macroeconomic management reached crisis proportions. No longer was it possible to trade in the time-honored manner on the old inventory of symbols, policy expedients, and promissory notes denominated in social change—though it must be acknowledged that in the absence of more far-reaching policy changes, some timely land redistributions (and stepped-up migration northward) helped keep the peace in the countryside and averted serious labor conflict. One gets the distinct impression that the fabric of Mexican development policy was swiftly unraveling by the time that López Portillo assumed the presidency and moved to restore the implied social compact of former times through his Alliance for Production. How much institutional damage had been done remained to be seen.

Economic Derailment, 1976–1982

The year 1982 was, as noted earlier, traumatic for Mexico. Besides marking the end of a presidential term that had become, like its immediate predecessor, ever more controversial in its ricochets of policy, the year included two substantial devaluations, nationalization of the entire Mexican-owned commercial banking sector, the imposition of exchange controls and a multiple exchange rate regime, and the start of negotiations on another IMF stabilization program. (Ironically, the administration had begun its work in the context of an IMF stabilization program that had been cobbled together to salvage the aftermath of the Echeverría period.) The end of free convertibility was particularly disconcerting, given the habituation of Mexicans to liberal policies in this field. But the seizure of domestically held dollar deposits and their conversion to pesos at a penalty rate made the situation much worse; in all probability, it left a legacy of mistrust that will bedevil the economy for years to come. The whole shift in policy configuration, in fact, made a strange conclusion to an administration that earlier seemed more or less favorably inclined to bringing Mexico into the GATT and that, at its inception, was welcomed with great relief by business as a significant improvement on the left-leaning and erratic leadership of Echeverría. When López Portillo took the oath, bathed in the glow of a prospective oil bonanza, few could have anticipated that the same leader would leave the executive mansion (for another no less elegant, to be sure) surrounded by so much economic distress.

In spite of the growth of petroleum reserves, production, exports, and revenues, the departing administration left as its legacy a huge fiscal deficit (around 18 percent of GDP), a drastically accelerating inflation (nearly 100 percent) that left Echeverría's record in the shade, and a troubling escalation of the external debt (to some $80 billion) with mounting difficulty in servicing it. The needs for external financing had risen so fast that they far outstripped export earnings brought in by the petroleum boom. Hampering the adjustment of policy was the fact that the need for external financing was intimately geared into the growth process itself. Real investment more than doubled between 1970 and 1981, so that, owing to a high import fraction in capital formation, imports were required in ever larger volume to support the strong investment rate that policymakers sought to maintain. Meanwhile, an again overvalued peso (despite the 1976 devaluation) had, in the context of a strong surge in domestic consumption spending, triggered a flood of consumer goods and services, hurt local import-competing industries while nipping the promising growth in new manufactured exports, and started up a fresh outflow of capital.

There was, moreover, growing evidence of the insufficiency, if not breakdown, of policies designed to help the lagging agricultural sector. A series of programs had been started in the Echeverría administration to try to undo years of inattention. Besides the stepped-up operations of the National Popular Staples Corporation (CONASUPO), three new strategies were launched during the 1970s: the National Plan for Impoverished Areas and Marginal Groups (COPLAMAR), the Integrated Rural Development Program (PIDER), and the Mexican Nutrition System (SAM). Especially refreshing was a willingness that surfaced under López Portillo to rethink the country's historical commitment to the collective agricultural enterprise known as the *ejido* and to consider modifications in that sacrosanct institution to promote higher productivity. Even so, the steady procession of governmental acronyms across the countryside never quite managed to spell success.

Still other problems were in evidence by 1982. Most reflected, in one way or another, the excessive hopes that had been placed on petroleum as, almost literally, a *deus ex machina* that would deliver the Mexican economy from the afflictions of the early 1970s. Yet, for all the initial determination of the government to avoid the structural distortions referred to as the *venezolanización* of the economy, the operative philosophy soon seemed to be "let the good times roll," even when the oil market began to weaken from the world oil glut. The growth of government spending was unbridled, rising in real terms by 20 percent in 1978, the year after the IMF program was concluded, and by over 13 percent each year between 1979 and 1981. So careless was the social use of oil revenues that one after another the elements of what had originally been an ambitious but not farfetched national development plan had to be revised or discarded. In short order, a country that had historically been distinguished by its diversified pattern of exports became overwhelmingly dependent (some three-fourths of export earnings) on foreign sales of a single commodity, with little headway having been made toward diversifying the country's export markets.

Both Echeverría and López Portillo had explicitly sought to strengthen the economy, and perhaps gain more policy space in the bargain, by diversifying the external sector's linkages abroad. Missions, ranging in scale from full presidential galas to more modest technocratic forays, sallied out to a variety of overseas destinations in search of new foreign suppliers of capital and technology. Export sales (including, proudly, sales of some items of Mexican technology) were pushed in a variety of Third World markets, for example, in Central America and the Caribbean, in Africa, and in India, and repeated efforts were made to expand Mexico's participation in markets of industrial nations other than the United States. Japan, not surprisingly, was wooed with special fervor, both as a customer and for its technology and capital. However, the structural modifications that such efforts could reasonably be expected to produce would be quite incremental and long term. In the shorter run, they tended to be much overshadowed by the rapid shift, thanks to petroleum, from a more diversified to a less diversified pattern of exports.

There were other casualties of the orientation to petroleum, such as López Portillo's early campaign against corruption. Although a number of investigations were initiated, these led to few prosecutions, and the effort was abandoned. Worse, the ready availability of petropesos lifted official peculation to spectacular new heights before the administration left office. The mere *mordida* ("bite"), to which everyone had long since been resigned, began to resemble an entire *comida* ("dinner"). From the standpoint of smaller and middle-sized businesses, those without preferential access to bank credit, there was still another snag—the significant "crowding out" effect that came from the "governmentalization" of loanable funds. According to some estimates, the public sector absorbed some 60 percent of bank credit in 1981 and 77 percent in 1982.

At the outset of the petroleum boom, the government had announced a policy of deliberately restrained production growth to avert inflation and extravagance and to harness the newfound subsoil wealth to national development priorities. The actuality of the case, however, was so different that by the end of the López Portillo term the erstwhile *deus* had, in the view of many, turned into an economic *bête noire*.

The Outlook

The object of the foregoing is not just to recount the elements that have gone awry in Mexican economic performance, although sorting out new relations and dealing with all the complications will constitute the chief task of both public- and private-sector decisionmakers for the presidential term now in progress. It is even more to the point to indicate that the situation confronting the country today has no precedents, not even near-precedents, from which extrapolation can reliably be made. Only the deterioration of agriculture promises to continue, and only the resumption by the state of its role as principal conductor of the economy leads back into a familiar institutional pattern. Many parameters have shifted, along with the variables, and government, firms, and households must now find their way, however painfully, over territory that is almost entirely new. So, too, must those who would try to see the implications from afar.

Finding a way through the current stabilization program may be particularly difficult as the compression of aggregate demand will inevitably intensify all the tensions that have built up through past years. For the time being, the government can undoubtedly capitalize on the universality of the economic crisis, claiming global conditions—the prevalence of recession and trade contraction—as extenuating circumstances. Few developing nations are, after all, in demonstrably better shape. Thus, while disaffection among working-class voters may lead some into the ranks of the Left and while middle-class defections may swell the membership of the rightist parties, political losses can probably be contained. In the longer run, the effect of the IMF policy regimen may, for all the customary allegations that such programs favor private enterprise, turn out to be a significant factor in reinstating the primacy of the political in the Mexican scheme of things.

Part of the agenda is not too hard to distinguish. In one form or other, management of the external debt will dominate the near-term future, although already Mexico has given a new wrinkle to development economics by adding to the concept of disguised unemployment that of disguised default.

Be that as it may, debt difficulties, along with the larger problems of which they are a part, will almost certainly prove salutary by tempering future national policies with a much greater degree of economic realism. The ultimate guarantor of recovery will be the wealth represented by the country's petroleum and natural gas reserves—that and the tremendous resources contributed by a half-century of rapid development. Technical, scientific, managerial, organizational, and other skills are far more abundant than they ever were before, and pending a collapse that is greater than anything one can reasonably envisage at present, these, together with the buildup of informational resources (including those gathered as externalities through proximity to the United States), should constitute the basis for a resumption of the interrupted expansion. Constriction will not, in other words, come from real resource scarcity if consumption is managed in any reasonable way.

Pressed by circumstances that can no longer be skirted and by the demands of the stabilization program, the government will also have to move seriously toward such goals as fiscal reform, raising agricultural productivity, and dealing with unemployment by a program of converting labor into rural and urban infrastructure. The decentralization of public services, begun during the 1970s, will surely be carried forward. Maintenance of a moderately undervalued peso will doubtless be tried, at least sporadically, in order to strengthen the balance of payments and again encourage export diversification in manufactures and services. The nationalized banking sector gives the state one more means of spurring export expansion—and, of course, of widening its base of political support among a hard-pressed business community. While the heavy costs inflicted on private savers by the imposition of exchange controls at the time of the last devaluation will probably require that government keep a watchful eye on trade and exchange markets to guard against a major resumption of capital flight, it is by no means clear that other new capital exports can be prevented or that the old exported capital will be repatriated.

Beyond these measures, it seems likely that the most prominent developments will lead away from the neoliberal orientation that has found so much favor of late in South America. The dismantling of the extensive system of politically determined prices, a process that has already begun at the insistence of the IMF, may tend to "depoliticize" the economy in one sense and deflate the cushion the state has traditionally held out to the more privileged segments of the working class and the middle class as well as to the business sector (the groups that have probably benefited most from consumption-related subsidies). But the adjustment of pricing will simultaneously place public enterprises on a much more solid financial footing and enable them—and the parastatal sector in general—to participate in accumulation more actively by laying the groundwork for self-financed expansion. The devaluations and import restrictions have tended to fall most severely on the larger firms of the private sector, while the nationalization of banking cut off their privileged access to loan capital where it did not actually bring in the state as a co-owner. Consequently, it should be the refurbished state sector that will take the lead in the accumulation model implied by the second stage of import-substitution industrialization, that is, the deepening of the industrial structure by a cautious expansion into intermediate and capital goods industries. The relational output associated with this pattern of renewed expansion via the parastatal sector should be socially stabilizing, for the major beneficiaries are almost certain to be organized labor and the professional and administrative middle class. Since the lower socioeconomic groups will not necessarily be worse off (the lot of the peasantry could conceivably improve) and inasmuch as private wealth, the focus of so much dissension anyway, is the most probable candidate for footing the bill, it is hard to see how what lies ahead could be other than a net gain for systemic stability.

Cooperation between the state and foreign capital, of necessity intensified by this development, should pose few political difficulties. The "commanding heights" of the economy having been secured for national purposes, the state can probably afford to take a more relaxed position in its dealings with multinationals. The growing sophistication of the Mexican technocracy, which has already overtaken the old-line *políticos* in key public bureaucracies, should work to the same end through strengthening the self-confidence of the Mexican government. A regime based on interventionism, when combined with middle-class comforts, is apt to be fairly moderate in its nationalism, especially when the anticipated foreign participation brings so many needed assets: the more complicated technologies required for the second stage of import-substitution industrialization, the equity-capital resource transfers that will have to substitute for the understandable chariness of bankers in supplying more loan capital, and, perhaps above all, the marketing expertise and international sourcing networks that could hasten development of Mexico's potential as an export platform in manufacturing. Arrearages in royalties and difficulties in repaying various credits may in many instances lead to conversion to equity as a means of settling accounts, and this, too, will maintain foreign involvement in the economy in a way that helps manage current problems. Given the unassailable position of national control over Mexican economic processes, save for constraints emanating from the country's engagement with the world economy, it is even conceivable that association with GATT may be placed back on the agenda.

In short, the most probable projection, in spite of all the problematic factors in the present and the vicissitudes of the recent past, appears to be a return to the state-led model of growth that has served pretty much as the historical paradigm for modern Mexico. Although the wild scramble that occurred in the 1970s after the bashing of the national piñata beclouded old certainties and raised new anxieties, the institutional framework that was forged in revolutionary struggle and tempered by decades of changing circumstances seems about as durable as any around.

Notes

1. For policy in the field of human resources development, see Clark Gill, *Education in a Changing Mexico* (Washington, D.C.: Government Printing Office, 1969); Charles N. Myers, *Education and National Development in Mexico* (Princeton, N.J.: Princeton University, Industrial Relations Section, 1965); Thomas Noel Osborn, *Higher Education in Mexico* (El Paso: Texas Western Press, 1976); Russell G. Davis, *Scientific Engineering and Technical Education in Mexico*, Education and World Affairs, Occasional Report no. 3 (New York, 1967); and Josefina Vásquez de Knauth, *Nacionalismo y educación en México* (Mexico City: El Colegio de México, 1970).

2. Key studies for understanding the incorporation of urban and rural labor into the Mexican political establishment are Joe C. Ashby, *Organized Labor and the Mexican Revolution Under Cárdenas* (Chapel Hill: University of North Carolina Press, 1967); and Moisés González Navarro, *La confederación nacional campesina* (Mexico City: Costa Amic, 1968). For a view of more recent developments, see Howard Handelman, "The Politics of Labor Protest in Mexico," *Journal of Interamerican Studies and World Affairs* 18 (August 1976): 267–94; and, for some tempering of the customary corporatist interpretation, Mark Thompson and Ian Roxborough, "Union Elections and Democracy in Mexico: A Comparative Perspective," *British Journal of Industrial Relations* 20, no. 2 (July 1982): 201–17. Broadly insightful for this aspect of institution-building is the near-classic Frank Tannenbaum, *Mexico: The Struggle for Peace and Bread* (New York: Alfred Knopf, 1950).

3. For an exploration of the continuity between the Cárdenas episode and subsequent administrations, see William P. Glade, "Revolution and Development: A Mexican Reprise," in idem and Charles W. Anderson, eds., *The Political Economy of Mexico* (Madison: University of Wisconsin Press, 1963).

4. Political strongman Plutarco Elías Calles, who was president in 1924–1928, controlled his three successors, none of whom served a full term. Since the election of 1934, all chief executives have served their complete terms, and none has been able to dominate the administration of his successor.

5. Sanford Mosk, *Industrial Revolution in Mexico* (Berkeley and Los Angeles: University of California Press, 1950).

6. Among the earliest writers, after Mosk, to explore the implications of business interest groups was Frank R. Brandenberg, "Organized Business in Mexico," *Inter-American Economic Affairs* 12 (Winter 1958): 26–50. Since then a number of good studies have appeared: Merle Kling, *A Mexican Interest Group in Action* (Englewood Cliffs, N.J.: Prentice-Hall, 1961); Marco Antonio Alcazar, *Las agrupaciones patronales en México*, El Colegio de México, Jornadas no. 66 (Mexico City, 1970); and the

definitive work by Robert J. Shafer, *Mexican Business Organizations: History and Analysis* (Syracuse, N.Y.: Syracuse University Press, 1973).

7. Typical of the outlook that prevailed in Mexico in that period is Manuel Germán Parra, *La industrialización de México* (Mexico City: Imprenta Universitaria, 1954).

8. John F. H. Purcell and Susan Kaufman Purcell, "Mexican Business and Public Policy," in James M. Malloy, ed., *Authoritarianism and Corporatism in Latin America* (Pittsburgh, Pa.: University of Pittsburgh Press, 1977), incline to the view that the state is paramount, while Dale Story, "Entrepreneurs and the State in Mexico," *Technical Papers Series* (Austin: University of Texas, Institute of Latin American Studies, Office for Public Sector Studies, 1980), stresses the autonomy of business groups. Actually, the two positions may to some extent be reconciled if they are taken as statements about longer-run and shorter-run relationships, respectively. Relevant also is Dale Story, "Trade Politics in the Third World: A Case Study of the Mexican GATT Decision," *International Organization* 36 (Autumn 1982): 767–94.

9. John F. H. Purcell and Susan Kaufmann Purcell, "State and Society in Mexico: Must a Stable Polity Be Institutionalized?" *World Politics* 32 (January 1980): 194–227, offer the interesting view that the balance resulting from this process of political development is actually quite precarious and that the fragility of the ruling interest coalitions is itself a major constraint on policy options.

10. The balancing of interests—for no one would claim that Mexican policy has been framed in complete disregard of the several political actors—is depicted succinctly but helpfully in the introduction of Jorge I. Dominguez, ed., *Mexico's Political Economy: Challenges at Home and Abroad* (Beverly Hills, Calif.: Sage Publications, 1982). As several sections of that book (and Story's article on GATT) indicate, there is not always internal coherence on the state side of policy bargaining, so that a bureaucratic politics model is often of use in ascertaining how particular decisions were reached.

11. Earlier time series show a slight decline in aggregate output for 1953, but the latest revised estimates have shown a very small gain for that year.

12. Among the convenient secondary sources of information on long-term Mexican growth are Clark W. Reynolds, *The Mexican Economy: Twentieth-Century Structure and Growth* (New Haven, Conn.: Yale University Press, 1970) and the more analytic René Villarreal, *El desequilibrio externo en la industrialización de México, 1929–1975* (Mexico City: Fondo de Cultura Económica, 1976).

13. William P. Glade, "Prices in Mexico: From Stabilized to Destabilized Growth," *Proceedings of the Academy of Political Science* 31, no. 4 (1975): 188–200 (special issue: C. Lowell Harris, ed., *Inflation: Long-Term Problems*).

14. Harry K. Wright, *Foreign Enterprise in Mexico: Laws and Policies* (Chapel Hill: University of North Carolina Press, 1971); and Ewell E. Murphy, Jr., "The Legal Framework for Foreign Investment in Mexico" (Paper for Symposium on Private Investments Abroad, Dallas, Tex.: International and Comparative Law Center, 1980).

15. Raymond W. Goldsmith, *The Financial Development of Mexico* (Paris: OECD Development Centre, 1967); Dwight S. Brothers and Leopoldo Solis, *Mexican*

Financial Development (Austin: University of Texas Press, 1966); and Robert L. Bennett, *The Financial Sector and Economic Development: The Mexican Case* (Baltimore, Md.: Johns Hopkins University Press, 1965).

16. An early attempt to provide an overview of this development is William P. Glade, Jr., *Las empresas gubernamentales en el desarrollo económico de México* (Mexico City: Problemas Agrícolas e Industriales de México, 1959). For a path-breaking, if controversial, effort to trace the growth of federal activity through its fiscal dimensions, see James W. Wilkie, *The Mexican Revolution: Federal Expenditure and Social Change Since 1910* (Berkeley and Los Angeles: University of California Press, 1967).

17. For a study that explores their larger systemic implications, see Charles W. Anderson, "Bankers as Revolutionaries: Politics and Development Banking in Mexico," in Glade and Anderson, *The Political Economy of Mexico*, pp. 103–85.

18. See Nacional Financiera, *Nacional Financiera, S.A., and the Economic Development of Mexico, 1934–1964* (Mexico City, 1964); Calvin P. Blair, "Nacional Financiera: Entrepreneurship in a Mixed Economy," in Raymond Vernon, ed., *Public Policy and Private Enterprise in Mexico* (Cambridge, Mass.: Harvard University Press, 1964), pp. 191–240; and Robert T. Aubey, *Nacional Financiera and Mexican Industry* (Los Angeles: University of California, Latin American Center, 1966). The industrial promotion function, it should be noted, did not really commence until 1941.

19. Miguel S. Wionczek, "Electric Power: The Uneasy Partnership," in Vernon, *Private Enterprise in Mexico*, pp. 19–110.

20. Merilee S. Grindle, *Bureaucrats, Politicians, and Peasants in Mexico* (Berkeley and Los Angeles: University of California Press, 1977).

21. Among the scholars who have noted, encouragingly, the more representative or democratic tendencies, see Robert Scott, "Mexico: The Established Revolution," in Lucien Pye and S. Verba, eds., *Political Culture and Political Development* (Princeton, N.J.: Princeton University Press, 1965); Robert Scott, *Mexican Government in Transition* (Urbana: University of Illinois Press, 1959); William P. Tucker, *The Mexican Government Today* (Minneapolis: University of Minnesota Press, 1957); and Martin Needler, *Politics and Society in Mexico* (Albuquerque: University of New Mexico Press, 1971).

22. Excellent for its portrayal of the flexibility of the policy process is Robert J. Shafer, *Mexico: Mutual Adjustment Planning* (Syracuse, N.Y.: Syracuse University Press, 1966).

23. For one of the many treatments emphasizing the seamier and more authoritarian side of Mexican political development, a view that emphasizes betrayal of revolutionary objectives, see K. F. Johnson, *Mexican Democracy: A Critical View* (Boston: Allyn & Bacon, 1971).

24. A voluminous literature now exists on these aspects of the system, some of the writing offering fairly spurious "coffeehouse" analyses based on a mixture of gossip and paranoia. Much, however, is quite well founded and helpful. For good examples of the latter, see Evelyn P. Stevens, "Mexico's PRI: The Institutionalization of Corporatism" (Paper delivered at the American Political Science Association Convention, Chicago, 1974); Vincent Padgett, *The Mexican Political System* (Boston: Houghton Mifflin,

1976); B. Anderson and J. Cockcroft, "Control and Cooptation in Mexican Politics," *International Journal of Comparative Sociology* 7 (March 1966): 16–22; José Luís Reyna, "Redefining the Authoritarian Regime," in idem and Richard Weinart, eds., *Authoritarianism in Mexico* (Philadelphia, Pa.: Institute for the Study of Human Issues, 1977); David Ronfeldt, *Atencingo: The Politics of Agrarian Struggle in a Mexican Ejido* (Stanford: Stanford University Press, 1973); Martin Greenberg, *Bureaucracy and Development: A Mexican Case Study* (Lexington, Mass.: Heath Lexington Books, 1970); Richard R. Fagen and William S. Tuohy, *Politics and Privilege in a Mexican City* (Stanford: Stanford University Press, 1972); Susan Kaufman Purcell, "Decision-Making in an Authoritarian Regime," *World Politics* 16 (October 1973): 28–54.

25. The most helpful books on this aspect of Mexican political style are Roderic A. Camp, *Mexico's Leaders: Their Education and Recruitment* (Tucson: University of Arizona Press, 1980); and Peter H. Smith, *Labyrinths of Power: Political Recruitment in Twentieth-Century Mexico* (Princeton, N.J.: Princeton University Press, 1979). Complementary to their analyses is a fine local-level study by William S. Tuohy, "Centralism and Political Elite Behavior in Mexico," Papers of the Latin American Development Administration Committee, Comparative Administration Group, American Society for Public Administration (Austin, Tex.: Institute of Latin American Studies, 1970).

26. Three incisive essays by Daniel Cosío Villegas provide as good a picture as any of the place of presidential power: *México: El sistema político mexicano*, Political Inquiry: Mexico, no. 1 (Austin: University of Texas, Institute of Latin American Studies, 1972), *El estilo personal de gobernar* (Mexico City: Cuadernos de Joaquín Mortiz, 1974), and *La sucesión presidencial* (Mexico City: Cuadernos de Joaquín Mortiz, 1975).

27. The concept used here is similar to the class and authority relations at both micro- and macro-levels that are summed up in the notion of relations of production, but I have preferred the term "relational output" to point to its character as a collective good that has both consumption and investment implications and, like other forms of output, is subject to trade-offs and diminishing returns. The investment implications of relational output were well caught in J. R. Commons's concept of "industrial goodwill."

28. Carlos Tello, a leader of the nationalist-statist camp, argues that the main policy failure was not so much a sin of commission as one of omission, the failure to impose more rigorous controls on the financial system and, in effect, to move into a much more closed economy model (see *La política económica en México, 1970–1976* [Mexico City: Siglo XXI Editores, 1979]).

7 Colombia

National Front and Economic Development

Bruce Michael Bagley

For more than a quarter of a century—since the creation of the National Front arrangement in 1958—Colombia has been viewed as a model of democratic stability and economic growth in Latin America. Only Venezuela and Costa Rica can match or surpass Colombia's record of twenty-five years of uninterrupted "democratic" rule, and neither proved capable of weathering the 1981–1983 international recession as successfully as Colombia. In fact, with declining but still positive growth rates (2.5 percent in 1982, 1.5 percent in 1983) and a manageable foreign debt (U.S. $10 billion in mid-1983), Colombia alone among the major industrializing Latin American countries (Mexico, Venezuela, Brazil, and Argentina) managed largely to escape the crisis that threatened widespread economic collapse and political instability throughout the region during 1982 and 1983. Although in mid-1983 Colombia confronted serious problems (an unprecedented industrial recession, low commodity prices for its agricultural exports, heavy pressures for devaluation, a widening balance of trade deficit, a soaring fiscal deficit, and severe capital flight), no Latin American country was in a better position to take advantage of international economic recovery during the mid-1980s.

This chapter offers an explanation of how and why Colombia has been able to achieve its enviable record of growth with stability. It also seeks to identify the major short- and medium-term problems, both economic and political, that the country must overcome if that record is to be sustained and to analyze the factors that have enabled the Colombian state to adopt and implement policies favorable to economic development.

The central thesis advanced runs counter to much conventional wisdom currently in vogue about Colombia. Rather than a functioning democracy as most analyses have maintained, this essay views the Colombian system as a particular brand of authoritarianism: an inclusionary authoritarian regime. It argues that Colombia's economic growth and political stability have been achieved at the cost of severe restrictions on democratic political participation. It concludes that the absence of effective channels of participation produced a growing crisis of political legitimacy over the decade of the 1970s, which in the 1980s could threaten the regime's stability.

The National Front: Democratic or Authoritarian?

The National Front, or *Frente Nacional*, was a bipartisan political arrangement between Colombia's traditionally dominant Liberal and Conservative parties to share power equally for a period of sixteen years (1958–1974) while excluding all other political parties from the system during the same period. It was designed to end the partisan strife (*La Violencia*) that had wracked the country since the late 1940s and to replace the military dictatorship of Gustavo Rojas Pinilla (1953–1957) with a civilian government. Among its major features were (1) alternation of the presidency between the two parties every four years for sixteen years, beginning with a Liberal and ending with a Conservative; (2) parity between the two parties in all elective and appointive posts; and (3) a two-thirds majority requirement to approve legislation in all decisionmaking bodies from the national congress to municipal councils.[1] This arrangement, unique in the annals of Latin American politics, has commonly been interpreted as a mechanism for the restoration of democracy in Colombia because it returned the army to the barracks after five years of military rule and because it restored political party activity, elections, and formal democratic freedoms (speech, press, assembly, and so forth). But most analysts recognized that the bipartisan arrangement incorporated a series of artificial, antimajoritarian and antidemocratic elements.[2]

In recognition of the Frente's limitations, the social science literature analyzing it has been replete with adjectives used to modify the term *democracy*, such as restricted, controlled, limited, oligarchical, elitist, elitist-pluralist, and consociational.[3] While these adjectives connote important analytic differences, their common denominator is the underlying insistence that the Front arrangement, despite its imperfections, constituted a democratic regime. Because the restrictions were temporary in nature (scheduled to end in 1974 with the programmed dismantling of the Front arrangement), most analysts felt comfortable in labeling the Front a variant of pluralist democracy. The regular holding of elections, the rotation of the presidency between the traditional parties, and the absence of the military from politics tended to confirm that the country was gradually becoming more democratic. When in 1974 the dismantling (*desmonte*) of the Front restrictions and the return to fully competitive elections were completed without military inter-vention or a return to violence, the sense that Colombian democracy had "matured" or "come of age" became entrenched as conventional wisdom.

The basic flaw in these analyses is an excessive focus on the formal aspects of democracy and failure to understand the dynamics of power and policymaking within the Colombian system. The National Front leadership adopted many forms and symbols of pluralist democracy, but in practice economic resources and political power remained highly concentrated in a small, relatively cohesive ruling class. The appearance of pluralism was maintained by the publicly ferocious competition among different fractions of the bloc-in-power represented in the political arena through the various factions of the traditional parties and an array of functionally and regionally specific interest groups. Such intra-ruling class competition did not, however, constitute pluralism in any real sense of the term. The Front rules guaranteed that the traditional party leaders—and the dominant class interests that they represented—would retain control of the state apparatus and its patronage potential. Elections were reduced to struggles over bureaucratic quotas among the factions within each party. Subordinate ethnic (Indians, Blacks) and class (peasants, rural workers, the urban poor, and segments of the working and middle classes) groups were systematically denied influence over state policy yet found themselves obliged to bear most of the costs of Colombia's accelerated economic growth during the 1960s and 1970s. Rather than an effort to create a framework for democratic political participation, the National Front was consciously designed as a system of political control from above to secure the conditions for rapid capitalist modernization.

While successful in reducing partisan violence and fostering growth, the Front also limited the possibilities for socioeconomic and political reform. The inability of the dominated classes to aggregate and articulate their demands effectively within the system produced rising political discontent (reflected in high abstention rates, the growth of opposition groups such as the Movimiento Revolucionario Liberal [MRL] and the Alianza Nacional Popular [ANAPO], peasant land invasions, civic and worker strikes, and guerrilla violence). Successive Frente presidents dabbled with symbolic redistributive reforms while in practice resorting almost continuously to their state-of-siege powers and the military to govern the country. The dismantling of the Front and the return to competitive elections in 1974 did little to remedy the deepening crisis of the regime. The parties, rooted in clientelism and patronage and riven with intense factionalism, had seen their ideological identities blur and their grass roots wither during the "safe" years of the Front. Elections and the electoral process remained mired in bossism and were increasingly divorced from the critical problems facing the country. The first two post-Front presidents (both Liberals) continued to invoke state-of-siege powers to rule as had their Front predecessors. In 1978 the Julio Turbay Ayala administration adopted by executive degree a harsh National Security Statute that significantly curtailed civil liberties while broadening the role of the military in the governance of the country. This 1978 statute—adapted from similar legislation used in the Southern Cone countries—was the Turbay administration's response to the intensification of left-wing guerrilla activities in both urban and rural areas during the late 1970s. It was accompanied by stepped-up antiguerrilla campaigns by the Colombian military and by the rise and spread of right-wing death squads carrying out vigilante justice against suspected subversives. Upsurges in common criminality (for example, kidnapping for profit) and drug-related violence and corruption also contributed to the Turbay administration's decision to adopt a hard-line strategy.

From this perspective, rather than a progressively more democratic and institutionalized regime, the Colombian system appears as a weakly institutionalized brand of inclusionary authoritarianism (at the outset of the Front) that became increasingly exclusionary and repressive during the 1970s in the face of the regime's deepening legitimacy problems. The transition to exclusionary politics has not yet been completed, nor is the trend irreversible. President Belisario Betancur Cuartas (1982–[1986]), in fact, came to power in August 1982 publicly committed, through democratic reforms, to reversing the trend toward militarization of the system. Whether successful or not in carrying out his ambitious "democratization" project, implicit in his diagnosis of the country's current political tensions is the recognition that the nation's political leadership failed over the previous two and one-half decades to sponsor the socioeconomic and political reforms required to institutionalize a stable democratic regime.

Origins of the Front

During the 1940s Colombia's traditional political regime (usually labeled an oligarchical democracy) broke down as a result of a fundamental conflict within the ruling class over the pace and direction of socioeconomic and political modernization. One segment, championed by the Conservative *caudillo* Laureano Gómez, sought to preserve the power and privileges of the traditional landowning class and allied agro-exporting interests through the installation of a hierarchical, authoritarian, and corporatist political system modeled on Franco's Spain. This segment did not seek to halt the process of capitalist modernization altogether, but rather to control its pace and direction. Gómez and the right-wing Conservatives were especially concerned with limiting and channeling popular participation in order to offset their party's minority position vis-à-vis the Liberals. A second segment of the ruling class, led by the Liberal *caudillos* Alfonso López Pumarejo and Jorge Eliecer Gaitán, sought to foster urban industry and modern commercial agriculture through Liberal mobilization of the electorate and the implementation of democratic and populist reforms. When superimposed on a fragile and traditional state apparatus, the conflicts between these two segments of the ruling class produced a crisis within the system and brought about the partial collapse of state authority. In 1948, following the assassination of the populist Gaitán, the situation finally degenerated into partisan warfare and anarchic rural violence—*La Violencia*.[4]

Designed to end the violence and restore political stability, the National Front agreement represented a compromise among the warring factions of the ruling class. This compromise was possible in 1958 because by the late 1950s the rapid expansion of capitalist agriculture had transformed many of the country's traditional landowners into commercial farmers and capitalist entrepreneurs, and many more were in the process of conversion. This change in the economic base of Colombian society reduced the relevance of the old antagonisms between capitalists and landowners within the bloc-in-power while promoting a new basis for their cooperation grounded in the common goal of accelerated capitalist development. In effect, the country's rapid economic transformation shifted the locus of economic and political power from the traditional landowners and agro-exporters to the capitalist class.[5]

Over the course of the *Violencia*, mobilized segments of the peasantry had grown increasingly independent of the control of the leadership of both traditional parties, the very elites who had instigated them to violence in the late 1940s and early 1950s. This tendency toward autonomy led elements in both parties to fear that the emerging class struggle in the countryside (especially in the zones known as "Red Republics") might escalate into a peasant revolution. Under these circumstances, most segments of the ruling class—landowners, commercial farmers, and urban industrialists from both parties—gradually came to the realization that they had to cooperate to restore political control or risk being swept from power altogether.[6]

The Rojas 1953 military coup against Gómez was initially supported by moderate Conservatives (especially the followers of former president Mariano Ospina Pérez [1946–1950]) and most Liberals, and it constituted a first attempt on the part of key elements of the ruling class to re-establish order and guarantee the conditions for capitalist growth. However, Rojas's independence from the traditional party leadership, his populist tendencies, his antibusiness economic policies, and his failure to promote the modernization and rationalization of agriculture ran counter to the interests of the ascendant capitalist class factions entrenched in both parties. Rojas attempted to develop among the military, the urban poor, and the working class a political base independent of the Liberal and Conservative parties. Although he achieved certain limited successes in this *Peronista*-style project, he was unable to loosen the traditional parties' sway over the majority of the Colombian population and was, therefore, vulnerable to the attacks launched by the party leaders against his government. Unable to mobilize sufficient popular or military support, Rojas was deposed in a bloodless military coup in 1957 carried out by an interim military junta committed to the restoration of civilian government.[7]

The National Front emerged in 1957–1958 as a political reaction to both the violence and the Rojas dictatorship. In contrast to the Rojas military experiment, its orienting ideology was "controlled democracy" rather than "populist authoritarianism," and its institutions were republican rather than dictatorial. The Front assumed this form not because of any unshakable commitment on the part of the dominant classes to the principles of democracy, but because the symbols of formal democracy constituted powerful ideological instruments to oppose the Rojas regime and to reconstruct a stable and legitimate state responsive to the demands and requirements of the hegemonic capitalist class.

The Front as an Inclusionary Authoritarian Regime

Although the Front arrangement assumed the formal trappings of democracy, in practice it set in motion a very different political system: an inclusionary authoritarian regime.[8] The basic characteristics of this type of authoritarianism include (1) low subject mobilization; (2) restricted or limited pluralism; (3) executive predominance; (4) a patrimonial style of rulership; and (5) the absence of any well-defined political ideology.[9]

Low Subject Mobilization. With a majority of the country's approximately 12 million inhabitants still living in rural areas in the late 1950s, the demobilization of the peasant self-defense and guerrilla bands operating in the countryside was essential for the restoration of political peace at the outset of the *Frente* period. This was accomplished through a variety of mechanisms. Chief among them was the elimination of partisan strife for public office through the restriction of electoral competition and the depoliticization of the national police and the armed forces. By guaranteeing each traditional party half of all elective and bureaucratic posts, the Front in effect eliminated the need for either party to mobilize its followers on a sustained basis or to maintain armed bands. Elections became essentially symbolic exercises in which the basic outcome was not in question, although the relative strength of different party factions was. As a result of this demobilization, the political parties were weakened at the grass roots, voter apathy and abstention rates rose, and party identification declined steadily during the 1960s. The Front reduced the immediate problem of intense partisan strife, but created new problems of responsiveness to the electorate and legitimacy that returned to haunt the nation's leadership throughout the 1970s and into the 1980s.[10]

In addition to limitations on electoral competition, the Front leadership also launched a campaign of community organization (called *Acción Comunal*) in both rural and urban areas. Designed to improve local infrastructure and living conditions through cooperative, self-help programs, Acción Comunal also served to create or strengthen links between the central government in Bogotá and local communities. Acción Comunal and similar programs undertaken by the government, private sector groups, the church, and various international agencies established new lines of political control and patronage that were used to bind local communities and leaders to the national political system more effectively than in the past. Along with renewed political party activity, such "inclusionary" programs, designed to incorporate rather than repress popular participation, clearly distinguished Colombia's National Front from the bureaucratic authoritarian regimes of the Southern Cone.[11] However, during most of the National Front and much of the post-Frente period, the country (or large parts of it) was ruled under emergency decree powers granted to the president.[12]

Limited Pluralism. A fundamental limitation on Colombian democracy during and after the Front has been the extreme concentration of key resources—land, capital, credit, education, and income—in the upper strata of Colombian society. Such concentration, combined with widespread poverty and illiteracy in the lower strata, created severe barriers to effective political participation. Colombia's overall level of income inequality is high by international standards. In fact, with Gini coefficients in the range of 0.50 to 0.55 percent, the Colombian pattern is similar to that found in Brazil (an exclusionary authoritarian regime) and Mexico (an inclusionary authoritarian system). The top decile of income earners in Colombia accounts for roughly 40 to 50 percent of all income, while the bottom quintile accounts for only 2.5 to 5.0 percent. Prior to the early 1960s, Colombia's income distribution patterns were clearly worsening. In the mid- and late 1960s, some improvement occurred as a result of higher levels of economic growth and the adoption of reformist policies, particularly by the Carlos Lleras Restrepo administration (1966–1970). In the early and mid-1970s, despite signs of increased concern with income distribution by successive administrations, the deterioration resumed, although at higher income levels. Since the onset of the global economic recession in 1979–1980, income distribution patterns appear to have deteriorated further.[13]

The Front arrangement further limited political competition by excluding all but the traditional party elites from serving in elective or bureaucratic posts. In effect, this restriction guaranteed that the Liberal and Conservative parties would be in a position to block or filter out demands that did not correspond to the dominant interests within the system.[14]

This did not preclude all pluralism. Indeed, the absence of inter-party competition actually fostered intra-party conflict. Factionalism (a traditional phenomenon in Colombian politics) flourished during the Front as different regional and sectoral elites competed within the framework of each party for bureaucratic power and privileged access to policymaking. Nevertheless, the range of interests represented within the bargaining process was effectively limited, for unless a group was able to organize within one or another of the two traditional parties, it was essentially excluded altogether from the political process.[15]

Factionalism did permit limited opportunities for nontraditional parties to gain indirect participation in the system despite their formal exclusion from politics. Leftist groups like the Communists, for example, allied themselves with the MRL faction of the Liberal Party during the early 1960s and thus were able to elect some of their members to Congress as representatives of the left wing of the Liberal Party. Another example of pluralism within the Front was that of the populist and anti-Frente ANAPO led by former dictator Gen. Gustavo Rojas Pinilla. In the mid- and late 1960s, ANAPO organized factions within both the Conservative and Liberal parties and was able to make important political inroads at the congressional, departmental, and municipal levels in the elections of 1966, 1968, and 1970 in spite of the formal constitutional monopoly of the two traditional parties. Indeed, in 1970, Rojas ran for the presidency as a Conservative against the official Frente candidate Misael Pastrana Borrero and came very close to winning. The fact that anti-Frente candidates such as Rojas could run for president under the Front rules indicates that the system was not hermetically sealed to opposition groups.

The ANAPO phenomenon, however, also suggests the limits to pluralism under the National Front system. Many observers contend that Rojas actually won the presidential race in 1970 but was denied his rightful victory through electoral fraud perpetrated by the top leadership of the two traditional parties. Since this incident, a variety of analysts (including the M-19 guerrillas, who derive their name from the date of these allegedly fraudulent elections) have argued that it is impossible to challenge the hegemonic position of the traditional parties through elections.

At least one author has used the term "elitist pluralism" to describe patterns of interest representation in Colombian politics during the Front.[16] The major producer and employer associations (representing dominant and allied class interests) have enjoyed privileged access to policymaking circles while subordinate classes such as the peasantry, rural workers, and the urban poor have had little or none.[17] The organized working class occupies an intermediate position in this system of interest representation. The two traditional labor confederations—the Confederación de Trabajadores de Colombia (CGT) and the Unión de Trabajadores de Colombia (UTC)—have historically been tied to the Liberal and Conservative parties, respectively. The price of such access has, however, been severe limitations on their autonomy and independence and, hence, on their capacity to press for working-class demands through the political process.[18]

A final major limitation on political pluralism involves the media. While the press is formally free in Colombia, in practice most of the country's newspapers and newsmagazines are closely tied to one or another faction of the two traditional parties and serve as spokesmen for them. There is no tradition of investigative reporting. Direct government censorship has been infrequent and temporary, but the print media have accepted tacit limits on their freedom to criticize the government during the Front and in the post-Front period. The state has also used its control over the availability of newsprint and of government advertising to enforce restraint. Radio and television have been subjected to direct censorship and state control through government licensing procedures.[19]

Inclusionary authoritarian regimes such as the National Front do not attempt to eliminate pluralist competition altogether but rather to restrict such competition to safe levels where only dominant and allied class interests are effectively represented. The Front and its successor arrangement have been quite successful in limiting pluralism, which has greatly increased the state's capacity to adopt policies that foster rapid economic development. The sacrifices demanded of the dominated classes in this process have been substantial, yet they have had no real channels through which to make their objections or demands heard within the system. The basic long-run problem with this type of interest representation has been that it has produced spontaneous and unchanneled political mobilization outside the system, which has undermined the stability and legitimacy of the entire political process.[20]

Two problems lie at the heart of Colombia's current legitimacy crisis. First, the political or governing class does not effectively penetrate the society as a whole; party politics and policy priorities have little resonance within the general population and do not respond effectively to their demands or necessities. Second, there is a growing vacuum of political leadership.

Bipartisanship has led to atrophy within the political parties themselves and has contributed significantly to rising levels of unresponsiveness and hence to instability. In spite of these problems, however, the dice appear to be loaded in favor of a continuation of present patterns of political control and electoral domination. There is no indication of major shifts in the near future, and it is probable that the basic pattern of shared traditional party hegemony will remain intact through the 1980s.

Executive Predominance. A central characteristic of inclusionary authoritarian regimes is the predominance of the executive. Under the Front arrangement, especially after the constitutional and administrative reforms of 1968, policymaking power has been vested in the president at the expense of Congress. Indeed, after 1968, the Colombian Congress exercised virtually no budgetary or policy-initiating powers whatsoever, although it retained enough residual authority to block executive initiatives and did so frequently in both the Front and post-Front periods.[21] As a result of growing centralization, the Congress became increasingly secondary to the economic development policies and programs launched by successive presidencies. Interest groups concerned with economic policy consequently focused their attention and energies on gaining access to and influencing executive branch authorities charged with making and implementing policy.[22]

Over the course of the Front, the planning and regulatory functions of the state expanded significantly. Nevertheless, in contrast with other major Latin American countries (for example, Mexico or Venezuela), the interventionist role of the Colombian state was relatively slight throughout the Front period and remains so today. Economic planning is essentially of the indicative (*concertada*) type carried out in cooperation with the private sector rather than imposed. This has meant that the Colombian executive simply does not have the capacity to guide or orient the economy as, for example, Mexican and Venezuelan authorities do.[23]

Instead of the statization trend observable in bureaucratic authoritarian regimes such as Brazil and Argentina or inclusionary authoritarian regimes such as Mexico, the tendency in Colombia has been toward "privatization"; that is, toward the parceling out of state authority to private sector groups that assume responsibility for policy implementation. Perhaps the most important example is the National Federation of Coffee Growers (a mixed entity composed of private producers and government officials but dominated by the large growers), which exercises virtually complete control over all aspects of coffee policy in Colombia, from production levels through pricing and export quotas. Coffee remains Colombia's principal (legal) export crop and foreign exchange earner, accounting for roughly two-fifths of all foreign exchange revenues.[24]

This trend is also noticeable in Colombia's approach to the proliferating semiautonomous state agencies; considerable care has been taken to incorporate key private sector representatives on their boards of directors. Even Colombia's Agrarian Reform Institute (Instituto Colombiano de Reforma Agraria; INCORA) included members of the agricultural sector interest groups such as the Farmers Association (SAC), even though SAC had opposed the agrarian reform. The explanation for Colombia's penchant for privatization versus the statization process apparent in countries such as Mexico, Venezuela, and Brazil lies in their differing economic and political histories. In comparison with Mexico and Venezuela, for example, Colombia has never had a nationalized state petroleum sector providing large sums for an expanded state role in the economy. The Colombian private sector developed prior to the emergence of the modern state, and its continuing political power has allowed it to play a central role in the economy. In both Mexico and Venezuela, in contrast, the state was a principal motor of economic expansion throughout the twentieth century, while the private sector assumed a secondary role. Equally important, unlike the Brazilian and Argentine militaries, the Colombian military never assumed permanent control over the state or a major role in the direction of the economy.

Two major exceptions to this privatization trend should be noted. First, at least since the 1930s the Colombian state has directly controlled most public services (water, electricity, transportation, and communications). Second, since the Alfonso López Michelsen administration's 1974 economic emergency decrees, all oil and natural gas concession contracts were replaced by mandatory joint ventures between private companies (foreign or domestic) and the Colombian state. In addition, the López government "Colombianized" the nation's financial sector and established stricter limitations on the participation of multinational corporations in this area of the national economy. In view of the multibillion-dollar joint venture between the Colombian government and the Exxon corporation to exploit the Cerrejón coal deposits in the Guajira region (expected to generate over $7 billion a year in foreign exchange earnings by the end of the 1980s), a major expansion of the state's role in the economy can be anticipated.

While privatization has allowed the Colombian economy to escape partially the treadmill of costly and inefficient state-run enterprises that have impeded other Latin American countries, it has also tended to reduce the impact of the state on the national economy. In combination with the formidable pressures the major interest groups are able to bring to bear on the executive, the trend toward privatization has significantly reduced the relative autonomy of the president and the state as a whole. As a result, reform-oriented presidents such as Liberal Carlos Lleras Restrepo (1966–1970) or Conservative Belisario Betancur Cuartas (1982–) have found themselves severely constrained in their efforts to introduce sorely needed social and economic reforms during their administrations. Indeed, the incapacity of the state to direct the development process more effectively has left it progressively paralyzed in the face of the severe social and economic disequilibria that Colombia's modernization process has generated over the past two decades.

Patrimonial Style of Rulership. The predominant style of rulership in Colombia is patrimonial or clientelistic. In both rural and urban areas, the society is organized into overlapping vertical chains of patron-client relations. At the apex of these chains or networks are the major economic and political elites who provide money, services, and patronage in exchange for information, personal loyalty, and political support. A given individual often is both client and patron. Such relations have their origins in the rural hacienda society of the colonial and early republican periods, but have been adapted to the contemporary urban environments.[25]

The two traditional parties in Colombia are rooted in the politics of clientelism. The lack of party coherence and the pervasive intra-party factionalism characteristic of the political system stem largely from the competition among individual factional leaders seeking to expand their bureaucratic power and thus the networks of political clients that they can support and control. Large numbers of voters go to the polls not to express their ideological preferences or to endorse specific programs, but to protect their jobs or improve their chances of obtaining patronage.[26]

The vertical, multiclass nature of such linkages makes the formation and maintenance of horizontal or class-based organizations exceedingly difficult. Ideological appeals are of little avail, as the history of the Colombian left attests. Unless politicians (called *caciques* or *gamonales* in Colombia) can deliver patronage, jobs, and political protection to their clientele network, they cannot sustain their political base. Political factions are often fluid and unstable, although there are a few prominent leaders (*caudillos* rather than *gamonales*) who retain the capacity to attract followers even after they have left office. This is especially true of ex-presidents such as Conservatives Mariano Pérez (now deceased) and Misael Pastrana Borrero and Liberals Alberto Lleras Camargo, Carlos Lleras Restrepo, Alfonso López Michelsen, and Julio César Turbay Ayala.

Among the costs of this personalistic and patrimonial pattern of leadership are governmental bureaucracies that are often overstaffed with expensive, incompetent, and inefficient appointees. Although a civil service does exist, it does not function, hence many capable individuals refuse to consider government careers. Scarce state resources go into misallocated patronage purposes. The system fosters corruption among government officials and generates high levels of cynicism and distrust of government among the public.

Absence of Ideology. A final characteristic of Colombia's brand of inclusionary authoritarianism is the almost total absence of ideological politics. Since the inauguration of the Front, Colombia's elites have been characterized by a high degree of consensus around a few core goals or objectives. The most central of these are the maintenance of political stability and the acceptance of rapid growth within a capitalist economic framework. Intense intra-elite disputes do take place over how best to achieve these national goals, but Colombian leaders have become renowned for their ability to compromise. Such elite cohesion has been a critical factor in limiting political polarization within the system as a whole and is one of the most remarkable features of the current regime. It is also one of the root causes of the paralysis of the political leadership and the growing illegitimacy of the political system.[27]

Economic Policy in an Inclusionary Authoritarian Regime

The closed and elitist character of the Colombian political process and the reduced role of the military have freed the country's economic policymakers from many popular pressures as well as from costly expenditures on military equipment and armaments that have beset other Latin American economies. As a result, following the major economic reforms introduced in 1967–1968 under the Liberal administration of President Carlos Lleras Restrepo, the country was able to achieve a remarkable economic growth rate of 5–7 percent per annum, which it sustained until 1979–1980, when the world economy plunged into recession. This striking success story was marred only by a short-lived downturn in 1975, brought about by the 1973–1974 oil crisis. The overall quality of economic decisionmaking in Colombia compares well with virtually any other Latin American country. This outstanding growth performance during the late 1960s and most of the 1970s was not an accident, but rather the result of technically sound, macroeconomic decisions made by successive National Front and post-Front governments in the context of a regime that freed them from the imperative of responding directly to lower-class demands for a more equitable share of the benefits of economic growth.

Colombia's economic development policies may be divided into three basic phases or periods. The first, beginning in 1958 with the inauguration of the National Front and extending through 1966 and the end of the administration of Conservative President Guillermo León Valencia, was the phase of import-substitution industrialization. The second, beginning in 1966 with the advent of Liberal President Carlos Lleras Restrepo and extending through the second oil crisis of 1979, was the phase of export-led growth. The third, beginning with the world recession of 1979–1980 and carrying through to the present, is one of recession and retrenchment.

The Import-Substitution Phase. At the outset of the National Front, Colombia was still a predominantly agricultural economy with the bulk of the population living and working in the countryside, many under precapitalist conditions. The internal market was limited. Coffee was the country's major export, and its dependence on this crop produced boom and bust cycles and chronic foreign exchange problems that severely inhibited the country's overall economic development.[28]

The administrations of Liberal Alberto Lleras Camargo (1958–1962) and Conservative Guillermo León Valencia (1962–1966) pursued classic (secondary) import-substitution industrialization policies consisting of combinations of high external tariffs, prior import deposits, exchange controls, and a selective import-licensing system. While average levels of protection were not unreasonably high, there were large variations among sectors, and many restrictions went considerably beyond reasonable needs to protect the country's infant industries, leading to serious economic distortions.[29]

By the mid-1960s, production had increased in areas such as steel and chemicals, but these products came on stream at protection-inflated prices that severely limited the possibilities for further growth. With the exhaustion of the "easy phase" of import substitution by the middle of the decade, the country was saddled with capital- and import-intensive sectors dominating industrial development. A steady drop in coffee prices over the 1960s made foreign exchange increasingly scarce, further reduced internal demand, and left the country with considerable excess industrial capacity. These problems were compounded by an exchange rate policy that severely overvalued the peso and made it virtually impossible for industrialists to export their products. The result was extremely slow economic growth that barely kept pace with the country's exploding population (rising at over 3 percent a year).[30]

In the agricultural sector, government policies proved more effective. Recognizing that the country was excessively dependent on coffee and that agricultural production was lagging, in late 1961 the Lleras Camargo administration pushed through Congress a major new agrarian reform (Law 135 of 1961) designed to diversify and modernize agricultural production. The provisions of this new law that sought to increase peasant access to land and credit were never effectively implemented because of the resistance of large landowners and their political allies, but the new legislation forced the country's farmers to rationalize land-use patterns and increase production and productivity. New sources of credit were provided for nontraditional crops, extensive infrastructural development was undertaken by the state, new technical assistance programs were launched, and the importation of modern agricultural machinery was made easier. As a result, both total agricultural output and farm income increased steadily during the decade despite a continuing stagnation of coffee prices on the international market. At the same time, patterns of land and credit concentration became more skewed, the peasantry suffered growing landlessness and poverty, and tensions in the countryside rose.[31]

From Import Substitution to Export-Led Growth. In 1967, President Carlos Lleras Restrepo began a series of reforms that substantially reoriented the country's economic development strategy. The centerpiece of these reforms was the decision to alter exchange rate management by institutionalizing a crawling-peg (or mini) devaluation system. This move produced a more realistic exchange rate policy, helped avoid disruptive (or maxi) devaluations, and greatly increased the ability of the country's industrialists to export their manufactured products. Stimulated by this policy adjustment and favorable international economic conditions, industrial exports jumped from U.S. $25 million in 1967 to U.S. $400 million in 1974.[32]

Additional tax stimuli for nontraditional (that is, noncoffee) exports were offered through the *Certificado de Abono Tributario* (CAT) mechanism. An import drawback system (called Plan Vallejo) that allowed inputs and machinery needed by exporters to be imported free of duty was also implemented, thereby reducing the disincentives to manufactured exports contained in the existing system of import protection. New low-interest credits were made available to enterprises involved in manufacturing for export.[33]

President Lleras Restrepo also reorganized and modernized the institutional structure of economic policymaking in the country. The planning capabilities of the state were increased through a strengthening of the National Planning Department, especially in areas such as control over foreign investment and the elaboration of national economic development plans. The president and his key ministers also took a more direct role in overseeing and coordinating economic policy through a reactivation of the National Council of Economic and Social Policy.

Alongside the more traditional instruments of state regulation (monetary, exchange, and financial policies), Lleras strengthened other state planning institutions that relied on fiscal and credit policies. The Institute of Industrial Development (IFI), for example, was used to channel cheap credit into key industrial sectors, the Export Promotion Fund (PROEXPO) to stimulate nontraditional exports, and the Agricultural Finance Fund to increase agricultural modernization and diversification.

The Lleras Restrepo government and subsequently the Pastrana and López Michelsen administrations also undertook to increase the pace of

agricultural modernization. New credits flowed into the commercial agricultural sector, additional infrastructure (irrigation systems, storage facilities,
farm-to-market roads) was built, and new crops and improved animal breeds
were introduced. While agricultural sector output increased by over 4 percent
a year during the 1970s, in 1971 most government efforts at land redistribution
were abandoned altogether, and peasant unrest increased dramatically. Nevertheless, agricultural production and productivity on the country's commercial
farms improved substantially, and the agricultural sector was increasingly able
to export and to meet the needs of the country's expanding urban industries.
The sugar bonanza of 1974–1975 and the coffee bonanza of 1975–1977, along
with the dramatic upsurge in illegal narcotics traffic in the 1970s (especially
marijuana and cocaine), also helped Colombia's foreign exchange position and
the overall vitality of the nation's economy during the mid-1970s.[34]

In place of the mild but highly controversial land redistribution program
promoted by the mainstream Liberals and Carlos Lleras Restrepo during the
1960s, first the Conservative administration of Misael Pastrana Borerro and
then the post-Frente Liberal governments of López and Turbay Ayala adopted
a rural development strategy geared toward increasing productivity and
standards of living in the rural sector without land reform. The major
institutional expressions of this alternative strategy were the Food and
Nutrition Plan and the Integrated Rural Development Program.[35] While
these programs may have been successful in improving the lot of the upper
ranks of the peasantry, they did not deal effectively with the growing problems
of landlessness and poverty among the lower strata of the rural population. As
a result, the exodus from the countryside to the major urban areas continued
and even intensified during the 1970s and early 1980s, the floating or seasonal
migrant population increased, and millions of Colombians crossed into
Venezuela in search of work and higher pay. Moreover, rising levels of peasant
unrest provided fertile conditions for agrarian struggles and guerrilla operations. With the downturn suffered by the entire agricultural sector after
1979–1980, unrest in regions such as the Caqueta and the Magdalena Medio
reached explosive levels during the Betancur administration.

In retrospect, the Pastrana government's 1971 decision to call a halt to a
decade of moderate land reform efforts in the Colombian countryside marked
a critical economic and political turning point in the nation's development
policies. At the economic level, it symbolized the adoption of a strategy of
agricultural modernization without serious attempts at redistribution. At the
political level, it revealed the resurgent political power of the large landowners
and their allies within the ruling coalition and the deepening political
impotence of the peasantry. The practical consequences of this shift in rural
development strategies were significant increases in discontent in the countryside. In response, the Pastrana government and its post-Frente successors

resorted to intensified state repression to maintain some semblance of order in the *campo*.[36]

In the early 1970s, under the guidance of economist Lauchlin Currie, President Misael Pastrana Borerro (1970–1974) implemented a new economic development strategy (called *Las Cuatro Estrategias*) based on urban construction and agricultural exports as "lead" sectors. The central thrust of this program was to provide additional financial resources to these two target sectors. Modern commercial agriculture was to provide cheap food to the urban population and inputs for industry while earning needed foreign exchange through exports. The urban construction sector was to provide employment for the rural masses moving into the cities, help solve the housing problem, and generate an expanding internal market for domestic industrial production. This new internal market was designed to stimulate new industries that would then allow the government to drop construction as a lead sector.[37]

To finance increased urban construction activity, Currie and his team proposed a new savings certificate (called *unidades de poder adquisitivo constante*—UPACs) that guaranteed a real rate of interest of 5 percent or more by compensating for inflation and new savings and loan associations (*corporaciones de ahorro y vivenda*) dedicated to financing construction. They also proposed new improvement taxes on urban property.[38]

This new economic program was implemented by presidential decrees during the early 1970s and undoubtedly contributed to the buoyancy of the Colombian economy during the first half of the decade. By 1974, the UPAC system had captured over 10 billion pesos in savings. It was, however, criticized for contributing to inflation (because of bottlenecks in the supply of construction materials) and for diverting scarce financial resources from industry and agriculture. Currie staunchly defended his development strategy against these criticisms; nonetheless, the program was effectively dismantled in 1974 when the López Michelsen government capped the interest rate allowed on UPACs, thereby limiting the funds available for construction activity.[39]

The López administration abandoned the urban construction strategy and adopted a more orthodox development policy based on increased agricultural and manufacturing exports accompanied by an emphasis on basic human needs and the poorest segments of Colombian society. In his first month in office, López became the first president to invoke the economic emergency powers granted to the president by the constitutional reform of 1968, which allowed him to legislate by decree for a period of up to 60 days. His new economic package included a major overhaul of the tax system to make it more progressive and efficient, including the implementation of a presumptive tax on nonproductive assets, new lines of credit for agriculture, and a liberalization of import restrictions. These policies, combined with favorable international prices for the country's agricultural exports, produced growth rates of over 7 percent a year and a period of economic bonanza from 1975 through the 1979 oil crisis.[40]

· The López administration also intensified Colombia's efforts to reduce its economic dependency on the United States. The first major steps had been taken by the Lleras Restrepo administration with Colombia's decision to join the Andean Common Market (Andean Pact) in 1969. López worked to broaden commercial and financial relations with the rest of Latin America, the European Economic Community, Japan, and the Eastern bloc countries, including Cuba. He also sought foreign credits from European commercial banks and the Eurodollar market, rather than more traditional U.S. sources. In 1975 his government terminated its relationship with the U.S. Agency for International Development (AID), a move made in anticipation of a planned AID phase-down in middle-income countries like Colombia. As a result of these policies, the United States absorbed a progressively smaller percentage of Colombian exports over the 1970s, dropping from the 60–70 percent range typical of the early 1960s to the 30–35 percent range in the early 1980s. A similar although less pronounced change occurred with imports. Exports to the Andean Pact countries of manufactured goods increased over the 1970s while the country's exports to the United States and Europe remained principally agricultural products and raw materials.[41]

In what was widely trumpeted as an act of economic sovereignty, López Colombianized the country's financial system. The heart of the reform was a requirement that foreign banks sell at least 51 percent control to Colombians at market rates over a specified phase-in period. While this reform did expand the economic bargaining leverage of the financial fraction of Colombia's capitalist class vis-à-vis international capital, the realities of Colombian financial dependence on the international financial system led to a multiplicity of quasi-legal, indirect, and informal arrangements (paper directorates, *prestanombres* [front men]) that in practice have largely nullified the nationalist thrust of the Colombianization process.[42]

The net result of the López administration's economic policies was to slow the pace of industrial growth. Because of the failure to control interest rates and the progressive overvaluation of the peso, investment capital dried up, production costs rose, and Colombia's overprotected industries became increasingly uncompetitive in international markets. During the euphoria of the coffee bonanza, the immediate effects of this industrial downturn were partially camouflaged through government deficit financing based on increased foreign borrowing, particularly during the Turbay administration. With the world recession of the early 1980s, however, Colombian industry experienced the deepest and most prolonged period of economic contraction in the country's modern economic history.

With the strong inflows of foreign exchange experienced by the Colombian economy during the 1970s, inflation became an increasingly critical problem. In the 1960s, rates hovered in the 10 to 15 percent range. In the late 1970s and early 1980s they reached the 25–29 percent level. Some efforts were made during the late 1970s to increase the quantity of imports licensed by the Colombian government in order to offset growing foreign reserves and the attendant inflation, but opposition from the country's major industrial groups prevented such measures from being implemented. Although the nation's economic policymakers proved capable of keeping inflation below the 30 percent level through 1983, the tradeoff was unemployment levels approaching 15 percent of the work force in the early 1980s.[43]

One result of inflation was the exacerbation of the country's already highly skewed pattern of income distribution. Inflation generated a price-wage lag and brought about a decrease in real wages in the range of 10 to 20 percent during the late 1970s and early 1980s. Capital received most of the profits generated by Colombia's economic expansion over the decade.[44]

Along with inflation and declining real wages, accelerated urbanization brought about by massive outmigration from the countryside (in part a consequence of the failure of the agrarian reform of the 1960s) heightened social and political tensions in both rural and urban areas in the late 1970s and early 1980s. The result was a renewed upsurge in popular protests and political discontent in both rural and urban areas during the late 1970s and early 1980s.[45]

The 1979–1983 Slowdown and Recession. Between 1978 and 1982, Turbay attempted to stave off the looming economic slowdown through increased government spending. Confronted with a private sector that lacked sufficient confidence to invest, he sought to offset accumulated reserves from the coffee bonanza with a countercyclical economic strategy that placed primary emphasis on the transportation, communications, mining, and energy sectors rather than on social programs.[46] The plan was vigorously applied during Turbay's term in office and roughly 90 percent of its targeted goals were achieved: public construction activity increased by 5.4 percent in 1979, 14.9 percent in 1980, 12.3 percent in 1981, and 5.8 percent in 1982.[47]

Turbay's strategy did not, however, succeed in reactivating the economy—an impossibility in the context of deepening international recession. The government entered the country's financial markets to compete with the private sector for investment capital, thus causing interest and inflation rates to rise and further discouraging productive business investment. From 1979 on, economic growth rates declined steadily, and in 1981 the country fell into recession. In 1980, GNP grew by 4.2 percent, in 1981 by 2.5 percent, and in 1982 by only 1.4 percent. The third figure represented Colombia's lowest rate of growth in the entire postwar period; in 1983 the growth rate was approximately 1 percent. While other Latin American economies such as those of Mexico, Brazil, Argentina, and Venezuela have suffered even more severely, Colombia's current situation is positive only by comparison.[48]

Upon assuming office on August 7, 1982, President Betancur inherited an extremely precarious economic situation. The industrial recession continued to deepen over the remainder of 1982 and throughout 1983, and agricultural exports remained flat. Unemployment rates rose to almost 20 percent in some cities, particularly the industrial center of Medellín. In large part because of Turbay's ambitious public construction program, the fiscal deficit reached 3.5 percent of GNP in 1982. The recession produced financial takeovers of a number of troubled industrial enterprises by banks and financial groups, several of which proved unable in 1983 to meet their obligations and entered bankruptcy, thus compelling the Betancur government to intervene to re-establish order in the financial sector. International reserves, which had stood at a robust $5 billion at the outset of 1982, dipped to approximately $3 billion by the end of 1983 as exports stagnated and capital continued to flee the country. The Betancur government found it increasingly difficult and costly to raise the international loans that it needed during 1983.[49]

Despite the severity of the crisis, in economic terms Colombia is better off than virtually every other Latin American nation. Several factors seem to account for the country's relative success. First, Colombia is endowed with a relatively rich and diversified resource and agricultural base. Second, with the exception of coffee (which now brings in less than 50 percent of the country's foreign exchange earnings), Colombia has not been dependent on any single export. As a result of economic diversification, Colombia has been more insulated from the international boom and bust cycles that have caused havoc in the economies of many other Latin American countries. Third, through the National Front pact and its successor arrangement, Colombia was able to establish a relatively stable political regime insulated from both the popular and military pressures that have severely distorted the economic policies of a number of its sister republics. Fourth, and closely related to the previous point, Colombia's technocratic elites have been able to adopt and implement over an extended period of time macroeconomic policies that encouraged investment and sustained growth. Put another way, they have had the freedom and skill to undertake moderate policies that avoided the extremes of excessive indebtedness and an overly open (vulnerable) or overly closed (subsidized) economy. Fifth, rapid growth in the 1970s, combined with a substantial decline in the rate of population increase (now approximately 2.1 percent per annum), allowed the country to provide jobs and thus forestall even more severe social and political tensions while simultaneously accumulating the substantial international reserves that gave the country considerable economic flexibility over the 1979–1983 period of slowdown and recession.

Against the backdrop of rising rural and urban discontent of the late 1970s and early 1980s, however, the current extended recessionary period poses major challenges to the continued stability of the political system. If popular expectations are not met, at least in part, social and political tensions will almost certainly continue to grow through the mid-1980s.

Contemporary Colombia and the Problem of Political Legitimacy

At least since 1974 and the "dismantling" of the National Front arrangement, and arguably well before, the Colombian political system has been caught in a continuing legitimacy crisis. The Frente itself, although probably necessary to end *La Violencia* and to restore political peace between the warring Liberal and Conservative parties, was essentially a formula for political immobility: it guaranteed that the pace of social and economic reform could proceed no faster than the conservative elements of the traditional Liberal-Conservative party leadership would permit.

In practice this meant that during the Front, reforms amounted to little more than "palliative, paternalistic. . . [measures], designed to alleviate severe stresses in the system and to respond to certain cues (such as anarchic rural violence) or to demands on the part of counter-elite groups, without at the same time yielding up any real share of effective control over the major power resources."[50] The agrarian reform died a silent death in the early 1970s, gutted by powerful landed and agro-industrial interests.[51] The urban reform was never approved by Congress because of the intense opposition of real estate, urban construction, and financial interests.[52] The upper ranks of the educational system remained essentially closed and elitist despite repeated "reforms" during the 1960s and 1970s.[53] Land, capital, and credit became more concentrated, and the gap between rich and poor grew larger. Some segments of the working class experienced either stagnation or relative declines in their standards of living.[54] Drug-related violence and corruption further undermined already weak institutions such as the court system, the police, the customs service, and even the military. Drug money is reputed to have financed congressional political campaigns for candidates from both parties and to have bought into legitimate businesses such as banks, insurance companies, industrial firms, resort hotels, and farms.[55]

The Front not only slowed socioeconomic reforms to a crawl, but by dividing all political offices equally between the two traditional parties, it also reduced elections to empty exercises and the political parties to mere dispensers of patronage split by factionalism and personalism, without ideologies, programs, or grass-roots organizations. The result was rising levels of voter abstention and cynicism during the 1960s, compounded by the emergence in the 1970s of an increasingly volatile urban vote, unaffiliated with either traditional political party.[56]

The dismantling of the National Front and the return to fully competitive elections in 1974 did not restore the legitimacy of the Colombian political system. Although Alfonso López Michelsen, the Liberal candidate, successfully mobilized the urban poor with a populist, reform-oriented campaign and won an overwhelming electoral victory over his Conservative rival, Alvaro Gómez Hurtado, his presidency was widely viewed as unsuccessful in addressing the critical socioeconomic and political problems of the system. Indeed, despite the economic boom during his term of office (1974–1978), there was a marked upsurge of guerrilla activity in both the countryside and the cities, widespread labor unrest culminating in a major nationwide strike on September 13, 1977, repeated accusations of influence-trafficking and corruption involving members of the López family, and insistent rumors of possible military coups.[57]

In the 1977–78 presidential race, Liberal candidate Julio César Turbay Ayala campaigned on a platform of "law and order," promising a tough response to the wave of strikes, kidnappings, guerrilla violence, and drug-related crimes that threatened the stability of the system. A traditional Liberal Party politician, Turbay did not hold any strong political-ideological convictions. He was, rather, a pragmatic, status quo–oriented leader supported by an extensive political machine. Within a month of his inauguration as president, he responded to the system's growing legitimacy crisis by promulgating a new National Security Statute that substantially increased the role of the military in the governance of the country. Since the dismantling of the National Front, the country had been ruled almost continuously under the state-of-siege provisions of the constitution. The 1978 National Security Statute further augmented the arbitrary arrest and trial powers of the armed forces, and reports of human rights abuses soon surfaced. During 1979, after the M-19 guerrilla group's January 1 raid on a military arsenal in the north of Bogotá in which 5,000 arms were stolen, mass arrests of suspected guerrilla sympathizers were reported, and there were abuses of political and civil rights on a scale previously unknown in Colombia.[58]

The use of extraordinary decree powers and the adoption of increasingly repressive measures revealed the underlying fragility and vulnerability of the regime. Unwilling or unable to sponsor the reforms needed to address the basic tensions of the society, Turbay opted for a hard-line, military response. At the domestic level, this approach was reflected in his government's "Southern Cone–style" National Security Statute and his regressive economic policies. In foreign policy, it was manifested in the close cooperation between the

Turbay administration and the Reagan White House and in Turbay's hostility toward Cuba and Nicaragua.[59]

Belisarismo Versus Turbayismo

Conservative Belisario Betancur's triumph over Liberal candidate and former president Alfonso López Michelsen in the 1982 presidential race was the first Conservative victory over the Liberals in fully competitive presidential elections since 1946.[60] Betancur won the election with the support of a broad-based coalition that reached beyond traditional Conservative support groups to incorporate segments of the urban poor and the working and the middle classes. He came to power with a reform-oriented, conciliatory political program that contrasted starkly with his Liberal predecessor's hardline approach. Betancur is less a partisan, machine politician and more a political maverick and a populist than Turbay; he also tends to be more progressive or reformist, less anticommunist, and warier of the United States than his predecessor, although he is certainly no leftist or radical.[61]

Paradoxically, early in his political career Betancur was a militant follower of ultra right-wing Conservative *caudillo* Laureano Gómez, whose political philosophy was similar to Franco's *falangismo*. Despite his close affiliation with the right wing of the Conservative party in the 1950s and early 1960s, after the death of Laureano Gómez in 1965 Betancur began to drift, both politically and ideologically, away from the *Laureanista-Alvarista* faction, now led by Laureano Gómez's son Alvaro Gómez Hurtado. In 1970 he ran for president (and lost) as an independent Conservative on an essentially populist platform against the official *Frente Nacional* candidate, Misael Pastrana Borrero (an *Ospinista* Conservative).[62]

In 1978, Betancur campaigned for president again, this time as the official nominee of the Conservative Party, and lost narrowly to the Liberal candidate Julio César Turbay Ayala. As in 1970, his campaign was reformist and populist, and he ran particularly well in the country's major cities, garnering votes from Liberals and Independents as well as Conservatives.[63] In 1982—his third presidential bid—Betancur won handily over former president Alfonso López Michelsen and a severely divided Liberal Party. The *Alvarista* Conservatives united behind his candidacy as did the mainline *Ospina-Pastranista* faction. But support for Belisario was not limited to the Conservatives; he successfully courted independent, Christian Democratic, *Anapista*, and even some Liberal voters as well, especially in the large urban centers. Since the 1930s, the Liberals have been the majority party in the country. Without a concerted attempt to develop a following broader than the customary Conservative Party constituency, no Conservative could have been elected to the presidency in 1982.[64]

Belisario Betancur is a nationalist, a mild reformer, and a populist; he has an independent streak, more than a dash of anti-American sentiment, and a tendency toward activism and state interventionism. In class terms, he represents the "progressive" or "modernizing" faction of the Colombian capitalist class rooted in the agro-industrial and financial sectors of the national economy.

Belisarismo and the Crisis of Legitimation

To confront the regime's legitimacy crisis and the problem of guerrilla violence, Betancur recommended an end to the repressive policies of the Turbay administration, called for the elimination of the state-of-siege powers that Turbay had used to govern the country throughout his presidency, and proposed a general amnesty for the guerrillas if they would lay down their arms. Once in the presidential palace, he pushed his amnesty proposal through Congress and opened up negotiations with the various rebel groups operating in the country. He also launched a new political reform—labeled a democratic opening—designed to increase participation in the system.[65]

In terms of social policy, he put forward a variety of reforms in the areas of education, health, housing, and job training. Among the most ambitious and controversial programs was an initiative launched during the campaign proposing "low-income housing without down payment."[66] López ridiculed this initiative, characterizing it as nothing more than empty, populist promises. Nevertheless, such proposals proved attractive to the urban poor and working class, and Betancur shocked the divided Liberal Party by capturing a significant part of the urban vote even in Liberal strongholds such as Bogotá and along the Atlantic coast.[67] Because of the recession and the ballooning government deficit he inherited from Turbay, during his first year in office President Betancur found it difficult to finance his ambitious housing program and the other social reforms he had promised. As a result, in 1983 he confronted the classic problem of populist politicians: the inability to fulfill expectations raised during the political campaign. However, Betancur continued to enjoy extraordinary personal popularity.[68]

His leadership style—open, informal, direct—contrasted sharply with Turbay's more ponderous, pompous, and tradition-bound manner and bolstered his personal popularity. He set the tone of his presidency at his inauguration when he dressed in a business suit rather than the traditional cutaway.[69] Amnesty, moderate reforms, and stylistic changes constituted the

Belisarista alternative to the hard-line strategy that President Turbay had adopted to meet Colombia's continuing crisis of political legitimacy. The president's social programs such as low-income housing stalled for lack of adequate public financing. Most important, the country's overall economic outlook for 1983–1984 was at best one of very gradual recovery, a situation that appeared to place severe limitations on Betancur's ability to meet the high expectations his presidency had raised.[70]

Economic and Political Constraints: The Limits to Reform

Colombia weathered the 1981–1983 world recession better than most Latin American countries, but in 1983 signs of economic distress became increasingly evident. Low prices for Colombia's key agricultural exports (coffee, sugar, bananas, and even cocaine and marijuana), a severe industrial recession, particularly in the textile, auto, and appliance sectors, tightening international and domestic credit, growing balance of payments problems, and a soaring fiscal deficit spelled hard times for the nation's economy during 1983 and into 1984, even with a mild recovery in the United States.[71]

Betancur responded with new export subsidies, increased protectionism, state intervention in the banking system, and a declaration of a 50-day economic emergency in late 1982 and early 1983. The president's measures were designed to increase regulation of the troubled financial system, rationalize the tax structure, and control the growth of the money supply. The goals of the administration's economic program were to restore confidence in the country's financial institutions, stimulate moderate growth, and keep inflation in check while holding labor costs down. In February, shortly after the economic emergency decrees had been announced publicly, the Supreme Court declared them unconstitutional. This decision produced great confusion in the country's business circles and forced Betancur to make accommodations with the Liberals.[72]

Favorable international economic conditions during the mid-1970s, coupled with conservative economic policies, gave the Betancur administration an advantage over most Latin American leaders in meeting the general crisis. But unless the Colombian economy experiences a sustained recovery, President Betancur will face increasingly stark economic and political choices that will inevitably undermine the popularity of his government. The stability of the regime is not likely to be seriously threatened in the short term, but increasingly repressive measures to control worker and peasant discontent as well as renewed outbreaks of urban unrest, guerrilla violence, terrorism, and kidnapping may be forthcoming.

Betancur's problems with the economic situation he inherited have been compounded by the fragility of the political coalition that brought him to power and through which he has to govern the country.[73] In light of his reformist and populist inclinations, his relationship with the right-wing *Alvarista* Conservatives is delicate. The Alvarista presence within the governing coalition, along with resistance from the military to Betancur's amnesty, set political and ideological limits on the reforms that Betancur could successfully undertake during his first year in power. Not only did he have to perform a delicate political balancing act within his own party; the bipartisan legacy of the National Front required that he govern with parity Liberal participation.[74] In an unprecedented political maneuver, in his first months in office he chose not to negotiate directly with the Liberal Party leadership, particularly not with defeated presidential candidate and *jefe único* Alfonso López Michelsen, over Liberal participation in his administration. Instead, he maintained parity by incorporating dissident Liberal factions and leaders on an individual basis into his government.

Already badly divided by the 1981–1982 nomination fight and the acrimonious 1982 presidential campaign, the Liberals were further fragmented by Betancur's manipulation of the parity requirements. When the Supreme Court ruled his economic emergency decrees unconstitutional in early 1983, however, Betancur had to negotiate a new political pact with the Liberal leadership giving them an expanded role in his government in order to secure congressional approval of his economic package. This new accord appeared to place additional constraints on his freedom to pursue socio-economic reform.

The military also imposed important constraints on the Betancur administration. From the outset, the top military officials (including then–minister of defense Fernando Landázabal Reyes) were wary of the president's proposed amnesty because they felt it would undermine the authority and morale of the armed forces. They went along reluctantly because the president gave them an informal veto over the negotiations and because he offered them unprecedented new outlays for military modernization (approximately U.S. $2.5 billion over his four years in office).

One of the most ominous developments in Colombian political life in the early 1980s was the rise and spread of right-wing paramilitary death squads like the Muerte a Secuestradores (MAS), the Tiznados, and at least a half dozen other groups. Such organizations have carried out hundreds of assassinations of suspected guerrillas, labor leaders, and leftist sympathizers in the country over the past few years, reportedly with the backing and involvement of some military officers. The Betancur government denounced these groups publicly and began legal proceedings against some suspected members (including active and retired military personnel), but as of late 1983 had not won any convictions.

The Colombian military has remained subordinate to and supportive of the Frente leadership since 1958. Yet steadily over the 1960s and 1970s, the deepening legitimacy problems of the regime forced the civilian elites to rely more heavily on state-of-siege powers, the military, and the police to control the country. The Turbay administration's 1978 security statute represented a major step in this direction, for it formally granted the military extensive new powers of search and seizure, arrest, interrogation, and trial by military court. Although these formal powers were revoked with the end of the state-of-siege in mid-1982, the military still retains broad authority to press the campaign against the guerrillas. However, there is no reason to suspect that the armed forces might try to seize power from the civilian leadership in the foreseeable future. The costs in terms of political legitimacy, precarious as the legitimacy of the present regime may be, would be high while the benefits in terms of increased freedom of action would be minimal. In Colombia, the armed forces have obtained what they sought from the civilian authorities without the need to resort to coups.

The Colombian political system has been experiencing an increasingly intense legitimacy crisis for more than a decade. In the 1970s and early 1980s, first the López and then the Turbay administration resorted to progressively more repressive tactics to deal with the rising levels of dissatisfaction, violence, crime, and instability in the country. The role of the military in Colombian politics increased substantially as force became increasingly important in preserving the status quo.

During his first year in office, President Betancur attempted to reverse this repressive and exclusionary trend by offering an amnesty to the guerrillas, mild social reforms to the poor and working class, political reform to broaden participation, and a new style of leadership to the country. The international recession, however, severely limited the resources Betancur's government was able to muster to address the country's pressing economic and social problems. The military and conservative elements in both parties have opposed his proposed amnesty and restricted his room to maneuver in economic and social policy areas.

Notes

1. The National Front agreement emerged from a series of talks conducted between Liberal leader Alberto Lleras Camargo and Conservative chieftain Laureano Gómez (then in exile in Spain). These discussions produced first the Declaration of

Benidorm (signed by Lleras and Gómez on July 24, 1956) and then the Pact of Sitges (signed on July 20, 1957). The original provisions called for bipartisan cooperation to last for twelve years. Following Sitges, a Bipartisan Commission of Institutional Readjustment was named to develop these provisions into formal constitutional reforms. On December 1, 1957, the amendments were submitted to the Colombian people for approval in a national plebiscite, the first such plebiscite in Colombian history.

The two-thirds majority requirement was eliminated in the Constitutional Reform of 1968. Electoral competition was gradually resumed over a four-year period between 1970 and 1974: municipal-level competition in 1970, departmental in 1972, and congressional and presidential in 1974. Between 1974 and 1978 bureaucratic parity between the two parties was fully maintained. In 1978 the Turbay administration adopted a proportional approach to bureaucratic parity based on the percentage of seats held by each party in the Congress. Since assuming power in 1982, President Betancur has continued to give "equitable" treatment to the Liberals, but has not negotiated a prearranged formula.

For an analysis of the origins, structure, and dynamics of the Frente system up to 1966, see Robert Dix, *Colombia: The Political Dimensions of Change* (New Haven, Conn.: Yale University Press, 1967); for an evaluation of the Front through 1974, see the essays in Albert Berry et al., eds., *Politics of Compromise: Coalition Government in Colombia* (New Brunswick, N.J.: Transaction Press, 1980).

2. The bipartisan monopoly institutionalized through the National Front clearly reflected the political realities of the period. Colombia's political left did not then—nor does it today—hold any real sway over the bulk of the country's rural or urban masses. The National Front arrangement was approved by an overwhelming majority of the Colombian population (some 95 percent of those who voted) in the national plebiscite held on December 1, 1957. This consensus is even more impressive when one recognizes that almost 70 percent of the total number of eligible voters went to the polls, a turnout that has no equal either after or before the plebiscite. The Colombian Left has historically had an even more severe problem of popular legitimacy than the traditional parties.

Although the communist party and other socialist political groups were legalized once again under the Frente (after years of clandestinity), the fact that they were legally proscribed from directly running for or holding office during the Front period undoubtedly compounded their problems in developing mass bases.

3. Among the authors who have advanced one or another of these qualifiers are Alán Angell, "Ni populismo ni oligarquía en Colombia: Un caso excepcional en América Latina," *Acción Liberal*, no. 4 (1966); Dix, *Colombia*; James Payne, *Patterns of Conflict in Colombia* (New Haven, Conn.: Yale University Press, 1968); Saturino Sepulveda Nino, *Las elites colombianas en crisis* (Bogotá: El Catolicismo, 1970); Andrew H. Whiteford, "Autocracy, Oligarchy and Cultural Change in Colombia," in A. J. Field, ed., *City and Country in the Third World* (New York: Holmes & Meier, 1971); Miles Williams, "El Frente Nacional: Colombia's Experiment in Controlled Democracy" (Ph.D. Diss., Vanderbilt University, 1972); and John Bailey, "Pluralist and Corporatist Dimensions of Interest Representation in Colombia," in James Malloy,

ed., *Authoritarianism and Corporatism in Latin America* (Pittsburgh, Pa.: University of Pittsburgh Press, 1977).

Recently, a few analysts have labeled the Colombian regime a "consociational" democracy following Arend Lijphart's model of consociationalism. See, for example, Robert Dix, "Consociational Democracy: The Case of Colombia," *Comparative Politics* 12, no. 3 (April 1980): 303–22; and Jonathyn Hartlyn, "Consociational Politics in Colombia: Confrontation and Accommodation in Comparative Perspective" (Ph.D. Diss., Yale University, 1981).

4. For an analysis of the factors that led to the partial collapse of the state and *La Violencia*, see Paul Oquist, *Violencia, conflicto y política en Colombia* (Bogotá: Banco Popular, 1979). The *Violencia* was certainly not a uniform phenomenon throughout the country. A number of recent works demonstrate that it had different causes and took different forms in various regions and localities. For discussions of the specific regional characteristics of the violence, see, for example, Germán Guzmán, *La violencia en Colombia (parte descriptiva)* (Bogotá: Tercer Mundo, 1964); and Gonzalo Sánchez and Donny Meertens, *Bandoleros, gamonales, y campesinos* (Bogotá: El Ancora Editores, 1983).

5. Víctor Manuel Moncayo, "Notas para un analisis histórico del Frente Nacional," *Revista de Historia* 1, no. 1 (1975); and Salomon Kalmanovitz, "Desarrollo represivo acelerado," *Ideología y Sociedad*, no. 11 (1974).

6. E. J. Hobsbawn, "The Revolutionary Situation in Colombia," *World Today* 19 (June 1963): 246–58; and Richard S. Weinert, "Violence in Pre-modern Societies: Rural Colombia," *American Political Science Review* 60, no. 2 (June 1966).

7. On the Rojas dictatorship and the transition to the National Front, see Dix, *Colombia*, pp. 115–28; and Vernon J. Fluharty, *Dance of the Millions: Military Rule and Social Revolution in Colombia, 1936–1956* (Pittsburgh, Pa.: University of Pittsburgh Press, 1957). As Fluharty and others have noted, the Rojas government was never an exclusively military government. From the outset, the *Ospinista* Conservatives and some Liberals occupied important political posts.

8. The Frente created an authoritarian regime, but one of the inclusionary stripe, for it did not attempt to repress participation in the system altogether but rather to channel and control it. For a discussion of inclusionary authoritarianism, see Susan Kaufman Purcell, *The Mexican Profit-Sharing Decision: Politics in an Authoritarian Regime* (Berkeley and Los Angeles: University of California Press, 1977), pp. 1–11.

9. Ibid., pp. 3–5.

10. Between 1958 and 1978, Colombian voters went to the polls on thirteen different occasions. With important exceptions in 1970 (when former dictator Rojas Pinilla ran for the presidency) and 1974 (when López was pitted against Conservative Alvaro Gómez Hurtado), the basic tendency has been high abstentionism. In 1958, 69 percent of the electorate voted; in 1978, only 29 percent voted. Mid-term elections have generally attracted fewer voters than the presidential races. In the presidential contests, approximately 50 percent of the electorate on average has gone to the polls.

For analysis of party identification and electoral behavior during the 1960s and 1970s, see Rodrigo Losada Lora and Eduardo Vélez, *Identificación y participación política en Colombia* (Bogotá: Editorial Presencia, 1981); and Fernando Cepeda Ulloa and Claudia González de Lecarros, *Comportamiento del voto urbano en Colombia: Una aproximación* (Bogotá: Universidad de Los Andes, Departamento de Ciencia Política, 1976).

11. The Acción Comunal program did not constitute a corporatist form of interest representation but rather a clientelistic and personalistic one. The National Peasants Association (Asociación Nacional de Usuarios Campesinos—ANUC) created by the Carlos Lleras Restrepo administration in the 1967–1970 period came closer to corporatism, but when it threatened to escape government control in the early 1970s, it was first isolated and persecuted and then reduced to client status once again. Despite halting efforts during the 1960s and early 1970s, Colombia has never succeeded in establishing effective corporatist mechanisms of interest representation similar to those of the Institutional Revolutionary Party in Mexico.

On Acción Comunal and ANUC, see Bruce Michael Bagley and Matthew Edel, "Popular Mobilization Programs of the National Front: Cooptation and Radicalization," in Albert Berry et al., eds., *Politics of Compromise*; and Bruce Michael Bagley and Fernando Botero Zea, "Organizaciones campesinas contemporáneas en Colombia: Un estudio de caso de la Asociación Nacional de Usuarios Campesinos," *Estudios Rurales Latinoamericanos* 1, no. 1 (January–April 1978).

12. See Alfredo Vasquez Carrizosa, *El poder presidencial en Colombia: La crisis permanente de derecho constitucional* (Bogotá: Enrique Dobry Editor, 1979).

13. The discussion of income distribution patterns presented here is based on the essays in R. Albert Berry and Ronald Soligo, eds., *Economic Policy and Income Distribution in Colombia* (Boulder, Colo.: Westview Press, 1980); Gustav Ranis et al., "Income Distribution and Growth in Colombia" (Paper prepared for a conference on Distribution, Poverty and Development, Universidad de los Andes, Facultad de Economia, Bogotá, Colombia, June 2–4, 1977); Miguel Urrutia M. and Albert Berry, *La distribución del ingreso en Colombia* (Medellín: La Careta, 1975); Fabio Hernán Gómez, *Concentración del poder económico en Colombia*, Colección Documento de Trabajo, no. 13 (Bogotá: CIAS, 1974); and Gabriel Misas A., *Contribución al estudio del grado de concentración en la industria colombiana* (Bogotá: Ediciones Tiempo Presente, 1975).

14. On the internal dynamics of party politics and elections, see Mario Latorre Rueda, *Elecciones y partidos políticos en Colombia* (Bogotá: Uniandes, 1974); Gary Hoskin et al., *Estudio del comportamiento legislativo en Colombia* (Bogotá: Uniandes and Cámara de Commercio de Bogotá, 1975); Gary Hoskin and Gerald Swanson, "Political Party Leadership in Colombia: A Spatial Analysis," *Comparative Politics* 6 (January 1974): 395–423.

15. Gabriel Murillo Castano and Israel Rivera Ortiz, *Actividades y estructura de poder en los partidos políticos colombianos* (Bogotá: Universidad de los Andes, Departamento de Ciencia Política, 1973); and Gary Hoskin and Gerald Swanson, "Inter-Party Competition in Colombia: A Return to La Violencia?" *American Journal of Political Science* 17, no. 2 (May 1973): 316–50.

16. Bailey, "Interest Representation in Colombia," pp. 294–95.

17. Bruce Michael Bagley, "Political Power, Public Policy and the State in Colombia: Case Studies of the Urban and Agrarian Reforms During the National Front, 1958–1974" (Ph.D. Diss., University of California at Los Angeles, Department of Political Science, 1979).

18. The political weakness of the Colombian labor movement can be attributed to two basic factors. First, Colombia has a numerically small organized working class—about 17 percent of the economically active population. This is in part due to late industrialization (import-substitution industrialization took off in the depression in the 1930s) and in part to the dependent, capital-intensive pattern of industrial investment that has occurred since. Second, Colombian labor was organized from above at the outset of the industrialization process. The Liberal CTC was organized under the auspices of President Alfonso López Pumarejo in 1936 and the Conservative UTC under the tutelage of President Mariano Ospina Pérez and the Catholic church in 1946.

Because both of the party-affiliated confederations have pursued conservative, patronal bargaining strategies, they have begun to lose members to more militant organizations. The UTC is still the largest confederation, with about 25 percent of organized labor. The CTC, with 15 percent, has dropped from second to third behind the communist-oriented Confederación Sindical de Trabajadores Colombianos (CSTC), founded in the early 1960s. With some 20 percent of the organized work force, the CSTC is the fastest growing confederation in the country. The social-democratic Confederación General de Trabajadores (CGT), founded in the mid-1970s, is also expanding; although with less than 10 percent of organized workers, it remains the smallest of the major confederations. About 30 percent of Colombian workers are affiliated with independent unions.

For a recent analysis of the Colombian labor movement, see María Teresa Heran, *El sindicalismo por dentro y por fuera* (Bogotá: CINEP, 1981).

19. On the role of the media in Colombian politics, see Robert Pierce, *Keeping the Flame: Media and Government in Latin America* (New York: Hastings House Publishers, 1970), pp. 152–54; Daniel Samper, "Mediamaking South of the Border: Investigative Reporting Takes Root in Colombia," *World Press Review*, February 1983, pp. 33–35; and Charles David Collins, *Prensa y poder político en Colombia* (Cali: Universidad de Valle, CIDSE, 1981).

20. On current peasant movements and guerrilla struggles, see Bruce Michael Bagley, "The State and the Peasantry in Contemporary Colombia" (Paper presented at the meeting of the Latin American Studies Association, Washington, D.C., April 1982); on the labor movement and strike activity, see Ulpiano Ayala and Luz Amparo Fonseca, "El movimento huelguistico, 1974–1981," *Desarrollo y Sociedad*, Separata no. 1 (November 1981): 25–48; on *paros cívicos*, see Luz Amparo Fonseca, "Los paros cívicos en Colombia," *Desarrollo y Sociedad*, Cuadernos 3 (May 1981): 17–30.

21. For an analysis of the 1968 reform, see Jaime Vidal Perdomo, *Historia de la reforma constitucional de 1968* (Bogotá: Ediciones Universidad Externado de Colombia, 1970); on the role of the Colombian Congress, see Ernest A. Duff, "The Role of Congress in the Colombian Political System," in Weston Agor, ed., *Latin American Legislatures: Their Role and Influence in Nine Countries* (New York: Praeger, 1971); and

on the scope of presidential power in economic policymaking, see Roger W. Findley, "Presidential Intervention in the Economy and the Rule of Law in Colombia," *American Journal of Comparative Law* 38, no. 3 (Summer 1980): 423–73.

22. Bruce Michael Bagley, "Political Power, Public Policy and the State," pp. 417–56.

23. Israel Rivera Ortiz, "Colombia's National Planning Department" (Ph.D. Diss., State University of New York at Buffalo, Department of Political Science, 1976); and Gustavo Gallon G., *Concertación simple y concertación ampliada*, Serie Controversia, no. 105 (Bogotá: CINEP, 1982).

24. Bailey, "Interest Representation in Colombia," pp. 280–94; and Marco Palacios, *El café en Colombia, 1850–1970: Una historia económica, social y política*, 2nd ed. (Mexico City: El Ancora Editores, 1983).

25. For analyses of clientelism in Colombia, see Steffen W. Schmidt, "Bureaucrats as Modernizing Brokers? Clientelism in Colombia," *Comparative Politics* 6, no. 3 (April 1974); "Patrons, Brokers and Clients: Party Linkages in the Colombian System," in K. Lawson, ed., *Political Parties and Linkages: A Comparative Perspective* (New Haven, Conn.: Yale University Press, 1980); Nestor Miranda, *Clientelismo y dominio de clase* (Bogotá: CINEP, 1977); Alejandro Reyes Posada, *Latifundio y poder político*, Serie Colombia Agraria, no. 2 (Bogotá: CINEP, 1978); Eloisa Vasco Montoya, *Clientelismo y minifundio*, Serie Colombia Agraria, no. 3 (Bogotá: CINEP, 1978); Jorge Valenzuela Ramírez, *Producción arrocera y clientelismo*, Serie Colombia Agraria, no. 4 (Bogotá: CINEP, 1978).

26. Nestor Miranda Ontaneda and Fernan E. González G., *Clientelismo, 'democracia' o poder popular*, Serie Controversia, no. 41–42 (Bogotá: CINEP, 1976), p. 243; and Payne, *Patterns*, pp. 25–95 and 185–320. Vote buying and electoral fraud of all types are endemic to Colombian elections at the local, departmental, and national levels.

27. Fernando Cepeda Ulloa, "Pensamiento político colombiano contemporaneo" (Paper presented at the Congreso sobre el Pensamiento Político Latinoamericano, Caracas, Venezuela, June 26, 1983), 18 pp.

28. Salomon Kalmanovitz, *Desarrollo de la agricultura en Colombia* (Bogotá: Editorial La Carreta, 1978); and Orlando Fals Borda, *Historia de la cuestión agraria en Colombia* (Bogotá: La Rosca, 1975).

29. J. P. Wogart and J. Hanson, "Colombia: Industrial Growth and Development and Challenges for the 1980s" (Washington, D.C.: unpublished manuscript, 1983), pp. 2–3.

30. Ibid., pp. 3–5; see also Carlos Díaz Alejandro, *Foreign Trade Regimes and Economic Development*, vol. 9, *Colombia* (New York: National Bureau of Economic Research, 1976).

31. Kalmanovitz, *Desarrollo de la agricultura*, pp. 184–295; Fedesarrollo, *La política agraria en Colombia, 1950–1975* (Bogotá: Banco de Bogotá, 1974), pp. 27–69; and Bagley and Botero, "Organizaciones campesinas," *passim.*

32. Wogarth and Hanson, "Industrial Growth," p. 5.

33. On the development of Colombian industry, see R. A. Berry, ed., *Essays on Industrialization in Colombia* (Tempe: Arizona State University Press, 1983).

34. Ernesto Parra E. et al., *La economía colombiana, 1975–76*, Serie Controversia, no. 46 (Bogotá: CINEP, 1976); and idem, *La economía colombiana, 1971–81*, Serie Controversia, no. 100 (Bogotá: CINEP, 1981).

35. For critical analyses of the PAN and DRI programs, see Ernesto Parra Escobar and Clara Bruce Cantor, *El plan de desarrollo Lopez-I*, Serie Controversia, no. 39 (Bogotá: CINEP, 1975), 83 pp.; Centros de Investigación y Documentación Social, *PAN and DRI: Nueva forma de agresión imperialista* (Bogotá: CIDOS, 1979), 120 pp.; Rosemary E. Galli, "Colombia: Rural Development as Social and Economic Control," in idem, ed., *The Political Economy of Rural Development: Peasants, International Capital, and the State* (Albany: State University of New York Press, 1981), pp. 27–90; and Santiago Perry, *La crisis agraria en Colombia, 1950–1980* (Bogotá: El Ancora Editores, 1983), 202 pp.

36. Bagley and Botero, "Organizaciones campesinas," pp. 67–91.

37. A general statement of Currie's approach to economic development can be found in Lauchlin Currie, *Accelerating Economic Development* (New York: McGraw-Hill, 1965). For the Pastrana administration's plan of development, see Departmento Nacional de Planeación, *Las Cuatro Estrategias* (Bogotá: DNP, 1972).

38. On the UPAC system, see Lauchlin Currie, *Ahorro, corrección monetaria y construcción* (Bogotá: Universidad de los Andes, 1974); on the new improvement taxes, see W. A. Doebele et al., "Participation of Beneficiaries in Financing Urban Services: Valorization Changes in Bogotá, Colombia," *Land Economics* 55, no. 1 (February 1979): 73–92; Johannes F. Linn, "The Incidence of Urban Property Taxation in Developing Countries: A Theoretical and Empirical Analysis Applied to Colombia," Staff Working Paper no. 264 (Washington, D.C.: World Bank, August 1977), 106 pp.; William A. Doebele and Orville F. Grimes, "Valorization Changes as a Method for Financing Urban Public Works: The Example of Bogotá, Colombia," Staff Working Paper no. 254 (Washington, D.C.: World Bank, March 1977), 83 pp.

39. Many of the criticisms directed at the UPAC system are compiled in Departamento Administrativo Nacional de Estadística, "Acerca de los UPAC," *Boletín Mensual de Estadística*, nos. 262–63 (1973); Jesús Bejarano, "Currie: Diagnóstico y estrategia," *Cuadernos Colombianos*, no. 3 (1974); and CORP, ed., *Controversia sobre el plan de desarrollo* (Bogotá: Editorial La Oveja Negra, 1972).

40. For the López administration's economic development program, see DNP, *Para cerrar la brecha, plan de desarrollo social, económico y regional* (Bogotá: DNP, 1975). On the 1974 tax reform, see M. Gillis and C. E. McLure, Jr., "Taxation and Income Distribution: The Colombian Tax Reform of 1974," *Journal of Development Economics* 5 (1978): 233–58; on the "bonanza," see essays in E. Reveiz, ed., *La cuestion cafetera* (Bogotá: University de los Andes, 1980).

41. On Colombia's relations with international markets, see A. von Gleich and D. Pizano Salazar, eds., *Colombia en la economía mundial* (Bogotá: Carlos Valencia Editores, 1982).

42. Wogart and Hansen, "Industrial Growth," pp. 23–27; Ernesto Parra, *La economía colombiana, 1971–1981*, Serie Controversia, no. 100 (Bogotá: CINEP, 1981).

43. Ernesto Parra, *Colombia: Análisis económica, 1980–1981* (Bogotá: CINEP, 1982); and Salomon Kalmanovitz, "Reactivación y empleo," in CINEP, ed., *Debate económico* (Bogotá: CINEP, 1983), pp. 9–24.

44. Berry and Soligo, *Economic Policy*, p. 1; see also Marco F. Fierro, "The Development of Industrial Capital in Colombia," *Research in Political Economy* 3 (1980): 209–34.

45. Ulpiano Ayala and Alejandro Sanz de Santamaria, "Actividad económica, empleo, e ingresos," *Desarrollo y Sociedad*, Separata no. 1 (November 1981): 5–24; José Antonio Ocampo and Nohra Rey de Marulanda, "La recessión de 1981 y la situación laboral," *Desarrollo y Sociedad*, Cuadernos 3 (May 1982): 3–16; Jaime Carrillo Bedoya, *Los paros cívicos en Colombia* (Bogotá: La Oveja Negra, 1981), 306 pp.; Pedro Santana R. et al., *El paro cívico, 1981*, Serie Controversia, no. 101 (Bogotá: CINEP, 1982), 136 pp.; and Pedro Santana, *Desarrollo regional y paros cívicos en Colombia*, Serie Controversia, no. 107–8 (Bogotá: CINEP, 1983), 207 pp.

46. For the Turbay administration's development program, see DNP, *Plan de integración nacional, 1979–1982* (Bogotá: DNP, 1980). For analyses of the plan, see Edgar Reveiz R. et al., eds., *Controversia sobre el plan de integración nacional* (Bogotá: Universidad de los Andes and FENALCO, 1981), 356 pp.; and Jorge Ivan González, *PIN II, plan de integración nacional: Estado y bienestar en Colombia*, Serie Controversia, no. 96 (Bogotá: CINEP, 1981), 109 pp.

47. Edgar Reveiz, "Colombia: Crecimiento económico moderado, mejoramienito social y estabilidad política" (Paper presented at conference on Models of Political and Economic Change in Latin America, Vanderbilt University, Nashville, Tenn., November 3–5, 1983), pp. 45–50.

48. Ibid., pp. 47–48; see also Rodrigo Botero, "The Colombian Economy in the 1980's" (A discussion paper prepared for the U.S.-Colombian Policy Dialogue, The Wilson Center and Los Andes University, Washington, D.C., October 27–29, 1983), 9 pp.

49. Reveiz, "Crecimiento económico," pp. 49–54; Botero, "Colombian Economy," pp. 6–9.

50. Dix, *Colombia*, p. 389.

51. Assessments of Colombia's agrarian reform can be found in Ernest Duff, *Agrarian Reform in Colombia* (New York: Praeger, 1968); Herman Felstehausen, "Agrarian Reform and Development in Colombia," in AID, ed., *Agency for International Development Spring Review* (Bogotá: AID, 1970); Roger Findley, "Ten Years of Land Reform in Colombia," *Wisconsin Law Review*, no. 880 (1972); Victor Manuel Moncayo, "La ley y el problema agrario en Colombia," *Ideología y Sociedad*, nos. 14–15 (July–December 1975); and A. Eugene Havens et al., "Agrarian Reform and the National Front: A Class Analysis," in Berry et al., *Politics of Compromise*, pp. 341–80.

52. On the urban reform, see Maurucio Solaun, Fernando Cepeda Ulloa, and Bruce Michael Bagley, "Urban Reform in Colombia: The Impact of the 'Politics of

Games' on Public Policy," in F. Rabinovitz and F. Trueblood, eds., *Latin American Urban Research*, vol. 3 (Beverly Hills, Calif.: Sage Publications, 1973).

53. Rodrigo Parra Sandoval, *Analisis de un mito: La educación como factor de la movilidad social en Colombia* (Bogotá: Universidad de los Andes, Departamento de Educación, 1977).

54. See Albert Berry, "Rural Poverty in Twentieth Century Colombia," *Journal of Interamerican Studies and World Affairs* 20, no. 4 (November 1978): 363–73; and the multiauthor *La problemática urbana hoy en Colombia*, Serie Controversia, no. 7 (Bogotá: CINEP, 1982).

55. For an overview of the narcotics traffic in Colombia, see Richard B. Craig, "Colombian Narcotics and the United States," *Journal of Interamerican Studies and World Affairs* 23, no. 3 (August 1981): 243–70; on corruption, see Penny Lernoux, "Corrupting Colombia," *Inquiry*, September 30, 1979, p. 15; on the penetration of drug money into the political system and legitimate business, see Rogelio García Lupo, "Geopolítica de la cocaína: La ideología del narcotráfico," *El Espectador*, September 4, 1982, p. 1B; "Los dineros no amnistiados," *Guión*, no. 322 (August 26–September 1, 1983): 18, 23, 25; and "El pulso de la nación," *Semana*, no. 6 (August 30–September 5, 1983), pp. 22–27.

56. See Cepeda and González, *Comportamiento del voto urbano*; Fernando Cepeda, "El voto urbano," *El Tiempo*, March 15, 1980; and Gary Hoskin, "Post-National Front Trends in the Colombian Party System: More of the Same?" (Paper presented at the Sixth Latin American Studies Association Meeting, Pittsburgh, Pa., April 1979).

57. For critical evaluations of the López administration, see Ernesto Parra et al., *La economía colombiana, 1975–1976*, Serie Controversia, no. 45 (Bogotá: CINEP, 1977); Patricia Ardila Plazas, *El negocio oscuro del mandato claro*, Serie Controversia, no. 102 (Bogotá: CINEP, 1982); and Fernando Rojas et al., *Política laboral de López*, Serie Controversia, nos. 50–51, (Bogotá: CINEP, 1978).

58. See Alejandro Angula et al., *La pendiente anti-democrática*, Serie Controversia, no. 90 (Bogotá: CINEP, 1980). On the use and the misuse of state-of-siege powers in Colombia during and after the National Front, see Eduardo Umana Luna, *Un sistema en estado de sitio: Ensayos* (Bogotá: Imprenta Nacional de Colombia, 1977); the National Security Statute is discussed in Amnesty International, *Informe de una misión de Amnistia Internacional a la República de Colombia* (London: Amnesty International, 1980), pp. 9–36.

59. On the growing reliance of the Colombian state on repression, see Fernando Rojas H., *El estado en los ochenta: Un régimen policivo?* Serie Controversia, nos. 82–83 (Bogotá: CINEP, 1980); Alfredo Vasquez Carrizosa, "El futuro de la democracia en Colombia" (Paper presented at the Conference on Democracy and Development in Colombia, Johns Hopkins University, School of Advanced International Studies, Washington, D.C., November 6–7, 1981); and Jaime Torres et al., *Colombia repressión, 1970–1981*, 2 vols. (Bogotá: CINEP, 1982).

For analyses of Turbay's foreign policy and his close relations with the Reagan administration, see Bruce Michael Bagley, "Colombia en el Caribe: El nuevo aliado norteamericano?" in Juan Tokatlian and Klaus Shubert, eds., *Relaciones internacionales en la cuenca del Caribe y la política exterior de Colombia* (Bogotá: Cámara de Comercio de Bogotá, Universidad de los Andes, and FESCOL, 1982), pp. 371–90; and Bruce Michael Bagley, "Regional Powers in the Caribbean Basin: Mexico, Venezuela, and Colombia," Occasional Paper no. 2 (Washington, D.C.: Johns Hopkins University, School of Advanced International Studies, Caribbean and Central American Program, 1983).

60. The assassination of the populist Liberal *caudillo* Jorge Eliecer Gaitán on April 9, 1948, and the subsequent spread of *Violencia*, aborted the presidential elections of 1949–50. The Liberals refused to run a candidate, and Conservative Laureano Gómez was elected unopposed to the presidency. The Rojas military coup of June 13, 1953, pre-empted the presidential elections scheduled for 1954. In 1958, the creation of the bipartisan National Front arrangement restricted electoral competition at the presidential level until 1974. In the first two post-Frente presidential elections (1974 and 1978), the Liberals won.

61. For an analysis of Betancur's 1982 campaign platform, see Francisco De Roux, *Candidatos, programas y compromisos*, Serie Controversia, no. 103 (Bogotá: CINEP, 1982).

62. In the 1970 elections, Pastrana was opposed by Betancur and two other Conservative candidates: Gustavo Rojas Pinilla (the former dictator and *jefe* of the ANAPO faction of the Conservative Party, and Evaristo Sourdis (an *Alvarista* from the Atlantic coast). By drawing votes from Pastrana, Belisario probably contributed to Rojas's near victory in the 1970 presidential race.

63. In 1978, Betancur received 2,356,620 votes versus Turbay's total of 2,503,601. On the 1978 elections, see Rodrigo Losada Lora, "El significado de las elecciones de 1978 en Colombia," *Coyuntura Económica* 8, no. 2 (1978): 183–201; and Rodrigo Losada L. and Georg Liebig, eds., *Las elecciones de 1978 en Colombia* (Bogotá: Fundación Friedrich Nauman, 1979). The campaign platforms put forward by Betancur and Turbay are summarized in Ernesto Parra, *Elecciones 1978: Plataformas económicas*, Serie Controversia, no. 36 (Bogotá: CINEP, 1978).

64. Mario Latorre, "Un desastre liberal y un nuevo conservatismo," *Estrategia*, August 1982, pp. 31–39; and Jonathan Hartlyn, "Colombia: Old Problems, New Opportunities," *Current History* 82, no. 481 (February 1983): 62–65, 85. Betancur's victory over López in the 1982 presidential race occurred within the context of a serious division in the Liberal Party. Betancur obtained 3,189,278 votes to López's 2,797,627. Dissident Liberal presidential candidate Luís Carlos Galan received 745,738 votes. The badly divided Liberals remained the majority party in Colombia despite Betancur's victory.

65. On the amnesty, see Presidencia de la Republica, *El Camino de la Paz* (Bogotá: Presidencia de la República, 1982). For the text of the political reform, see *El Espectador*, August 31, 1983, p. 10A.

66. For summaries of Betancur's social programs, see Joaquín Vallejo Arbelaez, "La política económica y social del gobierno de Belisario Betancur," in Eduardo Lora, ed., *La política económica y social del gobierno de Belisario Betancur* (Cali: Corporación

Editorial Universitaria de Colombia, 1983), pp. 19–32; and Gabriel Restrepo, "La política social en el plan de desarrollo," in ibid., pp. 89–102.

67. Latorre, "Un desastre liberal," pp. 33–39; and Hartlyn, "Colombia," pp. 62–64.

68. "Personaje del ano: Belisario, Presidente Amigo," *Guión*, nos. 290–91 (December 17, 1982): 31–32.

69. *New York Times*, December 4, 1982, p. 4.

70. According to an International Monetary Fund report released on June 21, 1983, Colombia's GDP would grow by 2.5 percent in 1983 with inflation in the 30 percent range (*Colombian Newsletter* [New York], no. 6 [June–July 1983]: 1). A more pessimistic scenario was put forward by Salomon Kalmanovitz, "Las posibilidades de la política económica en la coyuntura recesiva," in Lora, *La política económica*, pp. 47–68.

71. Alfonso Rojas Llorente, president of the Asociación Colombiana de Exportadores (ANALDEX), characterized the first semester of 1983 as the "worst six months of the current recession" (*Colombian Newsletter*, no. 6 [June–July 1983]: 2). In the first six months of 1983, Colombia's international reserve position fell approximately U.S. $1.2 billion to $3.6 billion while industrial production grew at a rate of less than 1 percent annually. Moreover, the nation's fiscal deficit continued to expand at an alarming rate.

72. On the economic emergency, see Mario Latorre, "La emergencia económica: Presentación para profanos," *Estrategia*, no. 65 (April 1983): 19–22. For an analysis of the tax reform as it emerged from Congress, see "En que quedo el régimen tributario," *Estrategia*, no. 68 (July 1983): 8–14. On the current problems of the economy, see José Antonio Ocampo G., "La recesión y la política económica," in Lora, *La política económica*, pp. 39–46.

73. The Liberal Party retained its majority status in the congressional elections held in March 1982. In addition, within his own party, Betancur had to balance the demands of the *Pastranistas* and *Alvaristas* against those of the *Belisaristas* and other minor factions.

74. Since 1978, parity has not been a legal requirement. Article 120 of the constitution requires that the major opposition party be given "equitable" treatment, but the term is open to multiple interpretations. Under Betancur, the level of interparty conflict has increased substantially as a result of Conservative-Liberal disputes over Liberal participation in the government.

8 Venezuela

Democratic Politics of Petroleum

John D. Martz

During the quarter-century since its emergence from the most recent of many dictatorships, Venezuela has constructed the most vigorous and vital participatory system in Latin America.[1] Powerfully energized by the juices of democracy, the nation has become a showcase of competitive, party-based, constitutional order for the Third World. It has even been suggested that the system is perhaps overly politicized; certainly it is a truism that the day after elections, campaigning commences for the next contest five years hence.[2] Furthermore, the wealth of petroleum has provided a powerful motor for generating national development and rationalizing political competition. The availability of oil and other natural resources has offered seeming security against retarded growth, social displacement, and political instability. Given these characteristics, the chaotic and mismanaged panorama that emerged in 1983 has understandably shaken Venezuelans' faith in their system and startled foreign observers.

As the country entered an election year, the outgoing administration of Luís Herrera Campins was beset with economic crises.[3] The massive foreign debt was estimated at anywhere from $24 billion to $35 billion—it was impossible to determine the figure. A minimum of $9 billion was due for repayment in 1983, some $3 billion of which was from the private sector.[4] By mid-April of that year, Finance Minister Arturo Sosa was forced to notify foreign creditors that although interest payments would continue, there would be an effective moratorium on payment of principal until July.[5] A complicated three-tier foreign exchange system decreed on February 28 produced mass confusion, while both government and opposition publicly dismissed out of hand the assistance from the International Monetary Fund (IMF) that appeared inevitable.[6]

In the words of one prominent Venezuelan commentator, "There must be examples of worse fiscal mismanagement than that of Venezuela in the last eight or nine years, but I am not aware of them."[7] The administration of Carlos Andrés Pérez (1974–1979) of the social-democratic Acción Democrática (AD) had spent more funds in its five years than had the republic in all its previous 143 years of independence. Although his Christian Democratic successor, Luís Herrera Campins of COPEI, came into office denouncing the "mortgaged" character of the state, initial austerity soon gave way to a new round of profligacy that increased the "mortgage" by nearly $30 billion. When the hemorrhaging of reserves forced the February 1983 suspension of the sale of dollars, the government dithered for another nine days before taking any action. Such was the climate of despair and frustration that rumors of incipient *golpes de estado* repeatedly surfaced. Both government and opposition leaders were compelled to issue public denials that conspiracy was afoot.[8]

The short-run questions revolved about rescheduling the foreign debt, management of the complex exchange system, possibilities of devaluation, consideration of a unilateral debt moratorium, and the inflationary and social repercussions of possible IMF terms for aid. Political speculation linked such matters to public opinion, especially as tied to the December 1983 elections and to personnel in a new government. At the same time, there were more basic issues, both for Venezuela and for the Third World. Fundamental developmental policy had been dependent upon petroleum wealth for decades, with its elaboration and management the responsibility of a civilian, popularly based administration since 1958.

Are there lessons from the Venezuelan experience, then, that might be instructive for development and the policy process in Latin America? Or is the historical domination of petroleum an indicator that the case is sui generis? What of the capacity of a party-dominated democratic system to administer— or to squander—the assets of material resources with which Venezuela is generously endowed? As we consider major facets of policy and the developmental process, it is important to bear in mind the policymaking qualities and abilities of Venezuelan democracy.[9]

Petroleum and the Politics of Democracy

The historical evolution of the Venezuelan petroleum industry is well known, and we need only recall its broad outlines.[10] It took shape under the

1908–1935 dictatorship of Juan Vicente Gómez. A precursor of its future magnitude was suggested by the fabled Los Barrosos strike in 1922, a blowout that produced 1 million barrels daily for nine days. Before the close of the decade, Venezuela was the world's leading oil exporter. *Gomecista* regulations controlled the length of concessions, with royalties running from 8 to 15 percent of market value.[11] There were modest revisions under the two milder military regimes in the decade after Gómez's death. The 1942 income tax law, Venezuela's first, also included a progressive tax on profits for oil corporations. The subsequent 1943 petroleum law (largely the work of North American oil experts) increased royalties and raised taxes. Larger concessions, running for 40 years, were also issued.

The impact of democratic politics was first manifested during the 1945–1948 *trienio*, a period of reformist government initiated by junior military officers in conjunction with the AD. The revolutionary junta adopted a 50/50 formula, which broke ground for the entire industry. A one-time tax of $27 million was also levied on the oil companies to bring the government's share of oil profits to the stipulated 50 percent. More broadly, the AD also moved toward the elaboration of petroleum policies that would be integrated into national developmental plans. What ultimately emerged was to constitute a pattern that the AD and other parties revived and expanded after the 1958 restoration of democratic rule following the military dictatorship of Col. Marcos Pérez Jiménez.

The major architect of petroleum policy was Juan Pablo Pérez Alfonzo, minister of development during the *trienio*, who "announced a policy of no further oil concessions and began collecting taxes in crude oil and offering the oil on a petroleum-short international market in order to raise the international price set by the companies."[12] He also moved to create an oil-financed reserve fund. Despite earlier AD statements that had spoken of nationalization, the AD concluded that such action would be unprofitable and it was better by far to rely on technology, marketing, and cooperation with the multinationals. Such would also be the thinking when the AD and its democratic confreres returned to the country in 1958. Meanwhile, the *Perezjimenista* era saw the dictator and his cronies amass personal fortunes via oil revenues. A new round of 40-year concessions in 1956–1957 alone produced some $675 million. Rómulo Betancourt, who became president in 1959, himself would later write that under Pérez Jiménez the nation had become a veritable "petroleum factory,"[13] as government income from oil tripled and came to represent two-thirds of the national budget.

No one was more conscious of the linkage between petroleum policy and national development than Pérez Alfonzo, who became minister of mines and hydrocarbons for the new Betancourt government in 1959. As he had observed in a policy memorandum penned in June 1954 during Washington exile:

> Venezuela has a great resource in its petroleum, but it is also faced with great responsibility. It must not impede use of this resource to satisfy the needs of other peoples, but in protecting its own national interest, it must never let the industry become dilapidated.
>
> Petroleum is the principal of all indispensable fuels in modern life. . . . The future of the product is absolutely certain; its prices will continue to rise. Venezuela needs to maintain and even to increase the income it receives from petroleum. With a policy of just participation, the exploitation of present concessions is enough for the country.[14]

This was also consistent with the thinking of other party planners as spelled out in 1958 doctrinal theses. Central to AD was the belief that petroleum held the key to balanced economic development.

Under the dictatorship, it was argued, the growth of the industry plus income from new concessions and sales merely financed the large volume of imports. Oil had represented up to 98 percent of the total value of exports while occupying barely 3 percent of the economically active population. Thus, the principle of state intervention and participation in the industry was central to national development. "Investments effected by foreign capital in our country. . . have converted it into a specialized producer of primary exports, to the detriment of the remainder of the national economy. These investments. . . basically benefit the industrial importers first and then, to a lesser extent, the country where the investment is realized."[15]

Such views were largely shared by other civilian leaders and political parties, excepting a small Marxist minority. David Blank is astute in contending that a broad-based national consensus had gradually emerged over petroleum objectives and strategies, which he summarized under four broad rubrics: (1) achievement of a "just share" of oil profits, realizable only through greater control over the industry; (2) the "sowing" of oil profits to achieve integrated national development; (3) conservation of proven reserves through the petroleum era, whatever its duration; and (4) encouragement of global conditions to assure stable markets and fair prices.[16] Certainly broad agreement gradually emerged between the AD and COPEI, with the multiparty system of the 1960s later evolving into a predominantly two-party configuration in the 1970s.[17] A telling illustration was contained in the Pact of Punto Fijo of October 31, 1958, in which the AD and COPEI were joined by the Unión Republicana Democrática (URD) of Jovito Villalba in a joint commitment to pluralistic democracy.[18]

Representatives of COPEI shared the belief that the state bore major responsibility for national development. Petroleum policy constituted a basic instrument for distributive justice.[19] It was only later that policy differences between the AD and COPEI, over instrumental rather than strategic factors, were perceptible. In the meantime, Pérez Alfonzo, for the Betancourt administration, maintained a system that taxed 65 percent of profits while creating a state oil corporation in 1960, the Corporación Venezolana del Petróleo (CVP). He also moved toward establishment of the Organization of Petroleum Exporting Countries (OPEC), of which he is rightly viewed as father and creator. The September 1960 founding of OPEC set as a major objective the establishment of a system "to ensure the stabilization of prices by, among other means, the regulation of production."[20] More important for our purposes, it was another pillar in the petroleum edifice being erected by the evolving system of parties and political democracy.

Under the AD-dominated coalition government (1959–1964), Venezuela sought to apply petroleum earnings in the most socially useful fashion while diversifying the economy to render the nation less dependent on oil exports. The prevailing domestic consensus on petroleum policy was particularly strong regarding the necessity to reduce excessive dependence on exhaustible resources. There was little discord over the perspective expressed by President Betancourt on February 15, 1961:

> We must dispel the happy theory that the oil derricks are producing an inexhaustible quantity of dollars and bolivars. The truth is that we are spending the proceeds of unrenewable, perishable wealth, and that we must spend it well, taking advantage of the extraordinary current situation of Venezuela to establish solid and durable bases for the Venezuelan nation. We are investing the funds that oil brings us to obtain increasingly greater returns from this wealth.[21]

The electoral victory of the AD in 1963 brought Raul Leoni to the presidency. With two schisms in the AD during the previous three years and a proliferation of competing parties, the reduced AD vote necessitated a new government coalition. This time COPEI chose to remain outside the administration, and Leoni therefore drew on the backing of the URD and the newly organized Frente Nacional Democrático (FND) of Arturo Uslar Pietri, a noted man of letters. Venezuela at the moment confronted a chilled relationship with the international petroleum industry. Several adjustments were negotiated during the life of the government, but the most important policy stemmed from the effort to apply retroactive taxation as a mechanism to affect or influence multinational marketing decisions. The oil companies resisted the notion, but their efforts to isolate petroleum policy were

unavailing, and it became inextricably involved in a major political controversy over national tax reform. During this time the domestic accord over
petroleum policy temporarily disintegrated. The pro-business FND was joined
by COPEI in opposing recommendations of the AD government, while the
fledgling democratic system also produced an ad hoc Committee of the Middle
Class, which helped lead the battle against the government proposals.[22]

The ultimate compromise forged by Venezuelan pluralism included a
modified form of increased income from back taxes, along with a five-year
system of so-called tax reference values (TRVs). The latter provided that,
beginning in 1967, all petroleum products exported from the country during
the next five years would receive "reference" prices for tax purposes. These
were negotiated in advance for the entire period, with the multinationals
committed to the TRVs regardless of prices on the international market.
Accompanying the arrangement on reference price taxes was an informal
agreement that the multinationals would increase production in exchange for
new incentives for exploration. In terms of democratic policymaking patterns,
the near crisis of 1966–1967 and its resolution dramatized the effective
interplay of diverse interests within the deepening pluralistic system. As
Franklin Tugwell observed, political change in Venezuela was in a sense
"catching up" with the AD and its petroleum policy. Evidently, "the freedom of
action obtaining during the Betancourt administration had been circum-
scribed by the progressive fragmentation of the party system, the partial
dissolution of the coalition mechanism, and the willingness of the domestic
private sector to ally with the petroleum industry against the state."[23]

The politics of democracy became still more crucial following the
December 1968 election to the presidency of Rafael Caldera of COPEI.[24]
Forging a brilliant electoral campaign that capitalized on a massive division of
the AD—out of which came the new Movimiento Electoral del Pueblo
(MEP)—Caldera became Venezuela's first democratically elected president to
reach office from the opposition. Yet his narrow margin of victory, with barely
29 percent of the vote, assured complications in the management of such
increasingly problematic areas as petroleum policy. COPEI was in the minority
in both the Senate and the Chamber of Deputies. Moreover, the oil industry
was undergoing important shifts both internationally and domestically. A
number of new policies were to be adopted during the Caldera years, two of
which deserve particular mention.

For one, the Congress in December 1970 adopted a new tax increase,
tied to a proviso that Venezuela could unilaterally alter existing TRVs for
export purposes at any time. The government's share of oil profits increased to
78 percent. In addition, congressional approval was extended to guidelines for
service contracts between the state's CVP and the oil multinationals; this
principle had already been accepted in theory during the Leoni period.

Perhaps most significant of all was the 1971 Hydrocarbons Reversion Law, which legislated the progressive return to Venezuela of all existing concessions on their expiration, beginning in 1983. This responded to a preoccupation, articulated by Pérez Alfonzo as early as 1962, that such assets as pipelines, refineries, and related facilities should be subject to reversion. When the measure reached Congress for debate, the now retired former minister argued that the reversion principle was not, as opponents charged, confiscatory. Since 1917 the large corporations had amortized two-thirds of their $5 billion investment in Venezuela and cleared $10 billion in profits. He further insisted that "the oil giants earned 30 percent of their fixed profits in Venezuela compared with only 11 percent in developed countries."[25]

The nation's basic fear was its prevailing inability to compel foreign oil interests to extend their investments in Venezuela. Moreover, "because the majority of the concessions were scheduled to revert to the state without compensation in a little over a decade, the companies had little or no incentive to invest."[26] The early initiative for reversion came not from the government but through a congressional alliance of the MEP and URD, to which the AD soon attached itself. President Caldera only later joined. As passed into law on July 30, 1971, the Hydrocarbons Reversion Law directed that the companies provide an annual deposit amounting to 10 percent of the value of their installations, thereby guaranteeing their good condition when turned over at the conclusion of the 40-year concessions. The altered domestic political context had in turn influenced the policymaking process. With a new party now heading the administration for the first time in what was essentially a minority government, the system required strong initiative from Congress and from diverse political parties. If Caldera himself initially wavered "between his accommodationist inclinations and the opposition's frontal attacks on the oil industry," he eventually moved vigorously in questioning multinational explanations and in interpreting their actions for himself.[27] A sympathetic biographer of COPEI would also remark that while opposition forces had assumed the early leadership in the reversion debate, one of the ultimate byproducts was the arrival of the Christian Democrats "firmly in the Nationalist camp, calling for greater Venezuelan control over the country's resources."[28]

The course of electoral history was again to insert partisan considerations into petroleum policymaking. In December 1973, Carlos Andrés Pérez and the AD swept to a resounding victory over COPEI's Lorenzo Fernández and ten lesser candidates.[29] Suddenly the presumably weakening and fragmenting multiparty system swung drastically toward two-party dominance as COPEI and the AD together received some 78 percent of the congressional and 85 percent of the presidential vote. The AD won an outright majority in both houses of Congress and gained control of three-fourths of Venezuela's municipal councils. Pérez, unlike his predecessor, enjoyed exceptional power and authority in the shaping and implementation of policy. Events soon proved that the Venezuelan vocation for democracy, as Betancourt often put it, would underline the systemic impulse toward consultation, debate, and dialogue. This was never more true than with the movement toward the historic act of nationalization enacted on January 1, 1976.

At dawn on that date, standing on the site of Zumaque Number 1, in 1914 the first commercial well in Venezuela, Andrés Pérez formally proclaimed the nationalization of the massive petroleum industry.[30] As I wrote elsewhere, it was evident from the outset "that the 1976 nationalization was moderate and non-radical. . . both compensation and association agreements with international oil interests were central elements in the action."[31] For our purposes, the nature of the quest for policymaking consensus on the terms of nationalization is crucial. If an authoritarian military ruler might have dictated sweeping action unilaterally, this was neither possible for nor desired by the leaders of Venezuelan democracy, even in the wake of Pérez's enormous popular victory.

Nationalization and Consensus-Building

By the 1970s, there was an accumulation of evidence testifying to Venezuelan successes in evolving policies that extracted substantial benefit for the nation from foreign corporations. It was also true that, in Paul Sigmund's words, there was "an almost irresistible combination of factors leading to a 'nationalization situation.'"[32] There were two crucial elements: the approaching expiration of most existing concessions and OPEC actions in raising prices and limiting production. It became obvious that the conditions that had argued strongly against nationalization in an earlier era were now being overtaken by events. As Pérez came to power, a new national consensus over nationalization was taking shape.

During the 1973 campaign, petroleum policy was denied electoral salience.[33] Carlos Andrés Pérez was typical in the refusal to play politics with oil: "*No voy a petrolizar las elecciones.*" As his official platform promised, a Pérez presidency was committed to undertaking those studies necessary to advance the date of reversion; any decision to nationalize would require a "national consensus."[34] His *Copeyano* opponent agreed; Fernández viewed any such decision not as "the fruit of emotional impulses but rather, the product of careful studies that will permit us to act in the most appropriate form and at the most opportune moment."[35] Only the two principal leftist candidates were inclined toward prompt nationalization, although neither was blind to the difficulties in absorbing the eighteen existing enterprises and operating within a single industry-wide structure. The "easy" electoral solution was to call for CVP control of the industry. Jesús Ángel Paz Galarraga of the MEP coalition, to which the Communists were attached, advocated state control and the termination of service contracts.[36] The more radical José Vicente Rangel described himself to interviewers as "an advocate of accelerating the process of reversion . . . the major weight of which would fall to the CVP."[37] This sounded little different from Pérez.[38]

In his March 12, 1974, inaugural address, the new president addressed the issue, underlining his personal commitment to a broad political consensus.

> Today we see the necessity of advancing the process to fix once and for all a new nationalist and national petroleum policy. It will be the National Congress that says the final word, but not by exercise of a simple parliamentary majority; rather, by decision of the entire nation. . .
>
> I will proceed to name a broad commission, composed of persons representative of national life, who will advise the government in the study of alternatives to be examined prior to submission to the consideration of this sovereign congress. In this fashion I hope to obtain effectively the cooperation of all Venezuelans in the search for that great national consensus that must be possible for the transcendental decisions that we are to adopt.[39]

Executive Decree Number 10, issued ten days later, called for creation of the Comisión Presidencial de Reversión Petrolera. President Pérez attended the initial meeting in May 1974 to enumerate the tasks of the commission: administrative formulas for the transition to state ownership, resolution of compensation questions (companies were to be paid just compensation as consistent with national law), and maintenance of welfare benefits for the oil workers. He proposed that the major subsidiaries (Creole, Shell, and Mene Grande) retain their own organizational identities following nationalization. All the operating companies should be placed under one broad supervisory authority acting on behalf of the state.[40] He requested completion of the official report by the close of the year, and it was indeed delivered to Miraflores Palace on December 23, 1974. The following March, Pérez, on the first anniversary of his inauguration, sent to Congress the proposed Law on the Nationalization of the Petroleum Industry.

The degree of consensus on the commission itself was considerable. The only real point at issue proved to be that of compensation for the companies. The final report called for payment in bonds at net book value (cost less depreciation and amortization) after deductions for taxes, workers' benefits, and the like. Compensation amounts were to be reviewed and endorsed by the Supreme Court. The minuscule communist party opposed compensation, but the more powerful leftist Movimiento al Socialismo (MAS) announced that while Venezuela was not morally obligated to the companies, the party was willing to approve compensation. As the forum for debate moved from the commission to the halls of Congress, however, domestic harmony broke down. The major point of contention revolved about the possible role of non-Venezuelan enterprises, as contained in Article 5.

In the commission report, all petroleum activities were to be the responsibility of so-called "state entities" formed by the government and subject to Senate approval. While seeking thereby to reserve and protect the industry for the state, such entities could "enter into necessary agreements" in the form of contracts with other companies, so long as ownership rights were retained for Venezuela. The Pérez administration, however, felt that such provisions in the commission version would unduly limit governmental flexibility, especially as related to exploration and development of the huge untapped Orinoco Tar Belt resources. Consequently, the government's draft bill, presented to Congress in March 1975, differed from the commission report in one particular. It provided authorization for the government to sign "agreements of association" subject to prior congressional approval and to the maintenance of state control of majority interest in any resultant partnerships.[41]

This proposed revision produced a political firestorm that raged for several months. COPEI led the attack on the redrafted Article 5, arguing that such joint agreements of association would restore multinational control. On March 21, the party contended that although it was hostile neither to foreign nor domestic capital, it viewed Article 5 as weakening the nationalization while "wounding the nationalist conscience of all Venezuelans in their traditional desire to take the nation's primary resources into their own hands." Rafael Caldera, exercising his role as a lifetime senator, was to synthesize *Copeyano* objections in addressing that body toward the conclusion of discussions in August. The former president cited his own experience that petroleum corporations had ignored Venezuelan aspirations for greater sovereignty. In fact, it seemed that "each time they have been able to obstruct [those] aspirations they have done so, and that far from being good colleagues or good partners...they have tried to erect obstacles, to create barriers in Venezuela's path."[42] Although Venezuela would need foreign technicians and would pay for such assistance, the distinction between mixed enterprises and technology was significant, with agreements of association being quite different from technological transfer.

Criticism from the Left was stronger. On March 20, the MAS announced fairly sweeping criticisms of the entire document, although attention again centered on Article 5. The party saw the possibility of a pseudo-nationalization within which the participation of both foreign and domestic private capital might reach enormous proportions. As a result, the riches of petroleum would remain the patrimony of the privileged, with the impoverished masses denied their fair share. Similar doctrinal and ideological attacks were voiced from the Partido Comunista de Venezuela, the Vanguardia Comunista, and the Movimiento de Izquierda Revolucionaria. In addition, there was heightened public concern over the future exploitation and development of the Orinoco Tar Belt, from which both COPEI and the leftist parties wished to exclude foreign companies. The earlier consensus on terms of nationalization having been shattered by Article 5, partisan battle lines were drawn up.

To critics of the government, the redrafted provision would open the door to foreign participation—most especially for the lucrative refining and marketing operations—and thereby would assure enduring subordination of Venezuelan to international interests. Should there be development of the Orinoco Tar Belt, moreover, presumably massive profits would be available to the international firms. In response, the Pérez administration insisted with equal conviction that there was limited national experience with transportation, marketing, and distribution. Given the historical vertical organization of the international oil industry, foreign involvement was inevitable. Furthermore, it would help to assure that the efficiency and profitability of petroleum in Venezuela would not suffer unduly at the time of reversion to the state. Above all else, any such agreements of association were dependent on full congressional review and approval, with foreign participation restricted to a minority role and, in any event, limited to a maximum of fifteen years.

Carlos Andrés Pérez had been prompt to note that the responsibility for the "single modification" of the commission's recommendations had been his, and he urged that consensus be maintained. His more vocal critics, however, contended that the oft-reiterated promise of achieving broad nonpartisan support had been revealed as the flimsiest of deceits. In effect, however, Pérez had consciously opted for consensus when he chose earlier not to proclaim immediate nationalization by executive decree on his inauguration. It would have been legal, constitutional, and politically feasible. Instead, the president selected a path whereby the inevitable impact of domestic politics and the requirements of systemic pluralism assured months of often impassioned debate before the terms of reversion could be finalized. The game of democratic politics constituted a major complication for the adoption of Article 5 and of the entire document.[43]

For COPEI, there was an understandable partisan concern that the AD would claim sole credit for the historic act. Some party leaders therefore argued for enthusiastic support of government proposals, so that the credit would at least be shared. Majority opinion, however, held that the party should voice a staunch opposition in hopes of tarring the AD government with an "antinationalistic" brush. This was also seen as promising some advantage for the subsequent 1978 election campaign. COPEI would presumably adopt the posture of having outdone the AD in terms of patriotic dedication to national interests as reflected by the conflicting attitudes toward Article 5 and its detailed provisions.

In the meantime, the AD itself was cautious in its endorsement. The party hierarchy was frequently at odds with Carlos Andrés Pérez and his presidential advisers throughout his term, and it viewed Article 5 in particular with some concern. Although Betancourt and party president Gonzalo Barrios strongly backed the government, the AD's Comité Ejecutivo Nacional supported the administration bill only with a strong accompanying emphasis on the importance of congressional approval for any and all relevant actions. AD oil expert Arturo Hernández Grisanti, a Pérez Alfonzo protégé, had registered personal misgivings, while Pérez Alfonso spoke from retirement with disapproval of Article 5 and the proposed role of foreign interests. Fearing the measured pace and incrementalism of the Venezuelan process as envisaged by the government, Pérez Alfonzo compared it with the gradualistic takeover of the copper industry in Chile, thus "giving the transnationals time to render more difficult the functioning of the eventually nationalized administration."[44]

The interplay of politics in Congress was intricate and elaborate. In May, the once-powerful URD, reduced to merely one senator and five deputies, sought public attention by redrafting Article 5 in conjunction with Adeco legislators. When both the MAS and MEP objected, they turned to COPEI in the quest for a new consensus. This, too, proved abortive, and a break in the congressional logjam appeared possible only when COPEI and the AD undertook direct negotiations with one another. By August, it was evident that congressional consensus was not viable. The Pérez administration therefore pushed ahead with the use of its legislative control. The only remaining act in the scenario was a final expression of conflicting views, personified by Venezuela's three leading public statesmen—ex-presidents Betancourt and Caldera, and AD president Gonzalo Barrios. Rafael Caldera's summation before Congress strongly defended his own administration's oil policies while criticizing Carlos Andrés Pérez. He saw the fight over Article 5 as having induced phantoms of fear among the citizenry. His eloquence concluded with a moving call for national unity through invocation of the spirit of Bolívar.[45] Barrios then rose to decry partisan politics, stressed the government preference for dialogue and participation, and minimized the significance of agreements of association. The next day, on August 6, 1975, Betancourt supported Article 5 while noting that agreements of association would be only occasional and modest arrangements, always controlled by Venezuela. Finally,

> I conclude by expressing my absolute faith in the success of the takeover by the state, once the law has been approved. . . . All we Venezuelans, including

those who in the exercise of democratic rights now dissent from specific aspects of the law about to be approved, will lend their efforts to administrative success for the country with its basic source of wealth...we men and women of this land must act with a high sense of responsibility.[46]

Pérez signed the Petroleum Industry Nationalization Law on August 29. Claiming unanimity of national opinion and choosing to ignore partisan differences of opinion, he characterized nationalization as the precursor of a new economic order. He promised not to undertake joint ventures during his term and proclaimed that no longer would the Third World be exploited by inadequate payment for its primary products. His closing peroration pledged "our irrevocable purpose of showing that a just society is possible only through respect for human freedom. We are committed...to a grandiose work of taking the initial steps for the economic liberation of Venezuela, and I invite my countrymen to achieve the task that is ours. Let's get to work!"[47]

Managing the Nationalized Industry

Transitions to national ownership customarily engender declines in productivity and inefficiency, and at least temporary reductions in profitability. The Venezuelan action was the first successful oil nationalization since the 1938 Mexican action. In addition to the dissatisfaction of several of the companies over compensation, which was to be negotiated, there were Venezuelan preoccupations over the agreements of association. Moreover, there was unmistakable apprehension that accompanied nationalistic pride in the action, for given the importance of petroleum to national development, there were latent fears about Venezuela's capacity to operate the industry effectively. In time the transition would prove exceptionally smooth, and the economic problems of the 1980s came in spite of, rather than because of, Venezuelan management of the oil industry.

Within its first two years of operation, the nationalized sector was seen to have avoided "most of the pitfalls that have become associated with nationalization of foreign mineral investments."[48] The 22 concessionary companies were reorganized as fourteen entities under the holding company structure of Petroleos de Venezuela (PDVSA). These were later reduced to four. From its founding in January 1976, PDVSA became the eleventh largest non-U.S. corporation in the world; assets included twelve refineries, thirteen tankers, and over 6,000 miles of pipeline. Virtually all of the 23,000 work force were retained after nationalization, including 500-plus foreigners. Operating companies functioned much as before, with non-Venezuelan technicians remaining in place. Furthermore, PDVSA proceeded under an extensive grant of operational autonomy. As its president remarked at the beginning, PDVSA "has been structured and operates as a commercial company...which seeks to obtain maximum economic benefit for its sole shareholder, the Venezuelan State."[49]

Perhaps the single element most crucial to what might be termed the "democratic management of the industry" was the commitment by Venezuela's political parties to a maximum of administrative discretion and financial self-sufficiency.[50] There was little margin for error in operational capacity, given the industry's domination of the economy. With oil regularly accounting for two-thirds of government revenue, at least 90 percent of export earnings, and one-quarter or more of gross national product, Venezuela could ill afford the kind of wasteful management characteristic of most of its national public enterprises. Both the structures and operating dynamics of PDVSA within the politics of democracy required uncommon sensitivity to principles of rationality and nonpartisan decisionmaking.

The independence of PDVSA from domestic politics was to be neither achieved nor defended without continuing debate. Both partisan and bureaucratic conflicts were inevitable. A determination that PDVSA be truly autonomous was reflected at the very outset through the nomination of Rafael Alfonzo Ravard as its first president. A retired general who had built a remarkable record of technical and managerial skill during lengthy service heading the Corporación Venezolana de Guyana (CVG), Alfonzo Ravard was a no-nonsense leader who stressed administrative competence and professionalism while skillfully minimizing partisan interference. Enjoying great support from the private sector as well as an international reputation, the general secured Pérez's initial commitment to noninvolvement by political forces. PDVSA was to operate as a commercial company for the benefit of the state. It also was soon to confront the first of numerous challenges to its untouchable status.

Public hearings in early 1977, for instance, sharpened the conflict over PDVSA secrecy regarding corporate and technological concerns. Industry officials argued that business and contractual matters could not be a matter of public knowledge. Ranking *Copeyanos* and *Adecos* were inclined to accept the contention, albeit reluctantly, until the crises of the 1980s led to further pressure for detailed PDVSA accountability to the legislature. In the meantime, there were perhaps more serious breaches in the consensus within the executive branch. The relationship between the minister of energy and mines and the PDVSA president was ambiguous from the outset and has never been fully clarified. PDVSA executives have understandably downplayed the need for significant involvement by the ministry, while authorities for the latter have questioned the "holding company" status assigned to PDVSA.

Personality clashes and rival ambitions among policymakers have also added fuel to the fire. At the outset in 1976, Minister of Energy and Mines Valentín Hernández Acosta expressed disapproval of the planning and supervisory authority that devolved on the industry. He saw the elaboration of PDVSA responsibilities as threatening to diminish the role of his ministry. As he remarked shortly after nationalization,

> The experience that we have had is that the ministry had more troubles...with the CVP than with the concessionary companies...The ministry will have, with the Ministry of Finance, the responsibility for guarding the tax reference values of oil insofar as they affect the government of Venezuela...we cannot let Petroleos de Venezuela treat the subject from the purely commercial point of view without taking into account national policy on prices as well as the commitments Venezuela has accepted in international organizations like OPEC.[51]

The rivalry was to become more acute under the Herrera presidency, as Minister of Energy and Mines Humberto Calderón Berti and other cabinet-level officials periodically engaged in power moves against Alfonzo Ravard. Even earlier, however, the dynamics of political pluralism were operating to diminish the technologically based economy of the industry. This stemmed in no small part from the rapid expansion of PDVSA operations following nationalization. After completion in 1978 of the two-step consolidation into four competitive concessionaires, PDVSA announced the completion of industry reorganization. That same year the PDVSA assumed responsibility for the state petrochemical company. PEQUIVEN, as the reorganized entity was called, had been known for incompetence, inefficiency, and gross mismanagement through several successive administrations. PDVSA confounded pessimists by turning it around so that by 1983 it was no longer operating at a deficit.

In the meantime, the questioning of industry autonomy had almost imperceptibly grown. Accumulating economic pressures further sparked a movement that threatened a politicization of industry management. In April 1981, Gonzalo Barrios for the AD issued a press statement sharply critical of the PDVSA, singling out alleged extravangances in its investment program. He was followed by Octavio Lepage, interior minister under Pérez, who promised private congressional hearings by the Senate Committee on Hydrocarbons, which he chaired.[52] Further questioning focused on contracts tied to exploitation of the Orinoco Tar Belt. Partisan factors were aggravated when *Calderista* elements of COPEI were slow to defend oil policy identified with President Herrera, an antagonist of Caldera's.

Congressional debates recurred in May and June 1981. The AD, previously a champion of PDVSA operations, argued the advisability of greater congressional control, while *Herreristas* somewhat disingenuously called for greater supervision by the minister of energy and mines. The administration also adopted executive directives requiring the industry to divert increasing resources to the promotion of socially oriented programs and demanding greater use of domestic services and capital goods, notwithstanding considerations of cost and efficiency. In August, the PDVSA Shareholders Assembly announced a decision to decentralize operations. MARAVEN (essentially the European concessionaires) officials were to be moved to Puerto La Cruz in the east; the concessionaire's director, not informed of the move in advance, promptly resigned in protest. At the same meeting there was a restructuring of the PDVSA Board of Directors in a fashion unsympathetic to Alfonzo Ravard, although he himself received another two-year reappointment.

At the close of 1981, a harbinger of yet broader conflicts in developmental policymaking surfaced with the annual report of the Banco Central de Venezuela (BCV). BCV president Leopoldo Díaz Bruzual had challenged many administration policies while serving as president of the Fondo de Inversiones Venezolano (FIV—Venezuelan Investment Fund). After moving to the BCV in April 1981, he has sought personal fiscal influence within PDVSA. His annual report bluntly charged the industry with producing more new employees than new wells. Alfonzo Ravard, scarcely a novice at bureaucratic battles, retorted that "El Búfalo" was misinformed on basic factual points, but could be expected to learn in time.

The PDVSA also provoked acquisitive resentment for its control of reserves, estimated by early 1982 at some $9-10 billion. Planning Minister Ricardo Martínez confessed to an interest in drawing on PDVSA funds as a means of servicing the foreign debt. Others also coveted these resources, especially as the nation's economic situation deteriorated further. Yet the industry for a time was successful in defending its interests. Not until September 1982 did the Herrera administration call for $4.51 billion of PDVSA reserves to be placed under BCV control. The action was defended as a means of improving Venezuela's sagging financial image with the outside world, an argument that proved specious. But the PDVSA had been dealt a setback, and Díaz Bruzual had prevailed.

El Búfalo contended that the industry's reserves effectively belonged to all Venezuela and thus should be used for a multitude of developmental purposes. General Alfonzo Ravard, unwilling to accept any dilution of PDVSA independence, retaliated through the special joint committee established to work out details of the financial shift. By November 1982 he had secured agreement that PDVSA would retain control over collections and receivables, along with the right of free use of income earned through domestic sales. The PDVSA could also acquire foreign exchange for imports or other external obligations from the bank at any time.[53] Notwithstanding these relative successes, the petroleum industry, by 1983, had largely lost its previously sacrosanct state. Whatever the advisability of this change, it tellingly illustrated the continuing vigor and influence of democratic politics in Venezuela. With the economic shocks of 1983, it became an increasingly crucial question whether the industry could maintain sufficient independence while interacting with domestic political forces and contributing to a crippled, yet still very vital, democratic system.

Petroleum and National Development

The notion of employing petroleum earnings to develop the nation and diversify the economy dates back to the 1940s. Symbolized by the phrase *sembrar el petróleo*, it has received at least verbal recognition by both democratic and authoritarian regimes. Since 1958 it has been a watchword of the developmental outlook of the political elites. The difficulties in realizing the broadly based developmental objectives have been underlined by the experience of the past decade. It was first under Carlos Andrés Pérez that a truly massive program to build swiftly a modern industrialized state was undertaken. Government revenue per barrel of oil exported rose from $2.29 in 1973 to $9.45 in early 1975, over 300 percent in little more than a year. The Pérez government created the FIV in May 1974 as a means of setting aside nearly half of Venezuela's petroleum earnings. Through the FIV and other state agencies, it was hoped that economic growth might combine public and private sector investment.

The Fifth National Plan (1976–1980), announced in spring 1976, represented an ambitious attempt to achieve balanced national development. It was overly optimistic in projecting an annual growth rate of 8.2 percent; the figure in 1977 and 1978 fluctuated around 7.4 percent, after which it dropped precipitously. Key sectors expanded less rapidly than anticipated, and non-traditional exports were also overestimated. When a slackening of petroleum income appeared at the close of 1976, the administration indicated a willingness to employ foreign borrowing as a means of financing new programs. The AD was critical, but had limited influence on the administration. The government continued to plow funds into agriculture without altering the record of failure that had marked previous administrations.[54] By the close of the Pérez years, notwithstanding progress on some fronts, there were uncorrected structural and systemic distortions. The flood of petrobolivars was also encouraging a higher level of corruption than Venezuela had previously known.

With the passing of the Pérez period, it was evident that whatever its political accomplishments, Venezuelan democracy had not effectively met many basic challenges.

> The system had not extended its economic largesse and natural resources on an equitable basis to large numbers of the population. . . the social agenda remained unfilled. With the rise of new sectors, the continuing migration from rural to urban settings, and the rapid population increase, it remained to be proved that the political and economic progress that had taken place could be translated into benefits for the great mass of the citizenry.[55]

When COPEI won the 1978 elections and Luís Herrera Campins took office, the new president denounced his predecessor at the inauguration ceremonies on March 12, 1979, voicing the now renowned charge that reckless spending in the previous five years had "mortgaged" Venezuela's future. The attack provoked national debate,[56] widening the AD–COPEI gulf and underlining the mounting developmental problems. At the same time, there was broad realization that the economy was overheated, requiring stabilization and a cooling-off period. Herrera's call for austerity and fiscal discipline was hailed as appropriate to the moment.

The new finance minister, Luís Ugueto, advocated tight credit policies to attack inflation while the alleged extravagance of the Pérez government was being brought to an end. During the first two *Herrerista* years, these efforts were pursued somewhat irregularly, and economic stagnation accompanied a slight reduction in the inflation rate. The Sixth National Plan (1981–1985) was presented to Congress in August 1981. It stressed industrial development, electricity and steel, improved transportation and communications, income redistribution, and agricultural self-sufficiency.[57] The public was assured that the corner was to be turned by the close of 1981.

In fact, the economy remained sluggish, with agriculture growing a mere 2.8 percent and manufacturing 0.8 percent. Government planners began speaking of economic growth of no more than 3 percent for 1982. President Herrera's commitment to a form of modified Thatcherism was diluted by constant feuding among his major economic advisers, which Herrera seemed disinclined to resolve. Public opinion, while favoring efforts to curb wasteful spending and to rationalize government investments, was also feeling the decline of growth rates to virtually zero after two decades of rates ranging from 4 to 8 percent. By 1982 it was unclear if the period of economic "stabilization" and recession might be converted into renewed growth and a revival of productivity. Within twelve months it was recognized that Venezuela was adrift in a sea of economic perils, of a magnitude unknown for at least three decades.

By 1983 it was unarguable that the decade-long spending spree was over. Gross domestic product had actually decreased by 1.5 percent; the foreign debt was between $25 billion and $34 billion. Oil production and prices both fell as a consequence of the international glut and new OPEC decisions. In July 1982, President Herrera had accepted the need for a 10 percent reduction in the budget as a response to falling oil revenues. There were at least three major problem areas: (1) changes in the international oil industry that far exceeded the expectations of policymakers, (2) misjudgment and error in managing fiscal and monetary policy, and (3) failures in the policymaking process that centered on the administration itself.

More modern refining and marketing strategies were also put into place. Traditionally Venezuelan petroleum has been predominantly light, and so PDVSA began stressing the export and sale of heavy oil to avoid premature depletion of the light. This grew in significance as economic stagnation was further aggravated by the reduction of revenues experienced by oil producers in the face of falling international demand. The world glut also encouraged greater government intervention in PDVSA, as previously discussed. In addition to the 1982 transfer of PDVSA reserves to the BCV, the incipient fiscal emergency threw into question the capacity of PDVSA to finance its vast developmental requirements. It had planned to spend $37 billion from 1983 to 1988. By the close of 1982 it was announced that the existing annual level of $3.5 billion would remain fixed rather than grow, thereby implying a five-year cut of some $20 billion. The scaling-down was directed particularly at the Orinoco Tar Belt. An earlier plan to devote some $7 billion by 1988 was shelved, with the completion date moved into the 1990s. Alfonzo Ravard was still bullish about the ability to meet cash flow requirements, however. "I believe we have enough. . . to invest in our petroleum and to continue making substantial contributions to the country."[58]

The fall in oil prices to some $27.50 per barrel by late 1982 affected the general economy. At this price, Venezuela would earn some $14 billion annually, versus the 1981–1985 national plan's projected $20 billion. Furthermore, government targets of 2.2 million barrels of daily production— including 1.79 to be exported—proved unrealistic. Official figures were revised downward to 2.02 and 1.6 million respectively, only to be rendered meaningless by OPEC decisions.

The January 1983 meeting of the oil exporters in Geneva failed to establish a consensus. Humberto Calderón Berti returned home with the belief that Venezuela should give renewed attention to such non-OPEC producers as Mexico. In his words, "OPEC can no longer play the role of a swing producer in the oil market. I think we have to begin talking to the non-

OPEC producers and to the consumers."[59] The climate further deteriorated in February 1983, when Great Britain, Norway, and then OPEC member Nigeria lowered their prices. For Venezuela, where the government budget at the moment was roughly $22.5 billion and oil revenues had dropped to $16.2 billion, each dollar reduction per barrel would mean some $500 million, or 2 percent of the budget. Reducing exports by 100,000 barrels per day would cost around $1 billion. When March talks in London lowered the price of marker crude to $29 per barrel, it meant a loss of some $2.6–2.8 billion for Venezuela.

Policymakers found the situation both complex and ambiguous. International market conditions and OPEC decisions were largely beyond Caracas's ability to affect more than marginally, although the nation remained influential within OPEC circles. If insight had been less than prescient in Caracas, the same was true of many petroleum industries the world over. What was more susceptible to rational planning and systematic management, however, was the overall economic situation as framed by fiscal and monetary realities. As one Venezuelan put it, the Pérez administration had engaged in building "lavish new industrial plants, but with inefficiency and at enormous cost overruns, partly caused by graft and irresponsible management, but mostly by the reckless overstretching of scarce human resources."[60] Then, the Herrera government, ignoring its own warnings about the recent quadrupling of public spending by its predecessor, accepted the market conditions accompanying the repercussions of the Iranian revolution as the price of oil reached $34 per barrel. The Herrera government "blithely forgot all its own remonstrances...and went down its own path to an even greater quagmire,"[61] spending in its first three years more than had Pérez in five. Such unwise management, less the product of conflict than of corruption and incompetence, has underlined the problems of policymaking in democratic Venezuela. It also redirects our attention to issues of policy and economic development.

Policy and Process in a Latin American Democracy

The fiscal and monetary fiasco of 1983 had been long in the making. The bonanza attitudes fostered by petroleum income encouraged both lax management and, at best, erratic implementation of policy. It was, for example, all too easy to forget campaign promises about the rescue of agriculture—wasting money in ill-conceived measures while importing basic consumer goods from abroad, often at government-subsidized prices. There also grew up a comfortable two-party domination of the policy process, wherein partisan conflict was more rhetorical than substantive. The stress upon consensus, nurtured during the Betancourt administration that initiated the democratic period, became an article of faith for a generation of party leaders. It also dulled the analytic and procedural capacities of bureaucrats and government workers.

The 1983 crisis followed years of problematic decisionmaking, dramatically spurred by Pérez's policies and the post-1973 spurt of petrobolivars. The president, initially committed to cautious management of increased wealth, soon fell prey to the temptations of building a modern industrialized nation overnight. Massive public works projects, grandiose plans ranging from a new national rail system to sophisticated industrial complexes, and a scholarship program sending thousands of young Venezuelans abroad each year—these and similarly impatient efforts to transform the nation were flawed by inefficient or dishonest management, cost overruns, and an absence of careful planning.

To be fair, it is true that many undertakings of the Pérez years were long overdue; others would only bear fruit long after the energetic president had completed his term in office. At the same time, the pattern of unchecked spending exceeded partisan boundaries, infusing the entire bureaucracy while contaminating the private sector. Endemic mismanagement was further encouraged by the statutory independence of many state-related agencies, which enjoyed authority to contract their own loans from both domestic and international sources. The Pérez government ultimately borrowed $15–20 billion.

By 1981, *Herrerista* pledges of frugality and austerity had been forgotten. Early in the year it was announced that the nation's public sector agencies had accumulated up to $10 billion in short-term foreign debt. The unexpected news helped provoke a turnover in the Directorship of Public Credit, as well as congressional action. A new Public Credit Law, adopted in August, authorized efforts to refinance $4.3 billion over an extended repayment period. It also plugged existing loopholes whereby autonomous government agencies had been able to negotiate new loans on the international market free from external review. Renegotiations subsequently refinanced nearly $1 billion on the Euromarket by the end of 1982. This failed to check the alarming rise in the international debt.

Manuel Rafael Riverto, the comptroller general, announced in September 1982 that the public debt had reached $35 billion (including $4.18 billion estimated at the margin of the Public Credit Law). The government disputed his figures, with President Herrera citing a total of $18.5 billion. As the new year unfolded, the fiscal and monetary situation became clearer. Foreign reserves stood at $12 billion, one-third lower than twelve months earlier. The IMF, employing Venezuelan data, presented its own estimate of the public debt at $20.7 billion; the short-term total was $6 billion. In February 1983, Finance Minister Arturo Sosa produced his own total of

$24.3 billion, including a $9 billion short-term commitment.[62] Still another source, drawing on Morgan Guaranty Trust, the World Bank, the Federal Reserve Board, and Geoffrey Bell and Company, reported in March that Venezuela's total debt at the beginning of the year was $28.5 billion, with the short-term component about $15 billion.[63]

Efforts to renegotiate the debt proved tedious and troublesome. Following informal discussions, Sosa announced on March 24 that the nation was calling a moratorium on debt repayments until July 1; during the interim, it would attempt to improve its own data while seeking to reschedule $9–10 billion of the short-term debt. He intended to renegotiate fully the $10 billion that would mature in 1983 and presented a host of additional, detailed proposals. International bankers were skeptical, and by mid-1983 the discussions were still under way.[64] Concomitant efforts to secure major relief from the IMF were foundering on the reluctance of the government, especially in an election year, to accept the IMF's demanding conditions.

There was even greater confusion and disarray with regard to monetary policy. Assumptions about the basic health of the currency and the absence of major liquidity problems were shattered by the February 1983 drop of foreign reserves to $8.5 billion. On February 20, 1983, the government announced the suspension of foreign currency transactions. For the next nine days the administration wrangled over its options while creditors, financiers, and citizens waited. Díaz Bruzual called for explicit devaluation; he was opposed by Sosa and by Planning Minister Maritza Izaguirre, who viewed devaluation as a guarantee of rampant inflation. Finally, on February 28, the government announced a compromise calling for a three-tier exchange system. The traditional 4.3 bolivars to one dollar would apply to "essential" imports, government purchases, and payments to students studying abroad. Non-essential imports would be at an intermediate rate, while luxury imports would be at a floating rate, which began at 7.5 to 1 but by June 1983 hovered around 11 to 1. There were controversial and confusing provisions for the different treatment of government, private, and non-Venezuelan debts.[65] While conflict about application of the preferential rate continued, the government debated and vacillated about the definition appropriate for imported whiskey.[66] Controversy between the BCV and the president over the rules for repayment of private debt typified the lack of coordination between and among administration policymakers, including the president himself. The administration program of banning selected imports while licensing others was not promising, for "such an approach requires that the government efficiently process applications for foreign exchange and monitor [the] flow of goods across the nation's borders. These are requirements that exceed the government's competence."[67]

By mid-1983 the Venezuelan panorama was littered with ambiguities and uncertainties. The fiscal and monetary situation was seriously troubled by a large foreign debt, a poorly planned system of currency exchange, and the effects of the world petroleum market. Beyond issues of policy judgment and administration decisions, however, lay the unmistakable evidence of policymaking incompetence and indecisiveness. Earlier, the Pérez government had forged a broad policy orientation and pursued it with reasonable consistency. Errors were less those of policy process than of actual substance. Under Herrera, however, the process itself was at fault.

Many of the internal disputes and inconsistencies have already been noted. At the beginning, Herrera staffed his economic team with Venezuela's "Chicago boys," most prominently Finance Minister Luís Ugueto. There was to be a reduction of subsidies, softening of tariff barriers, a selective withdrawal of price controls, and in general a free-market approach. Yet this current of thought and action was never fully backed by President Herrera, leaving Ugueto and his supporters constantly engaged in internecine skirmishes with other administration officials. Both the PDVSA and the Ministry of Energy and Mines periodically fought Ugueto's initiatives. Political pressures also caused a loss of will at important junctures, as when a lifting of price controls on important consumer products was followed by an inflationary wage increase to mollify organized labor. The public sector, which the president refused to court, became fully as antagonistic as the workers' federation (CTV). The latter could lobby effectively, as when it helped in passing September 1982 legislation increasing tariffs on more than 400 products—in direct opposition to Ugueto's recommendations.

The conflicts involving the BCV under Leopoldo Díaz Bruzual have also been cited, with the latter seeking to expand his own authority. Having ultimately won his battle with Ugueto, he then promptly was at odds with Sosa. His running dispute with Alfonzo Ravard and the PDVSA could only damage both the oil industry and its relationship to the central government. All such disputes were aggravated by Luís Herrera's unwillingness either to negotiate or to choose among and between high-level administration officials. The quixotic and erratically directed substance of policy thus added to the endemic problems inherited from Pérez and, to some extent, embedded in the experience of the entire democratic era in Venezuela.

As Venezuela has moved toward a two-party system, responsibility for development policy has fallen to COPEI and the AD. In the last decade, each of these has captured power and floundered over serious economic problems. Electoral advantage and partisan opportunism also played a part in the formulation and application of policy. For the dominant oil industry, only recently have domestic considerations become important. The trend toward politicization may prove a major difficulty in the years immediately ahead, yet that industry retains a quality of leadership and technical competence external to the character of the political system and absent in other policy areas.

The capacity to change, to learn by error, and to apply corrections lies at the core of the representative pluralistic system. As Venezuela faces its most severe economic challenges in more than a generation, there are few grounds to argue that authoritarianism would produce greater progress, development, or well-being. The consensual approach of the parties, which has so diluted the effectiveness of policymaking, may be diminished somewhat as the margin for error is reduced. The systemic capacity to employ petroleum for the good of the citizenry will be more seriously tested than in the past. At the same time, its impact as a tool to promote the post-1958 democracy cannot be ignored or forgotten. "Oil may have gone to Venezuelan heads, like a dangerous addictive drug, but it has also made Venezuela a modern, educated, healthy democratic country—the very qualities and advantages that are needed to face the present crisis."[68]

Notes

1. For a broad multiauthor overview, see John D. Martz and David J. Myers, eds., *Venezuela: The Democratic Experience* (New York: Praeger, 1977).

2. John D. Martz, "Los peligros de la petrificación: El sistema de partidos venezolanos y la década de los ochenta," in Enrique Baloyra Herp and Rafael López Pinter, eds., *Iberoamérica en los años 80: Perspectivas de cambio social y político* (Madrid: Centro de Investigaciones Sociologicas, 1983), p. 149.

3. The Venezuelan constitution permits a second presidency only after the lapse of two five-year terms. Thus Luís Herrera Campins, inaugurated in March 1979, was ineligible to succeed himself.

4. *Latin American Weekly Report*, May 20, 1983, p. 5.

5. *Washington Post*, April 1, 1983, p. 16.

6. *Wall Street Journal*, April 8, 1983, p. 1.

7. Carlos Rangel, "How Venezuelans Twice Squandered Their Oil Wealth," *Miami Herald*, March 20, 1983, p. 7.

8. See illustrative articles in *Journal of Commerce*, March 2 and 22, 1983.

9. For a review and projection through the 1980s, see Martz and Myers, "Venezuelan Democracy and the Future," in *Democratic Experience*, pp. 359–92.

10. Among a few of many convenient English-language sources, in addition to those cited later, see Edwin Lieuwen, *Petroleum in Venezuela: A History* (Berkeley and Los Angeles: University of California Press, 1954); Luís Vallenilla, *Oil: The Making of a New Economic Order* (New York: McGraw-Hill, 1975); and Stephen G. Rabe, *The Road*

to OPEC: United States Relations with Venezuela, 1919–1976 (Austin: University of Texas Press, 1982).

11. Paul E. Sigmund, *Multinationals in Latin America: The Politics of Nationalization* (Madison: University of Wisconsin Press, 1980), p. 228.

12. Ibid., p. 230.

13. Romulo Betancourt, *Venezuela: Política y petróleo*, 2nd ed. (Caracas: Editorial Senderos, 1969), p. 777.

14. Juan Pablo Pérez Alfonzo, *Petróleo: Jugo de la tierra* (Caracas: Editorial Arte, 1961), pp. 83–84.

15. Acción Democrática, *Tesis petrolera* (Caracas: Editorial "Antonio Pinto Salinas," 1958), pp. 24–25.

16. David E. Blank, *Venezuela: Politics in a Petroleum Republic* (New York: Praeger, 1984), p. 138.

17. See John D. Martz, "The Evolution of Democratic Politics in Venezuela," in Howard R. Penniman, ed., *Venezuela at the Polls: The National Elections of 1978* (Washington, D.C.: American Enterprise Institute for Public Policy Research), pp. 1–30; see also "Peligros de petrificación."

18. For a work stressing the collaborative nature of Venezuelan pluralism, see Daniel H. Levine, *Conflict and Political Change in Venezuela* (Princeton, N.J.: Princeton University Press, 1973), especially p. 43. See also John D. Martz, *Acción Democrática: Evolution of a Modern Political Party in Venezuela* (Princeton, N.J.: Princeton University Press, 1966), pp. 104–5.

19. Donald L. Herman, *Christian Democracy in Venezuela* (Chapel Hill: University of North Carolina Press, 1980), pp. 55 ff.

20. Ministerio de Minas e Hidrocarburos, *Venezuela and the OPEC* (Caracas: Imprenta Nacional, 1961), p. 13.

21. Romulo Betancourt, *Dos años de gobierno democrático* (Caracas: Imprenta Nacional, 1961), p. 404.

22. Easily the best account in English is found in Franklin Tugwell, *The Politics of Oil in Venezuela* (Stanford: Stanford University Press, 1975), pp. 88 ff.

23. Ibid., p. 96.

24. The best analysis of the 1968 race is David J. Myers, *Democratic Campaigning in Venezuela: Caldera's Victory* (Caracas: Fundacion La Salle, 1973).

25. George W. Grayson, "Venezuela's Presidential Politics," *Current History*, January 1974, p. 26.

26. Sigmund, *Multinationals*, p. 234.

27. Tugwell, *Politics of Oil*, p. 158.

28. Herman, *Christian Democracy*, p. 157.

29. The most extensive analysis of the campaign and elections is John D. Martz and Enrique A. Baloyra, *Electoral Mobilization and Public Opinion: The Venezuelan Campaign of 1973* (Chapel Hill: University of North Carolina Press, 1976).

30. The flag-raising over Zumaque was followed later in the morning by a presidential address at Cabimas, both of which the author attended.

31. John D. Martz, "Policy-Making and the Quest for Consensus: Nationalizing Venezuelan Petroleum," *Journal of Interamerican Studies and World Affairs* 19, no. 4 (November 1977): 483.

32. Sigmund, *Multinationals*, p. 253.

33. Martz and Baloyra, *Electoral Mobilization*, pp. 148–49.

34. Carlos Andrés Pérez, *Acción de gobierno* (Caracas: n.p., 1973), p. 39.

35. Lorenzo Fernández, *Directrices para una acción de gobierno* (Caracas: n.p., 1973), p. 8.

36. Nueva Fuerza, *Programa de gobierno* (Caracas: n.p., 1973), unpaginated.

37. *El Nacional* (Caracas), December 10, 1973, p. D-1.

38. See Martz, "Policy-Making," especially pp. 484–86.

39. Carlos Andrés Pérez, *Mensaje del presidente* (Caracas: Imprenta Nacional, 1974), unpaginated.

40. For documents, see José Agustin Catala, ed., *Nacionalización del Petróleo en Venezuela* (Caracas: Centauro Editores, 1975).

41. Venezuela, Congreso Nacional, *Proyecto de ley de nacionalización* (Caracas: Imprenta Nacional, 1975), unpaginated.

42. Rafael Caldera, *La nacionalización del petróleo* (Caracas: Ediciones Nueva Politica, 1976), pp. 68–69.

43. Sigmund, *Multinationals*, p. 241.

44. As quoted in "Nuevo enfoque de la situación humana y el petróleo," *SIC* (Caracas), March 1976, pp. 137–44.

45. Caldera, *Nacionalización*, p. 70.

46. Romulo Betancourt, *Dueño de su petróleo* (Caracas: Centauro Editores, 1976), p. 28.

47. Carlos Andrés Pérez, *Mensaje de nacionalización a la República* (Caracas: Imprenta Nacional, 1976), p. 15.

48. Sigmund, *Multinationals*, p. 247.

49. As quoted in Blank, *Petroleum Republic*, p. 156.

50. Ibid.

51. *Resumen* (Caracas), no. 125 (March 28, 1976): 20.

52. *SIC* (Caracas), May 1981, p. 231.

53. *Journal of Commerce*, November 5, 1982, p. 1.

54. John D. Martz, "Approaches to Agricultural Policy in Venezuela," *Inter-American Economic Affairs* 34, no. 3 (Winter 1980): 25–54.

55. Martz, "Evolution," in Penniman, *Venezuela at the Polls*, p. 27.

56. David J. Myers, "The Elections and the Evolution of Venezuela's Party System," in Penniman, *Venezuela at the Polls*, p. 224.

57. *Journal of Commerce*, August 3, 1981, p. 1.

58. *Latin American Times*, November 1982, p. 13.

59. *Washington Post*, February 22, 1983, p. 15.

60. Rangel, "How Venezuelans Twice Squandered Their Oil Wealth."

61. Ibid.

62. *Latin American Weekly Report*, February 11, 1983, p. 1.

63. *New York Times*, March 13, 1983, p. F-4.

64. *Journal of Commerce*, March 30, 1983, p. 1.

65. *Washington Letter on Latin America*, March 2, 1983, pp. 7–8.

66. *New York Times*, March 23, 1983, p. 17; see also *Miami Herald*, March 31, 1983.

67. *Wall Street Journal*, April 15, 1983, p. 5.

68. Rangel, "How Venezuelans Twice Squandered Their Oil Wealth."

9 Jamaica

Alternative Approaches

W. Raymond Duncan

The Questions Faced

Jamaica shows an exceptionally high level of political development not matched by corresponding economic growth. This situation has produced increased strains on the political system, as evidenced by escalating violence during the 1970s and strikes and protests during the 1980s. While Jamaica's government so far has avoided the revolutionary turmoil besetting Central America, lack of perceived economic progress by Jamaica's diverse interest groups undermines the consensus required for an effective development strategy. Jamaica's political leaders have grappled with this dilemma since independence in 1962, especially since 1972 when international economic conditions made even more difficult the quest of economic growth.

This chapter explores the interrelationships between politics and economic development in Jamaica in an effort to understand how and why a highly developed political system in a small Third World country has failed to produce acceptable levels of economic progress. A number of questions merit attention in this inquiry. How far and in what ways have the political ideologies, practices, and policies of Jamaica's leading political parties—the People's National Party (PNP) and the Jamaican Labor Party (JLP)—affected economic outcomes since the country's independence in 1962? How have the PNP and JLP utilized the state's resources to forge their economic politics? In what ways have economic outcomes in turn affected the political process in Jamaica? What limits on the politics of economic development are imposed not only by Jamaica's restricted economic resources and social forces at home, but also by the international economic and political setting?

These questions suggest that Jamaica is caught in several dilemmas associated with the politics of economic development. First, higher levels of political development generate increased demands on the economic system. Political development means more channels for interest expression, which allows different interest groups to demand more services from the state.[1] These include employment, housing, transportation, education, fresh water supply, sewage disposal, and other services. Thus, in a developed polity, the government must be able to generate more economic resources and attempt to distribute them equitably in order to meet political demands. The problem is that it may be far easier to forge the political determinants of development than the economic resources to match that level, the result undermining the political regime.

Second, a rapid increase in the scope and level of participation in a political system can suddenly overload the institutions of governance.[2] An increase in the scope and level of participation can occur when a particular political party or leader suddenly launches a process of mobilization and communication with the lower and lower-middle sectors of society in an effort to build support. This occurred during the 1972–1980 period in Jamaica under Michael Manley's emphasis on Democratic Socialism led by the PNP. A similar situation occurred in Chile under Salvador Allende (1970–1973). Results of this phenomenon—as evidenced by Allende's Chile—include heightened political instability, failing consensus, urban violence, inter- and intra-party feuding, and potential mismanagement of the economy.

Third, a high level of political development is no guarantee of implementation of an effective economic development strategy if other impediments to consensus building exist. Obstacles to economic strategy include lack of a common national identity, divisive class relations, and ethno-racial tensions. Jamaica is an appropriate setting to examine these problems, given its heterogeneous racial mixture, class frictions, and social system, where whites tend to be at the top, browns—or coloreds, in Jamaican terminology— in the middle, and black people on the bottom.[3]

Fourth, the policies of economic development in a small Third World country are constrained greatly by the country's limited resource endowment and its consequent dependence on bilateral and multilateral aid, export trade, and foreign investments. External economic forces limit the available policy options for the political leaders, impact greatly on the party system's ability to deliver and implement a satisfactory economic strategy, and create enormous conflicts for the political party in power. One of these conflicts is the necessity to meet externally imposed criteria if a major loan is to be granted, as in the case of International Monetary Fund (IMF) lending. Applying IMF conditions such as a drastic cut in real wages and retrenchment in the public sector undermined the very economic and social groups on which the party in power based its support. This happened to the PNP during 1972–1980.[4] These aspects of "dependency" plague many a small Third World country like Jamaica.

Jamaica is a "politically developed" country with a complex, sophisticated, and diversified political structure—including an effective two-party system coupled to trade unions, business associations, and other interest groups. Political development is connected with expanded popular participation in national life, legitimate rule through widespread support, governmental leadership committed to managing the resources of the country in ways to benefit increasing numbers of people, and elections and institutions allowing interest groups to express their demands. Political development is associated with an underlying political culture, with attitudes and values toward authority based upon popular notions of equality of opportunity to express demands, perceived efficacy of the country's political institutions, and the accepted legitimacy of its leaders chosen through elections.

Jamaica fits this description. Unlike many Latin American countries, Jamaican politics is shaped by a well-organized and strongly financed two-party system. Centered in the PNP and the JLP, this two-party system draws upon the liberal ideas, parliamentary institutions, and concepts of the rule of law inherited from previous experience as a British colony.[5] It is based upon regular and frequent elections, access to the polls, a fair counting of the vote, an articulate and literate public, a free and vigorous press, independent trade unions, and a wide range of civic and political organizations. Admittedly, this system is by no means free from political patronage and consequent inter-party conflict, which grew worse during the late 1970s.[6] But compared to the graft and corruption in many Latin American political systems, as well as their constraints on popular democracy, Jamaica must be rated high.

Jamaica's two major parties, the PNP and JLP, share a number of long-range goals that date back to their formation before independence was achieved in 1962.[7] These objectives, representative of a "politically developed" country, include the quest for national integration, national identity as a fully sovereign and independent country, increased control over domestic and foreign policies within the international arena, and a greatly improved standard of living. Not least among these goals, and running as a *leitmotiv* through them, is the drive to moderate the inequalities associated with the race and class relations of colonial rule.[8] Jamaica seeks equality of opportunity in economic, social, and cultural life, acceptable minimal levels of income, and a broad range of economic, social, and cultural rights, including the right to work.[9] Achievement of more equality—and of Jamaica's other national goals—quite clearly is conditioned by progress in economic development, which increases the economic pie and, presumably, equality in distribution. Both the PNP and JLP are deeply committed to economic development as the means to achieve their overall program.

While progress has been made toward equalitarian-oriented national goals, economic and social indicators, along with public opinion polls, suggest that neither the PNP nor the JLP has been capable of ensuring sustained consensus on how to proceed in the tasks of economic development. The lack of perceived progress in economic development to improve the living standards of lower-income groups in Jamaica lay behind mounting social and political unrest during the 1970s, which in turn worked against tourism, private investment, and overall productivity. The 1970s were marked by escalating street violence and crime, gang warfare, widespread political unrest, violent demonstrations, emigration of managerial, technical, and entrepreneurial personnel, and mounting labor discontent.[10] The general election of 1980, called by the PNP to seek support for its failing economic policies, followed the most violent campaign in Jamaica's history. The gap between Jamaica's equalitarian and nationalistic economic aspirations and the economic realizations, however, brought the JLP to power.

In grappling with how to produce economic growth through political power, the PNP and JLP began to take diverse views of the chief roles to be played by the state and party during the 1970s. The PNP began to advocate Democratic Socialism, pressing for increased state control and ownership, coupled with emphasis on social reform, political mobilization, and reduced dependence on foreign investment. The JLP, in contrast, advocated a more capitalist-oriented "open economy," with less governmental bureaucracy, more encouragement of direct private foreign investment in government-owned enterprises, expanded export sales, and encouragement of competition in the local market.[11] While the PNP is more concerned to use the state to advance directly the interests of Jamaica's lower-income groups, while restricting foreign investment with its "dependency" connotations, the JLP tries to structure a system of assurances and guarantees appealing to foreign investors.[12] Each party continues to face major obstacles in the implementation of these approaches to economic development.

Historical Perspective

The Economy

Jamaica's principal sources of income are bauxite/alumina mining, sugar, and tourism. The country is richly endowed with bauxite, lies close to U.S.

markets, and has a skilled work force, all of which explain the importance of bauxite mining. Since the 1960s, however, the country's manufacturing industries have also improved, which has made for a more diversified economy. Jamaica became one of the 35 upper middle-income countries of the world during the post–World War II period; it ranked sixth in per capita gross domestic product (GDP) in 1960 within Latin America and third in 1970. But massive economic problems began in 1972, and the country fell to twelfth place in Latin America's per capita GDP rankings by 1980.

When the PNP replaced the JLP in national leadership in 1972, Jamaica's economy reflected the previous two decades of rapid economic growth and structural change. The 1950s began a period of planned industrialization with emphasis on incentives to attract local and, especially, foreign investment. Both the PNP and the JLP pursued this policy of industrialization based upon direct private foreign investment until 1972, when the PNP moved into office and began its thrust toward Democratic Socialism. The planned incentive- approach to development resulted in a sharp rise in industrial growth—in mining, manufacturing, tourism, transportation, construction, and public utilities. Jamaica's GDP growth averaged 5 to 6 percent per year during the 1950s and 1960s, stimulated essentially by foreign investment and exports, led by bauxite.

Jamaica's reliance on the foreign sector for a major portion of its remarkable economic growth is reflected in a number of statistical indices. Between 1953 and 1972 approximately U.S. $1 billion flowed into Jamaica, especially in the transnational aluminum corporations that mined bauxite and refined alumina for export to the United States. This amount represented about 6 percent of Jamaica's GDP between 1953 and 1966, rising to approximately 9 percent of the GDP in the 1966–1972 period.[13] About 32 percent of all domestic investment and approximately 25 percent of all imports were financed by capital inflows during this twenty-year period, while foreign trade as a proportion of GNP grew from 53 to 64 percent.[14] These substantial links with the external economy form the backdrop to many of the difficulties that plagued the PNP government during 1972–1982.

Accelerated industrialization had produced many structural changes in the Jamaican economy by 1972 when the PNP came to power. The economy had become relatively diversified. Agriculture's contribution to the GDP dropped from over 32 percent in 1950 to 9 percent in 1972. Manufacturing, which accounted for 6.5 percent of the GDP in 1950, rose to 14 percent by 1972, and construction rose from 4 percent in 1950 to 12 percent by the early 1970s.[15] Where mining contributed almost nothing to Jamaica's economy in 1950, it took first place by the 1960s. During the 1970s, Jamaica became the second leading producer of bauxite, following Australia.

This diversification appeared to make Jamaica a very promising developing country at the outset of the 1970s, no longer dependent on agriculture, possessing a well-developed financial system, and an educated and skilled work force, and evolving as one of the world's largest suppliers of bauxite. The economy remained characterized generally by private enterprise, while trade unions were strong and collective bargaining had come to exercise a significant role in securing wage improvements for most of the labor force.

Yet beneath these outward manifestations of progress lay a number of forces that were to plague subsequent governments. First, while the decline of the agricultural sector's contribution to GDP between 1950 and 1972 suggested a modern diversified economy, it had negative consequences. Much of Jamaica's labor force remained in rural areas, which meant that the decline of agriculture lowered the standard of living for rural Jamaicans, who were still a majority (two-thirds) of the population.[16] A corollary was food dependence, which drained away for food imports funds that might have been invested.

Second, the growth in bauxite mining and in the urban industrial sectors failed to produce equivalent growth in employment. The mining, refining, manufacturing, and construction sectors were, of course, capital-intensive rather than labor-intensive, thus failing to increase employment opportunities proportionately to population growth and rapid urbanization.[17] Unemployment thus rose from 12 to 24 percent during 1962–1972, while both the relative and absolute income of the poorest 30 percent of the population actually declined between 1958 and 1968.[18]

Third, the mineral-led development program launched during the 1960s, which relied on the foreign-operated aluminum firms, met difficulties. Taxing the companies posed the problem of identifying the profits realized in Jamaica in an internationally integrated process of production. Liberal capital depreciation allowances had also been granted the aluminum industry, which made it difficult to tax their revenues, a complicated situation made even more difficult by intra-company transfer pricing. Added to these difficulties was Jamaica's reliance on imported raw materials and energy to sustain its industrialization program.

Jamaica's rapid economic growth of the 1950s and 1960s came to an end in the early 1970s. This occurred partly because of conditions in the external sector on which Jamaica has so strongly relied for its growth during the 1950s and 1960s. The year 1972 ended the second phase of expansion in the bauxite investment cycle, which greatly reduced the principal source of growth.[19] Next came the world economic crisis in 1973–1974. It was accompanied by the sharp rise in the real price of energy (oil), the decline in growth within the developed countries, including the United States, accelerated worldwide inflation and recession, and increased interest rates on international loans.

Jamaica plunged into deep recession during the 1970s, and the GDP steadily declined, reaching an accumulated decrease of 26 percent by 1981. Jamaica's foreign debt climbed from $192 million in 1970 to $1.7 billion in 1980. The balance of payments was in deficit throughout the period, reaching over $450 million by 1981. Real income fell, 1970–1980, by 25 percent, while the cost of living increased by 320 percent. Real investment fell by 65 percent, while unemployment rose from 25 to 31 percent. Meanwhile, owing to a PNP-imposed tax on bauxite mined by the foreign companies and the loss of skilled workers through emigration, the bauxite companies cut production by approximately 50 percent after 1974.[20] And because of horror stories of crime and violence, Jamaica's tourist industry took a nose dive. The JLP, as discussed below, inherited many of these externally related problems when it took office in 1980.

Social Forces

By the early 1970s, Jamaica's population reached about two million, growing at about 1.6 percent annually. Natural population growth had averaged between 2.5 and 3.0 percent annually since the early 1960s, but this was offset by emigration. In 1970, about 46 percent of Jamaica's population was under the age of fifteen, thus not contributing to the economy.

With an area of 4,400 square miles, the island had a population density of 455 persons per square mile in 1970. Less than half of Jamaica's land is cultivable, thus placing a far greater pressure on land resources than indicated by the population density figure. Since bauxite is the only exportable mineral deposit, Jamaica's population density creates a natural constraint on economic development. This situation helps explain the high rate of emigration since World War II. Emigration helps relieve population pressures, but it includes the departure of skilled workers from the bauxite industry—one cause of its declining production after 1972—and doctors, lawyers, engineers, dentists, and nurses, whose skills are greatly needed.

Jamaica's problems were compounded by the high rate of urbanization. In 1960, 23.6 percent of Jamaica's population was urban; in 1980 the urban proportion had risen to 69.3 percent, and in 1981 to 73.5 percent. These figures represent the highest urban growth rate in the Caribbean Basin and Latin America.[21] Jamaica's population concentrated in and around Kingston, a city with mounting socioeconomic problems.

In 1970, in central Kingston, only 14 percent of all dwellings had running water, 80 percent of all households shared toilet facilities with others, and 43 percent of all dwellings consisted of one room only.[22] For the average poor Jamaican living in Kingston, adequate police protection, water and sewage systems, and recreational opportunities were rarities. Breakdowns in public transport, deplorable health and postal services, crime, violence, and a high level of social tensions were the most obvious results of these conditions. Together with the strains created by the visibility of great income inequality, such a social context provided fertile ground for radical sentiments and for the emergence of widespread popular support for the leftist political leaders in the 1972 election, which brought Michael Manley to office.[23] The situation was ripe for disillusionment, more crime, and more violence when the PNP could not visibly improve conditions for the lower classes.

Race relations in Jamaica complicate politics and economic development. Whites and light-skinned nonwhites have dominated Jamaica's politics and economy, although fully 80 percent of the island's population is of African descent. Racial divisions thus take on class connotations.[24] In the words of one observer, "there is a clear, gross correlation between 'race' and class. Blacks are concentrated at the bottom of the economic and occupational pyramid. . .and light-skinned people become more common at the higher levels (though prosperous, well-educated and influential [black] Jamaicans are no rarity)."[25] Although Jamaican society is not about to fly apart in class conflict, racial stratification has at times contributed to the hostility of blacks toward whites and other, relatively affluent minorities.[26] Unemployment and low-class status of Jamaica's black population has contributed to weak "Jamaican" multiracial identity, pro-black and anti-white attitudes, and political movements outside the PNP and JLP two-party system such as the Rastafarian and Black Power movements.[27] Political leaders cannot ignore continued alienation from the two-party system, anti-white hostility, and low nationalism in pursuing their paths toward economic development.

Political Dynamics

Jamaica's political system is inherited from Great Britain. Even before independence in 1962, the country had evolved a functioning two-party system that provided for the institutionalized transfer of political power through regular and frequent elections. The system adheres to the rule of law and parliamentary institutions through which the prime minister and his cabinet are responsible to the legislature. This type of government is clearly different from models on the Latin American mainland derived from Spanish and Portuguese rule.

Jamaica's highly organized two-party system would suggest that the political system well represents the interests of Jamaica's broad masses. For much of Jamaica's post-independence period, this assumption is inaccurate. Until the PNP assumed power in 1972, politics tended to benefit the upper and middle sectors of Jamaican society as the two parties alternated in power. The JLP won the first parliamentary elections in 1944 and again in 1949. In

1955 the PNP replaced the JLP and ruled until 1962, when the JLP again took over until the 1972 elections. In this pattern of alternating power every two terms, both parties tended to follow a model of development based upon foreign investment and responded to sectional interest groups rather than addressing the problems of the broader population.

This resulted in large-scale alienation from the political system during the 1960s. Growing political apathy and riots in 1966 and 1968 expressed popular frustration. Indeed, as one observer notes, elections in Jamaica became increasingly violent over the years, beginning in the early period with mud-slinging and rock-throwing but by the 1970s leading to arson, bombing, and assassination. Increased crime and violence, growing social unrest, and the apparent failures of previous foreign capital development approaches led the PNP to take new steps—aimed directly at improvement of poor Jamaicans—following its victory in the 1972 elections.

Given the ineffectiveness of Jamaica's political leaders in improving the condition of the poor, new political movements have emerged since the 1940s. Although these movements have not seriously challenged the PNP's and JLP's dominant positions in the political system, they indicate the long-run potential effects of unemployment, racial tensions, and political alienation from the traditional parties.

While the Rastafarian and Black Power movements in the 1960s highlight the racial aspect of Jamaican politics, the rise of two Marxist-Leninist parties in the 1970s indicates new currents of leftism. These two parties are the Jamaican Communist Party (JCP), founded in 1975 and led by Chris Lawrence, and the Workers Party of Jamaica (WPJ), led by Dr. Trevor Munroe.[28] Of the two communist parties, the WPJ is the more influential, operating as a pro-Moscow party and estimated to control between 1 and 3 percent of Jamaica's popular vote.[29] The JCP and WPJ aligned themselves with the PNP candidate, Michael Manley, in the hotly contested general elections of 1980, but following Manley's defeat the PNP tried to distance itself from these communist parties.

Politics and Economic Development Under the PNP

As leader of the PNP in 1972, Manley had become concerned with the need for greatly increased equality, social justice, and self-reliance among the Jamaican people to free them from the psychology of dependence inherited from previous colonialism and slavery.[30] Attainment of these goals required a major restructuring of the economy to make income distribution more equitable, increase public ownership and worker participation in decision-making, and expand state control over foreign capital.[31] These goals, in effect, were a response to the increasing protests against inequality, unemployment, and huge foreign involvement in the economy in the first ten years of independence.[32] Once in office, the PNP moved toward policies aimed at immediate income redistribution, much greater state control over the economy, and more public sector projects. By November 1974, the PNP published its "Thirteen Principles of 'Democratic Socialism,'" the principal themes of which were "cooperation," "socialism as a way of life," "the right to private property," and "the mixed economy."[33]

Role of the State Under PNP Leadership

The PNP's new initiatives by 1974 included programs to create employment, youth skill training, adult literacy, health care, housing, food subsidies, rent restrictions, and equal pay for women. The government announced tight price controls and minimum wage legislation, coupled with policies of import substitution. In addition, it negotiated the nationalization of several important public utilities and some enterprises in the export agriculture sector.[34] By 1975 the government was active in programs for worker participation in the economy and for industrial development with major public sector intervention. Campaigning on its effort to bring the "pillars of the economy" under state control, the government emphasized its achievements in the 1976 national elections and won a decisive victory over the JLP.[35]

One of the more important new departures was expanded state control over the foreign-dominated bauxite industry. In April 1974, Manley insisted that the bauxite contracts be renegotiated. This action resulted in a special "production levy" imposed on the bauxite companies that increased Jamaica's revenues in one year from $25 million to $200 million.[36] The PNP, at the same time, began to buy back land owned by the bauxite companies, and it demanded a 51 percent share of mining facilities and the right to sell to Algeria, Eastern Europe, or any other market. The PNP also planned for a state-owned bauxite company, in partnership with Mexico, Venezuela, and Hungary. No less significant was the PNP-led formation of the International Bauxite Association (IBA), an international cartel of bauxite-producing countries (Australia, Guinea, Guyana, Jamaica, Sierra Leone, Suriname, and Yugoslavia).

Jamaica's agricultural sector underwent substantial tranformation as the PNP moved toward Democratic Socialism. The PNP pursued goals of import substitution to reduce food imports, increased food production to raise rural nutritional and income levels, and increased agricultural employment and levels of land utilization.[37] Following its socialist analysis that land had been maldistributed, the PNP redistributed land, developed "people" ownership through cooperatives and community enterprises (especially in sugar), expanded state involvement in agricultural production, and mobilized rural youth and stimulated youth projects to check the drift away from the rural areas. These approaches to agrarian reform led to land-lease projects, state-owned Food Farms, sugar cooperatives under worker management, pioneer farms that introduced socialist youth to farming under group participation, and extended credit to small farmers not associated with the state-managed enterprises.[38]

That these and other programs under the PNP version of Democratic Socialism seem reminiscent of the Cuban version of economic development planning should come as no surprise. During the Manley era, Jamaica began to exchange frequent visits of its top leaders with Cuba, including exchange trips by Manley and Fidel Castro, and a number of Cuban-inspired approaches appeared in Jamaica.[39] Cuba provided approximately 600 doctors, nurses, school-building teams, and mini-dam construction workers by 1980.[40] Cuba became very active in aiding the country in its water supply problems, housing, schools, agriculture, fishing, medical facilities, and sports training.

Manley maintained that these Cuban activities by no means indicated that Jamaica was turning toward communism, but simply that Cuba's experience with economic development based upon limited resources was applicable to Jamaica's conditions. However, the PNP also turned toward the Soviet Union and Eastern Europe for sources of support different from traditional "capitalist" dependency. Having restored relations between Jamaica and the Soviet Union, Manley visited the USSR in April 1979. This trip led to an agreement for the export of 50,000 tons of alumina per year to the Soviet Union between 1980 and 1983 and 250,000 tons thereafter. The PNP and the USSR also established a joint fisheries company, and Moscow granted a long-term loan to Jamaica to finance imports of Soviet goods. During the period of PNP rule, Jamaica also made trade agreements with Hungary and Yugoslavia. These arrangements, coupled with the greatly expanded relations with Cuba, led to the accusation by the JLP that the PNP was bent upon making Jamaica "another Cuba."[41]

Results of PNP Policies

The PNP's increased state control and ownership of resources was designed to generate the capital necessary to transform Jamaica into a socialist society. But due to the combination of external and internal pressures—some under the PNP's control and others not—Manley's plans fell far short of fulfillment. The economic record, as indicated above, reflects the worldwide pressures of energy price rises, inflation, and recession, which greatly affected Jamaica during 1972–1980. The effects of Manley's bauxite production levy led to temporary increases in government revenues, but the bauxite companies' cutback in exports from Jamaica seriously undermined this major source of revenue by 1976. Other multinational corporations also reduced their investments in Jamaica, and between 1973 and 1976 foreign capital inflow declined from 9.7 percent of the GDP to 0.9 percent. Meanwhile, the land reform program suffered from many problems, unemployment and inflation produced widespread discontent, and tourism declined precipitously.

Defenders of the PNP argue that Jamaica's problems during 1972–1980 were caused essentially by *external* factors. The argument is that the worldwide economic crisis beginning in 1973 caused Jamaica's import prices to double between 1972 and 1974, and subsequently to rise even more, and Jamaica severely felt the effects as a small energy- and food-dependent country.[42] The decline in foreign investment, stimulated by the bauxite companies' cutback in production, added to the country's distress. This argument blames IMF lending policies as the most important external cause for the failure of Democratic Socialism.

In terms of the IMF's impact on Jamaica, the argument is that its severe austerity measures undermined the PNP's popular support. While the PNP long resisted the temptation to borrow from the IMF—which represented the "imperialist" groups and a "dependent" relationship opposed by the PNP—it was forced to turn to IMF loans in 1977. It did so reluctantly after bitter ideological debates inside the party itself, which is not surprising in view of the requirements imposed by the IMF: a wage freeze, a nearly 40 percent devaluation of the Jamaican dollar, and a massive cutback in public spending—all injurious to the lower-income groups courted by the PNP since 1972. In pursuance of a second drawing in 1978, the country was required to further devalue the Jamaican dollar, increase indirect taxes, lift price controls, institute tax benefits for companies to stimulate production, allow unemployment to rise as jobs in the public sector were cut, and to scale down social programs in an effort to curb inflation. Erosion of PNP support accompanied these events, the result of severe austerity without the compensation of renewed foreign investment, increased employment, alleviation of the foreign exchange problems, and relief from the consumer goods shortages. Eventually the PNP broke off negotiations with the IMF and announced the beginning of an "alternative self-reliant economic path," but it was too late to restore support.

Internal Management Problems

The failure of Democratic Socialism can be blamed only partially on external factors, for the PNP experienced great difficulties in trying to manage politically the expanded economic roles of the state. First, the PNP's mass mobilization created high levels of expectations incompatible with Jamaica's resources or with the PNP's capacity to tranform the lopsided economic structure rapidly. While political motivation may be important as a stimulant to productivity, it cannot replace economic skills and incentives. In the pressure for rapid land and income redistribution, a conflict naturally arose between welfare goals and economic realities.[43] This situation reminds one again of Salvador Allende's Chile.

Second, the PNP's socialist goals frequently ran afoul of traditional party machinery, which operates through pork-barrel politics, clientelism, and the exchange of favors for political support. This became a real problem for such projects as the state-owned Food Farms, where politics eroded efficiently run and honestly managed organizations, despite the plans and goals of PNP bureaucrats.[44] The state Food Farms, for example, set up to reduce food imports and provide employment, lost millions of Jamaican dollars and were abandoned in 1976.

Third, traditional political patronage in Jamaica made the PNP's difficulties worse. Frictions between those rewarded by the PNP and JLP supporters led to more political violence with its attendant economic and political effects. The Manley era did not reduce this pattern of party political patronage.

Fourth, management fell victim to economic irrationality. Unskilled individuals were frequently given authority to oversee operations, unauthorized land seizures embarrassed the PNP and alienated middle- and upper-income groups, the behavior of many Jamaicans drove away tourists, and political activity consumed many work hours. In some cases, youths wound up on farms for essentially political motivations, without interest or experience in agriculture. In other cases, hotel employees were extremely unfriendly to "imperialist" guests.

Fifth, the PNP approach to economic development, by unleashing all the above trends, tended to alienate skilled management talent that might have been of help to the Manley government. Kaiser Aluminum Company's Jamaican subsidiary, for example, lost about 5 percent of its salaried staff each year through emigration.[45] Prime Minister Manley conceded in February 1980 that "there is no doubt that internally one of our biggest problems is management."[46] Even the telephone system was plagued with mismanagement and inefficiency, with frequent wrong numbers frustrating harassed administrators.

Division Within the PNP

Conflicts within the PNP contributed greatly to the ineffective management practices and other negative internal forces during 1971–1980. The PNP became increasingly divided between a radical left wing and more moderate elites. Democratic Socialism never achieved ideological clarity or programmatic consistency. Its "thirteen principles" called for the right of every Jamaican to own private property, a commitment to "build a socialist society," a mixed economy of public and private sector participation, a "rejection of capitalism," and a "faith in cooperation." Even PNP leader Michael Manley reflected this ambiguity. Manley first followed a moderate and orthodox approach to change, then became more leftist under pressure from the "radical leftists" within the PNP from 1974 onwards, only to become more orthodox again, reasserting control over the "leftists" during 1977 and 1978, and again turned leftward in 1980.[47]

Second, the struggle between "leftists" and moderates within the party created damaging disunity. Intra-party acrimony heightened over the IMF borrowing issue when the Left argued that the IMF demands constituted a "massive destabilization attempt" and a major "demoralization" for the government.[48] The PNP moderates could, of course, see no other path for the PNP to follow, especially in view of Jamaica's economic stagnation combined with its socialist expansion of the public sector. The defeat of the Left led to the resignation of some of its leftists, including D. K. Duncan, party secretary and minister of mobilization, and the emergence of Jamaica's second communist party, the WPJ under Trevor Munroe. PNP internal conflict was grist for the mill of JLP criticism of the failures of Democratic Socialism, and it contributed greatly to the waning of popular support for Manley after the 1976 elections.

Third, the presence of a strong "radical left" wing inside the PNP after 1974 led to some of the management problems discussed earlier. Well-known leftists, such as D. K. Duncan, Hugh Small, and others, occupying high-level cabinet posts, encouraged the expansive political mobilization that in turn stimulated excessive demands and impatience with Jamaica's slow economic transformation and resource redistribution. At the same time, middle- and upper-income sectors were put off by the country's leftward course, including its flirtation with communist Cuba. The PNP leftist elites also contributed to mismanagement by appointing less-qualified individuals with authority over the expanded public sector.

Finally, pressures by the radical left simply did not coincide with popular aspirations when judged by public opinion polls after 1976. While Manley's reformist policies were actually more populist than Marxist, their association with strong leftist rhetoric, alignment with Cuba, and "socialist" solutions found little broad support within the Jamaican polity. And although the PNP never defined precisely what it meant by a "socialist" system, it was clear by 1978 that a majority of the people were not prepared for "radical socialism." By then, leftist radicals such as D. K. Duncan and Trevor Munroe had become unpopular in Jamaica, and middle-class supporters of the PNP were disenchanted with Democratic Socialism. Only 19 percent of the urban working class favored government expropriation of land, and only 12 percent of them saw the private sector as "exploiters."[49] In one poll in January 1978, "governmental mismanagement" and "radical talk" consistently outweighed the "private sector" as the main reason cited for Jamaica's deteriorating economy.[50]

Defeat of Democratic Socialism in October 1980 Elections

The PNP was heavily defeated in the general elections of October 30, 1980, which brought to power a new government, headed by Edward Seaga, leader of the JLP. The collapse of the Jamaican economy, shortages of basic foods, widespread public dissatisfaction with Democratic Socialism, and mounting violence between rival gangs attached to the PNP and JLP precipitated this change in government leadership. The October 1980 election was called at a time when the PNP had clearly shifted back to a "leftist" ascendancy within its leadership. This trend was marked by the breakoff in further negotiations with the IMF, the re-election of D. K. Duncan as PNP general secretary in an unopposed election in September 1977, and the appointment of another leftist member within the PNP, Hugh Small, to the office of minister of finance and planning. At the same time, Mr. Manley announced that Jamaica would embark on a road of greater self-reliance.

The JLP effectively utilized these trends. First, Seaga claimed that he and the JLP could straighten out the complex economic and financial problems unsolved by Manley and the PNP. Seaga strongly opposed Manley's anti-IMF position and called instead for an economic strategy to restore the confidence of private investors that, in the long run, would create jobs. In addition to consistently portraying the PNP as a party incapable of managing the country's economy, Seaga hammered away at Manley's connections with Cuba. He insisted that the PNP was a communist-influenced party—as evidenced by its left-wing membership and the frequent trips to Cuba—and that the PNP was intent upon creating a one-party state in Jamaica. Only a return to free-enterprise policies under JLP management and a break in relations with Cuba (which undermined Jamaica's reputation with the West) would save the island from bankruptcy. This JLP campaign won 51 seats in October 1980 compared with 9 for the PNP—a near complete reversal of the 1976 elections.

The JLP in Power

The JLP's record in the politics of economic development may be compared to the PNP's experience during 1972–1980 in regard to the following issues: (1) the direction of change undertaken by Seaga's JLP in 1980; (2) the role of the state since then; (3) the JLP's economic and political management record; (4) continuing problems for the JLP in its approach to economic development; and (5) the prognosis for the future. The general conclusion to be drawn from this assessment is that Jamaica's small-island status, limited natural and human resources, and unavoidable dependency on the international economic system, especially its relations with the United States, continue to impede finding a successful formula for economic growth and equality despite the high level of political development maintained through the two-party system.

New Directions Under the JLP

The JLP emphasized private enterprise as the key to growth, reduction of the public sector, access to Jamaica's resources for foreign investors, and a pro-Western, anti-Cuban orientation in foreign policy. The major new priorities were to secure immediate financial aid for the Jamaican economy to forestall bankruptcy, to re-establish a strong U.S.-Jamaican relationship to attract massive foreign investment, and to stimulate free enterprise at home under competitive market conditions. At the same time, the Seaga government sought to "halt the expansionist movement of Communist imperialism in the Caribbean."[51]

In pursuit of these objectives, the JLP launched a coherent and integrated policy of capitalist development unabashedly linked to the international economy. The Seaga government immediately initiated talks with the IMF, which led to a $698 million loan to Jamaica over a three-year period. Thanks to the pro-Western and anticommunist stance of the JLP, Seaga obtained much more favorable conditions for this loan than the PNP had received. Equally important, the IMF stamp of approval paved the way for other substantial loans to Jamaica—from the World Bank, Western commercial banks, and through the Caribbean Group for Cooperation in Economic Development.[52]

Seaga also sought to attract foreign investors to Jamaica and renewed emphasis on tourism. He spoke of the "Puerto Rican" model of development followed by Jamaica in the 1960s—where foreign investors imported all their inputs except labor and produced essentially for export. In following this model, the Seaga administration began to dismantle import controls on a wide range of goods, including those traditionally produced by local businessmen. Jamaica's tourist development budget meanwhile was increased, and new air links were opened up between London and Montego Bay.

Pursuing his pro-U.S., anti-Cuban foreign policy, Seaga in October 1981 severed diplomatic relations with Cuba on the grounds that Cuba was interfering in Jamaica's internal affairs. This move brought to full circle a period that began when Michael Manley restored diplomatic relations with Cuba in 1972. Practically the whole of the JLP economic strategy became based upon strong ties with the United States. Seaga was the first foreign head of state to visit the White House after Ronald Reagan's election. From this time onwards, Seaga spoke of the need for a massive recovery program for the Caribbean along the lines of the Marshall Plan in Europe after 1945. This line of argument helped produce the Caribbean Basin Initiative subsequently announced by President Reagan.[53] By 1982, Jamaica had received $234 million in loans and direct aid from the United States, including $50 million from the aid portion of the Caribbean Basin Initiative.

Role of the State

In its commitment to capitalism and laissez-faire economics, the JLP sought to reduce direct government ownership in and direction over economic enterprises. Seaga established a "divestment committee" to attempt to reduce the number of public enterprises established during the Manley years, and it ended virtually all the multiple restrictions and licenses with which the Manley government had entangled the private sector. The JLP also improved tax collection, tightly controlled public spending, and terminated the public sector relief employment sponsored by the more free-spending PNP.

The JLP tried to reduce the state's direct role in the operation of the economy, aside from providing the most advantageous setting for foreign and domestic private enterprises. It ended the earlier import-substitution emphasis of the 1960s and 1970s and sought to restrict domestic consumption through a more "open" economy and expanded export sales. The policy was to provide export incentives, liberalize import restrictions, reduce bureaucratic regulation of the private sector, divest government-owned enterprises, and encourage competition within the local market. The JLP's political involvement in the economy, as stated by Seaga, was to "set the tone . . . set the climate and provide the policies" for an economic turnaround.[54]

Policy Outcomes

The Seaga administration began with high hopes, popular support, and private sector enthusiasm, but it soon faced major problems. At the outset, the intense political conflicts, violence, and polarization characteristic of the last years of Manley's rule faded, to be replaced by heightened consensus, faith in Seaga's "managerial" style, and confidence in the JLP's clear formula for economic recovery. With a bustle of new activity in construction, merchandise trade, and tourism—coupled with great increases in imported food, U.S.

economic aid, and the hope of more U.S. private foreign investment—Jamaica's future looked bright. The crime rate fell, some skilled personnel began to return to the country, and hopes ran high that business life would ignite and jobs were just around the corner. These attitudes persisted until late 1981 when the JLP's program for change began to erode.

Major problems soon beginning to plague the Seaga government illustrated the country's dependency on external economic forces and its limited resource base. The fall in world demand for aluminum during 1981 and 1982 triggered major cutbacks in the bauxite industry, with consequent large layoffs of bauxite workers. In part because of the U.S. recession, foreign investors demonstrated far less enthusiasm in Jamaica than anticipated, despite attractive terms such as a five- to fifteen-year tax holiday on all profits.[55] Most of the foreign loans, which greatly increased Jamaica's debt, went to debt repayments, with little left to finance imports for manufacturers. These weaknesses were accompanied by continued unemployment of about 27 percent and a negative trade balance by mid-1983. Added to these troubles were mounting strikes over wage demands and the weakening of popular confidence in Seaga's management.[56]

Midway through his term, Seaga faced growing problems, all of which were exacerbated by his difficulties with the IMF—not so dissimilar from those experienced by the Manley government. In May 1983, Jamaica failed the test set by the IMF for continued drawdowns of its three-year loan. This failure was the unexpected shortfall in Jamaica's balance of payments when scheduled loans from the World Bank, the Inter-American Development Bank (IDB), Japan, and the Organization of Petroleum Exporting Countries (OPEC) were delayed. The IMF's urging reductions in government spending did not help Seaga's position as a national leader in his turbulent relations with state employees. These had produced strikes and wage protests during 1983 and a fall in the JLP's popularity and credibility. In May 1983, the IMF, in an effort to ease some of the strains, waived the economic criteria that Jamaica had failed to meet.

The one bright spot lay in tourism, the biggest source of income after bauxite. This industry grew by 20 percent during both 1981 and 1982, sparked by a $6 million advertising campaign in the United States. Yet the boom in tourism did not produce an equal percentage growth in earnings because hotel rates were cut drastically to lure tourists. Nevertheless, the recovery of tourism must be counted as a positive aspect of the Seaga record since 1980.[57]

Continuing Management Problems

In addition to Seaga's problems with striking workers and the IMF, he began to face difficulties within the ranks of his supporters by mid-1981. The

Jamaican private sector became increasingly disenchanted over Seaga's removal of import controls, which exposed it to foreign competition. Local businessmen, especially small manufacturing companies, could not compete in cost and quality with imported goods. By early 1982, the powerful Jamaican Manufacturers' Association (JMA) was displeased with Seaga's emphasis on production for the export sector and the enormous competition this policy created for local producers. Open criticism by the JMA grew during 1982 because the private sector saw the Seaga government catering too much to foreign investors and not allowing Jamaican businessmen enough participation in policy formation.

The private sector also began to complain of corrupt practices in the Seaga administration. The Industry and Commerce Ministry, run by a JLP appointee, became the center of controversy between the government and businessmen over bribes involved in the procurement of import licenses. The private sector also implied that the government had deceived them regarding deregulation, factory closings, and the spending of scarce foreign exchange on imported goods.[58] By late 1982, over thirty Jamaican factories had closed, and those still open were working at just over one-third capacity.

By the summer of 1983, Jamaica was in deep economic trouble. The country's young population—56 percent under 25 years of age—meant strong pressure for more housing, employment, and other services in the next two decades. Jamaica's economic growth rate, running at 2 percent in 1980–1981, fell to 1 percent by 1983. Unemployment crept up to 27 percent in 1983, while a 30 percent increase in the price of gasoline was followed by a 40 percent increase in transportation costs, drugs, and soaps. Airline fares rose by 60 percent in 1983, and the overall price index was projected to grow by 40 percent in 1983–1984. These mounting economic problems, as shown in polls conducted by Carl Stone, indicated that Seaga's popularity was falling during 1982–1983, not only among public sector employees but also in the private sector. World economic recovery might, of course, brighten this picture.

Prognosis

How to overcome Jamaica's economic underdevelopment, with its dependent relationship in the international economic system and constrained resource base, continued unsolved after 1972. Neither the heavy state involvement in the economy followed by the PNP nor the laissez-faire approach of the JLP has achieved the goals associated with independence in 1962. The highly developed two-party system has facilitated a relatively smooth and institutionalized transfer of power from one government to the next, but its record in the politics of economic development is less impressive.

As the Seaga government moved to the midpoint of its term, its failures in economic policy began to set the scene for a PNP revival, just as the PNP's economic failures led to the massive JLP victory in 1980. Polls in October 1982 indicated that the PNP had overtaken the JLP in popular support, largely because the electorate perceived the PNP as "the more genuinely people-oriented party of the two," which would better protect the interests of the common man.[59] This rise in popularity may have also resulted from the PNP's move away from the communist WPJ and from its earlier "radical leftist" image after the 1980 elections.[60] Meanwhile the Jamaican electorate seemed to be moving toward more "issue" consciousness, which is less partisan and less confident in the middle-class leaderships of both the PNP and JLP. This trend suggested more unstable patterns of voting and party loyalty in the future. While the Jamaican political system has yet to deal effectively with the economy, it nevertheless has so far absorbed discontent into the electoral process without the breakdowns in authority and rise of revolutionary groups found in other small countries with dependent economies in Central America.

Despite the heavy economic burden on the Jamaican political system, it has demonstrated great capacity for democratic processes. Jamaica's political development has been important in offsetting the strains of economic growth that have crippled other governments in Central and South America. Even during the days of severe economic dislocation and political turmoil under Manley, the Jamaican middle class, unlike that of Allende's Chile, did not panic, nor did a complete and irrevocable polarization of opposed political groups occur. Admittedly political life was strained, but even the radical left did not want violence, unlike Chile's Movement of the Revolutionary Left during 1970–1973. Challenges to the democratic system occurred in Jamaica, especially in the high levels of urban violence and gun warfare in Kingston, but not on the scale found in Chile. There was only marginal threat of military intervention like that in Chile.

It remains to be seen whether the Seaga approach to economic growth is more promising than Manley's. One is strongly tempted to give Seaga the edge, however, owing largely to the government's stress on efficient management of the economic system, its cutback of bureaucratic bottlenecks, and its attempt to attract technological expertise to compete more effectively in the international market. The government is appropriately tackling the economy's infrastructure—roads, energy, and improved water supplies—while seeking a diversification of agriculture. U.S. offers to increase bauxite purchases, meanwhile, are welcome. But the problems of a small country in an unstable world economy persist.

Notes

1. See Martin Needler, "Political Development and Socio-economic Development: The Case of Latin America," *American Political Science Review* 62 (1968): 889–98. For other studies of the politics of economic development, see Charles W. Anderson, *Politics and Economic Change in Latin America* (New York: Van Nostrand Reinhold, 1967); Gerald A. Heegar, *The Politics of Underdevelopment* (London: Macmillan, 1974); Samuel P. Huntington, *Political Order in Changing Societies* (New Haven, Conn.: Yale University Press, 1968); and W. Raymond Duncan, *Latin American Politics: A Development Approach* (New York: Praeger, 1976).

2. Huntington, *Political Order in Changing Societies*, pp. 78 ff.

3. On the lack of national integration in Jamaica, see Fitzroy Ambursley, "Jamaica: The Demise of 'Democratic Socialism,'" *New Left Review*, July–August 1981, pp. 76–87; Irving Kaplan et al., *Area Handbook for Jamaica* (Washington, D.C.: Government Printing Office, 1976), chap. 4; and W. Raymond Duncan, "Caribbean Leftism," *Problems of Communism* 27 (May–June 1978): 39.

4. See Norman Girvan and Richard Bernal, "The IMF and the Foreclosure of Development Options: The Case of Jamaica," *Monthly Review* 33 (February 1982): 34–48; and Adlith Brown, "Economic Policy and the IMF in Jamaica," *Social and Economic Studies* 30 (December 1981): 1–51.

5. See Michael Manley, *The Politics of Change: A Jamaican Testament* (London: Andre Deutsch, 1974), chap. 2; Adam Kuper, *Changing Jamaica*, (Kingston: Kingston's Publisher's, 1976), chap. 15; and Kaplan et al., *Area Handbook for Jamaica*, chap. 7.

6. For a sharp criticism of party patronage in Jamaica, see Arthur Lewin, "The Fall of Michael Manley: A Case Study of the Failure of Reform Socialism," *Monthly Review* 33 (February 1982): 49–60.

7. Disturbances in 1938 began to indicate the depth of discontent with the colonial system, which in turn led Norman Manley, Michael Manley's father, to establish the PNP in 1938. It was linked to the Bustamante Industrial Trade Unions (BITU), named after the BITU's leader, Alexander Bustamante. Bustamante broke with Manley and founded the JLP in 1943, taking the BITU with him. The PNP shortly thereafter organized a group of trade unions separate from the BITU (Kaplan et al., *Area Handbook for Jamaica*, pp. 76–82).

8. One researcher, Wendell Bell, found deep concern among Jamaica's pro-nationalist leaders over the inequalities of race and class under colonialism and a determination to use the instruments of the state to lessen inequality after independence from Britain was achieved. These visions of equality and social justice carried over into the post-independence period as subsequent research by Bell and others indicates. See "A Preliminary Appraisal of Elite Performance," *Revista/Review Interamericana*, 7 (Summer 1977): 294–308; Wendell Bell and David L. Stevenson, "Attitudes Toward Social Equality in Independent Jamaica: Twelve Years After Nationhood," *Comparative Political Studies* 11 (January 1979): 499–532; Robert V. Robinson and Wendell Bell, "Attitudes Towards Political Independence in Jamaica

After Twelve Years of Nationhood," *British Journal of Sociology* 29 (June 1978): 208–33; and Wendell Bell, "Equality and Social Justice: Foundations of Nationalism in the Caribbean," *Caribbean Studies* 20 (June 1980): 6–36.

9. Bell, "Equality and Social Justice," pp. 18–25.

10. See Wenty Bowen, "Letter from Kingston," *Caribbean Contact* 6 (May 1978): 1–2; and idem, "Confrontation Politics in Jamaica," *Caribbean Contact* 6 (February 1979): 7. Confrontations and crime were evident in Jamaica during the 1960s and at the outset of the 1970s. See Richard Nolte, Letter on Jamaica, Institute of Current World Affairs (April 30, 1970); and Henry Giniger, "Jamaicans Tense as Voting Nears," *New York Times*, February 20, 1967.

11. Anthony Payne, "Seaga's Jamaica After One Year," *World Today* 37 (November 1981): 434–40; and Francis Pisani, "The New Jamaica," *World Press Review*, March 1981, pp. 27–29.

12. Carl Stone, "Seaga Is in Trouble," *Caribbean Review* 11 (April 1983): 5–7.

13. Girvan and Bernal, "The IMF," p. 36.

14. Ibid.

15. Kaplan et al., *Area Handbook for Jamaica*, p. 323.

16. Kuper, *Changing Jamaica*, p. 16.

17. Ibid., p. 17; and Girvan and Bernal, "The IMF," p. 37. On the failure of agricultural production to keep pace with population growth and the growing need to import food, see Kaplan et al., *Area Handbook for Jamaica*, pp. 245–55.

18. Girvan and Bernal, "The IMF," p. 37. For a socioeconomic analysis of Jamaica's unemployment and low-income problems, see Arthur J. Furnia, *Syncrisis: The Dynamics of Health. An Analytic Series on the Interactions of Health and Socioeconomic Development: Jamaica*, U.S. Public Health Service, Office of International Health, Division of Program Analysis (Washington, D.C.: Government Printing Office, 1976).

19. Girvan and Bernal, "The IMF," pp. 37 ff.

20. Winston A. Van Horne, "Jamaica: Why Manley Lost," *World Today* 37 (November 1981): 428–33.

21. "Jamaica," *Economic and Social Progress in Latin America: The External Sector* (Washington, D.C.: Inter-American Development Bank, 1982), p. 346.

22. L. Alan Eyre, "Quasi-Urban 'Melange' Settlement and Its Problems" (Paper presented at the meeting of the Caribbean Studies Association, Santiago, Dominican Republic, January 1978).

23. Duncan, "Carribean Leftism," p. 38.

24. Rex M. Nettleford, *Identity, Race and Protest in Jamaica* (New York: William Morrow & Co., 1972), pp. 24–25.

25. Kuper, *Changing Jamaica*, p. 64.

26. See Carl Stone, "Race and Nationalism in Urban Jamaica," *Caribbean Studies* 13 (January 1974): 5–52.

27. Ibid.; and Carl Stone, *Class, Race, and Political Behaviour in Urban Jamaica* (Kingston: University of the West Indies, Institute of Social and Economic Research, 1973), pp. 123–55.

28. The WPJ program calls for agrarian reform to end the system of large private landownership, democratic control of the economic and political life of the country, and the need for strengthening relations with socialist countries in economic and technical areas (see *Caribbean Contact*, February 1979, p. 7).

29. *Bridgetown Advocate News*, March 9, 1982, p. 1.

30. Manley, *Politics of Change*, pp. 37–51, 76–123.

31. Ibid.

32. Girvan and Bernal, "The IMF," p. 37. As Derek Heaven of the Foreign Ministry explained to the author in January 1978, the PNP program was a reaction to the traditional capitalist system, which had not worked in Jamaica before 1972, especially in light of Jamaica's small size, high rate of unemployment, its ties to multinational corporate interests, and the maldistribution of wealth. The PNP, he stated, simply recognized the need to "reorder the economy," "provide more opportunities for more people to enjoy their fruits of labor," and "expand equality of opportunities" (Interviews, Kingston, Jamaica, January 1978).

33. Norman Girvan of the National Planning Ministry reported to the author in 1978 that Jamaica was on the verge of an "explosion" in 1972, which led the PNP toward its formula of Democratic Socialism. Girvan noted that Jamaica's approach to economic development involved a form of "mixed economy" and that it was a far cry from the Cuban model. The PNP model, he said, was a "progressive" movement with many currents in it, but united by the belief that Jamaica must be brought into the twentieth century (Interview, January 1978).

34. The government entered into a number of related industries, including a flour mill, Jamaica Omnibus Services, Radio Jamaica, the Jamaica Public Service Company (electricity), and some hotels. See Wendell Bell, "Foreign Policy and Attitudes of Elites in Jamaica: The First Twelve Years of Nationhood," in Richard Millett and W. Marvin Will, *The Restless Caribbean: Changing Patterns of International Relations* (New York: Praeger, 1979), p. 162; and *Kingston Daily Gleaner*, November 22, 1976, pp. 1, 18.

35. Government of Jamaica, *Green Paper on Industrial Development Programme: Jamaica, 1975–1980*; and Rex Nettleford, *Report on Worker Participation in Jamaica* (Kingston: Government of Jamaica, February 1976). See also Prime Minister Michael Manley's discussion of the nation's economic survival in *Kingston Daily Gleaner*, May 21, 1976, pp. 15, 19 ff; and the unveiling of the PNP national development plan in November, *Kingston Daily Gleaner*, November 22, 1976, p. 1.

36. Winston A. Van Horne, "Why Manley Lost," *World Today* 37 (November 1981): 430–31; Girvan and Bernal, "The IMF," pp. 38–39; Arthur Bonner, "'Heavy Manners' in Jamaica: Michael Manley's Race with Time," *Nation*, January 1977, pp. 81–82; and Brown, "Economic Policy," pp. 22–37.

37. Carl Stone, "Socialism and Agricultural Policies in Jamaica in the 1970s," *Inter-American Economic Affairs* 4 (Spring 1982): 3–29; "High Wind, Low Yield," *Economist*, February 10, 1980, p. 80; and Bonner, "'Heavy Manners' in Jamaica," p. 82.

38. Stone, "Socialism and Agricultural Policies," pp. 5–10.

39. Prime Minister Manley traveled to Cuba in June 1977, and Fidel Castro visited Jamaica in October 1977. Meanwhile, a number of high-ranking Jamaican govern-

ment officials regularly traveled back and forth to nearby Cuba. See Havana Radio Broadcast, June 19, 1977; and David D'Costa, "Fidel Speaks Straight to Our Heart," *Jamaican Weekly Gleaner*, October 28, 1977, p. 8; see also W. Raymond Duncan, "Jamaica," in Robert Wesson, ed., *Communism in Central America and the Caribbean* (Stanford: Hoover Institution Press, 1982), pp. 117–30.

40. See U.S. Central Intelligence Agency, National Foreign Assessment Center, *Communist Aid Activities in Non-communist Less Developed Countries*, by year; Tad Szulc, "Confronting the Cuban Nemesis," *New York Times Magazine*, April 5, 1981, pp. 36 ff; U.S. Congress, House, Committee on Foreign Affairs, *Impact of Cuban-Soviet Ties in the Western Hemisphere*, Hearings, Spring 1980 (Washington, D.C.: Government Printing Office, 1980).

41. By October 1977 the opposition JLP was accusing Michael Manley of being an "agent of Cuban imperialism" (*Jamaican Weekly Gleaner*, October 28, 1977, p. 1). But as Norman Girvan argued in an interview with the author in January 1978, the PNP was in great need of technically trained assistance from wherever it could get it, including Cuba, owing in part to the enormously high rate of emigration of skilled Jamaicans.

42. Girvan and Bernal, "The IMF," p. 38.

43. Stone, "Socialism and Agricultural Policies," p. 8.

44. Ibid., p. 15; and Van Horne, "Jamaica: Why Manley Lost," p. 430.

45. John Huey, "Sinking Island," *Wall Street Journal*, February 25, 1980, p. 1.

46. Ibid.

47. Anthony Maingot, "The Difficult Path to Socialism in the English-Speaking Caribbean," in Richard Fagen, ed., *Capitalism and the State in Latin American Relations* (Stanford: Stanford University Press, 1979), p. 283.

48. This "radical" leftist position was taken by Norman Girvan, at the time director of the National Planning Agency (see *Caribbean Contact*, June 1977, p. 7).

49. As early as 1974 Carl Stone had concluded that "in Jamaica there is neither a will to achieve the socialist alternative nor the necessary political supports to sustain it even if such a will existed" (*Electoral Behavior and Public Opinion in Jamaica* [Mona, Jamaica, 1974], p. 96, as quoted in Maingot, "The Difficult Path to Socialism," p. 284). See *Jamaican Weekly Gleaner*, February 13, 1978, p. 17, and January 30, 1978, p. 8, for the poll results.

50. Carl Stone, "Poll," *Jamaican Weekly Gleaner*, January 16, 1978, p. 1.

51. Jamaican Labour Party, "Change Without Chaos," (Kingston, October 1980), as cited in Payne, "Seaga's Jamaica After One Year," p. 438.

52. In the U.S. fiscal year ending September 1981, American assistance to Jamaica rose 300 percent, from U.S. $23 million to U.S. $93 million. In fiscal year 1981–82, U.S. aid rose to $112 million, with Jamaica the second highest recipient of U.S. aid per capita after Israel.

53. *Business Week*, October 18, 1981, p. 162.

54. *Caribbean Contact* 8 (February 10, 1981): 7.

55. Most U.S. investments in Jamaica by late 1982 were small, involving less than $500,000 (*Business Week*, October 18, 1982, p. 163).

56. *Latin America Weekly Report*, April 29, 1983, p. 4; and *Latin America Regional Reports: Caribbean*, May 13, 1983, p. 1.

57. See "Tourism Lives Again," *Jamaica News*, March 1983; and James Nelson Goodsell, "Profitable Tides of Surf-Loving Tourists Return to Jamaica," *Christian Science Monitor*, March 7, 1983, p. 11.

58. *Business Week*, October 18, 1982, p. 163.

59. *Latin America Regional Report: Caribbean*, December 10, 1982, p. 2.

60. As evidence of the PNP's rightward trend, D. K. Duncan resigned as general secretary, saying that the PNP had become a "watered-down version of the JLP" (*Latin America Regional Reports: Caribbean*, February 25, 1983, p. 5).

10   Costa Rica

Problems of
Social Democracy

Robert Wesson

Costa Rica has liked to call itself the Switzerland of Central America. This is somewhat unrealistic as Costa Rica has a good deal of poverty and landholding and wealth are concentrated, although less so than in most Third World countries. But Costa Rica is the most democratic state of Latin America and one of the most democratic in the world. Since 1948 the opposition has usually won elections, the elected legislature is very strong, civil liberties are fully observed, and the constitution is designed to check political power. In some ways it is exceptionally democratic; for example, officeholders, from the president down, are forbidden to engage in partisan politics, and there is no military organization even potentially capable of exerting influence. The roots of democracy go back to Spanish colonial times when the isolated farmers of the Central Plateau worked their land with their own hands for lack of Indians to enserf; and democracy became and has remained a matter of national pride, almost the essence of being Costa Rican, a prime distinction of mostly European Costa Ricans over the mostly Indian peoples of neighboring countries.

Democratic politics have consequently been the determinant of economic policies if not outcomes, at least since the patriarchic old republic, governed by coffee growers, was overtaken by modernization and modern demands. The president elected in 1940, Rafael Angel Calderón Guardia, was a candidate of the aristocracy, supported by the church and his conservative predecessor, León Cortés. However, having become conscious of needs that he saw as a physician, he undertook a populist program, especially social security and labor legislation, inspired by social Catholicism, the Mexican populism of Lázaro Cárdenas, and Franklin Roosevelt's New Deal—a social and re-distributive program ahead of both the social-economic development of Costa Rica and the growth of an organized working class. Calderón soon found himself at odds with the upper classes; in compensation, in 1942 he allied himself with the well-organized communist (Popular Vanguard) party. The Communists had opposed his election but were eager to join with a "bourgeois" party after the invasion of the Soviet Union, and they became politically respectable when the Soviet Union became an ally in World War II. On the other hand, Calderón alienated many of the oligarchy by the expropriation of German and Italian landholdings.

Calderón's effort to realize the economic implications of political democracy, alienating the privileged classes and relying on new forces, unions, and the organized pro-Marxist left, was in the tradition of populist politics in Latin America, with variations in Chile (1970–1973), Brazil (1961–1964), Guatemala (1948–1954), and other countries. It has ordinarily led to economic troubles, deepening class divisions and tensions, and a military coup. After the first flush of popularity of his reforms, Calderón likewise encountered increasing problems. The costs of government soared; and there were many charges of waste, jobbery, and corruption.[1] Calderón, who became more authoritarian, increasingly aligned himself with the Communists as the middle classes followed the upper into opposition.

Unable to succeed himself, Calderón in 1944 advanced the candidacy of a stand-in, Teodoro Picado, whose election was widely regarded as fraudulent.[2] Picado relied even more than Calderón on the Communists. Unaccustomed acts of violence, beatings, and intimidation polarized the country; and many small farmers and people of the middle class became frightened. Liberal intellectuals who agreed with most of the *Calderonista* program but who were repelled by the misuse of the state formed an opposition movement; this developed into a social-democratic party and allied itself with the oligarchy to combat the communist-populist power.[3] The onset of the cold war in 1947 increased tensions and deprived the communist alliance of respectability, as Vanguardia Popular faithfully sided with the Soviet Union against the United States.[4]

Costa Rica did not have a military coup because the army—about 300 men in early 1948[5]—was too small and amateurish. However, in 1947 rising violence led to a middle-class general strike, under the pressure of which the government agreed to an independent electoral tribunal. This tribunal awarded the election of 1948 to the conservative candidate, Otilio Ulate, over Calderón. When the *Calderonista*-communist majority in the Assembly annulled the election, José Figueres Ferrer, a dynamic young planter whom Calderón had (illegally and contrary to Costa Rican political mores) exiled in 1942 and who had allied himself with various antidictator movements in the Central American–Caribbean area, seized the awaited opportunity to rebel.[6] The regular forces were unenthusiastic in collaboration with communist-led workers' battalions,[7] and the chief defenders of the *Calderonista* cause were the Communists. Figueres won fairly easily.

His victory largely eliminated the communist issue for the next three decades. Figueres, during the eighteen months when he governed by right of victory before turning the presidency over to Ulate, severely crimped the coffee-exporter aristocracy by nationalizing the banks and imposing a 10 percent capital levy (which he was mostly unable to collect).[8] He also oversaw the writing of a new constitution that introduced full adult suffrage and reinforced the democratic order, including abolition of the army. He set the country on a course toward social-democratic welfarism.[9] Unlike Calderón's communist-supported populism, this welfarism was not associated with the idea of revolution and did not seem threatening to the social order.

In the elections Figueres held for a constituent assembly, his followers fared poorly. However, he organized an effective National Liberation Party (PLN); and Figueres dominated Costa Rican politics for a generation, serving as president 1953–1958 and 1970–1974. The PLN has remained the chief political force to this day, having been defeated in three presidential elections as much by its divisions as by the appeal of its opponents. The PLN has almost always held a majority in the Assembly and has dominated the bureaucracy. Other parties, from conservative to the communist, have been successful when they could unite to take advantage of mostly personalist quarrels within the PLN.

The PLN, a middle-class party with its greatest strength among the employees of the public sector, has been both anti-Marxist and mildly anticapitalist,[10] desirous of economic equalization and checking the role of capital, especially foreign, while collaborating with it and with the United States.[11] The division of Left versus Right was largely left behind as the *Calderonistas*, once allied with the Communists, and the *Ulatistas*, representatives of the old landholding elite, forgot their mortal differences and joined more or less consistently against the PLN. The non-PLN administrations of Mario Echandi (1958–1962) and José Joaquín Trejos (1966–1970) were rather conservative, but they could only slow, not turn back, the growth of the welfare-interventionist state. The administration of Rodrigo Carazo (1978–1982), a former PLN leader who headed an oppositionist coalition, was fully as interventionist as the PLN.[12] The result of the war of 1948 was thus not the rejection of the populist program but its further development under anti-Marxist banners.[13]

The Welfare State

Up to 1978 the social-democratic republic was remarkably successful in many ways. From 1950 to 1977, the economy grew at an average rate of over 6 percent per annum. Prices were practically stable from 1957 to 1968,[14] and in the following years inflation was moderate except for 1974, the year of the first petroleum crisis, which showed a rate of 46 percent.[15] Medical services of fair to good quality, with all costs covered by the state, were made available to virtually everyone; preventive medicine was eventually so successful as to make a surplus of hospital beds, especially for children. Paramedics attached to over 400 village centers were supposed to carry hygiene and disease prevention to all homes at least once per six weeks.[16] Life expectancy grew to approximate that in the United States. Pensions gave a modicum of security to all.[17] Social security was extended to the self-employed, costs for the poor being covered by the state. In 1974 Costa Rica became one of the few countries to give (small) pensions to the aged and disabled even without their having been under the contributory social security system.[18] Housing was subsidized for the poor.

The educational system was also greatly expanded. Nine years of education were made obligatory in 1973. Secondary school enrollment doubled, 1970–1974,[19] and the number of university students rose from 18,870 in 1970 to 44,000 in 1979, overcrowding facilities under pressure to admit all applicants.[20] The number of professional school graduates increased, 1970–1977, from 3,539 to 55,008.[21]

Per capita real GNP grew 4.6 percent yearly from 1961 to 1965, 7.3 percent from 1966 to 1974, and 8.9 percent in 1977.[22] Meanwhile the trade balance remained fairly stable, and nontraditional products (other than coffee, bananas, sugar, and beef) grew from 27 percent of the total in 1970 to 45 percent in 1980.[23] Unemployment, which was low for Latin America, declined in 1973–1976 from 42,981 (of a work force of 585,332) to 40,921 (of 616,788).[24] Modernization of the economy raised the share of GNP attributed to industry and mining from 13.2 percent in 1961 to 22.0 percent in 1978.

The number of persons under social security grew, 1969–1977, from 776,592 to 1,783,964.[25] Infant mortality declined from 80 per thousand in 1960–1970 to 45 per thousand in 1970–1980 (the Central American average being 112 in the latter period).[26] The number of preschool centers tripled, 1970–1976. Free breakfast and lunch for small children, pregnant women, and lactating mothers by June 1977 reached over 500,000 people, a quarter of the population.[27] The general death rate declined from 14 per thousand in 1945–1949 to an amazing 3.8 in 1981.[28]

The life of the peasants was revolutionized by roads and buses, water supplies, electricity reaching into all corners, telephones in villages, agricultural extension services, health and sanitary services, and television, which has found its way into most peasant homes. A land reform begun in the early 1960s benefited about 10 percent of the population, furnishing plots, in practice almost gratis, to some 40,000 families.[29] A result of this social change, and at the same time a cause of further change, was a sharp fall in the birthrate from 1969 to 1977 by virtue of no official population policy but by the actions of the lower echelons of the health services, private organizations, and changes of values.

Until the recent crisis, which has struck less-advantaged classes harder than the wealthier, Costa Rica seemed to have made remarkable progress toward fulfilling the promises of social democracy. There were benefits for the masses, both in redistribution (especially through the social security system) and in health and other services. The economy was considerably modernized. By the late 1970s housewives were complaining that they could not find domestics, and coffee growers were hiring pickers from Nicaragua. The condition of women was much improved, partly because of opportunities for state employment. The once dictatorial *paterfamilias* lost status, and women probably enjoyed more equality than in any other nonradical country in Latin America.

The democratic consensus was effective. Upper-class conservatives resisted redistributive policies, but they accepted defeat.[30] The universalization of social security, which laid fixed levies on all incomes including the self-employed and professionals and helped mostly the poor at the expense of the affluent, was propelled not by pressure of the masses but by bureaucrats. It met little resistance[31] because the elite accepted the need for economic justice for social peace.[32]

The Crisis

It was hoped, not without reason, that Costa Rica could call itself a developed country by 2000 A.D.[33] But the years of progress were the prelude to economic disaster. In 1978 the ascending curve halted and thereafter skidded downwards; by 1979 there was already a sense of crisis.[34] A primary sign of trouble was the ballooning fiscal deficit, which amounted to 11.7 percent of revenues in 1970, 22 percent in 1977, 40 percent in 1978, and 60 percent in 1979 and 1980.[35] Financing the deficit took 18 percent of available credit in 1971, 62 percent in 1979.[36] The balance of payments deficit went from a bearable $41 million in 1978 to $82 million in 1979 and leaped to $456 million in 1980.[37] The trade deficit grew from $97 million in 1977 to $356 million in 1980.[38] International reserves were wiped out. The government began borrowing wildly, and the public foreign debt went from $141 million in 1966 and $227 million in 1970 to $812 million in 1977, $1,869 million in 1979, and $2,679 million in 1981.[39] The public foreign debt amounted in 1978 to 62 percent of the GNP,[40] about 100 percent of the GNP in 1981. The amount of private sector foreign debt could only be guessed, but it was well over $1 billion in 1981.[41] In late July 1981 Costa Rica suspended payments on its foreign debt and became probably the worst credit case in the Third World.

The colón collapsed. It had been rather stable for many years, having weakened, 1950 to 1980, only from 6.25 to 8.60 per dollar; and borrowing in 1979–1981 was motivated partly by the urge to maintain the 8.60 rate. In 1981 the Central Bank lost nearly 3 billion colones buying dollars at ¢36 to ¢42 and reselling to government agencies at ¢8.60 or ¢20, making up the difference by issuing currency. The money supply grew by 53 percent in 1981.[42] In 1981 the dollar shortage drove the free rate rapidly up. In December 1981 the official rate was set at ¢20 per dollar, but the street rate was already much higher. It rose to ¢63 by July 1982.

Even people of modest condition began putting spare money into dollars, while the more sophisticated sent savings to Panama or the United States. Many firms and individuals that had contracted dollar loans in the boom years now found themselves obligated for dollars costing up to seven times as much in colones, and failures multiplied. The real value of domestic credit shrank by 50 percent in two years up to mid-1982, that available to the private sector decreasing by 60 percent.[43] Deficits came to 6.5 percent of GNP in 1976–1978, 10 percent in 1979, 12.5 percent in 1980, and about 17 percent in 1982, compared to 2–3 percent in the United States. Growing uncertainty led to capital flight and retrenchment; available credit was further reduced as inflation discouraged savings and capital sought security abroad. The nationalized banks did not press borrowers because of political considerations, fear of unemployment, and desire to avoid visible losses (partly because the powerful bank workers' union wanted paper earnings); and over half their portfolios became overdue by mid-1982.[44]

The rise of consumer prices was calculated at 8 percent in 1978, almost double the average of the several preceding years. But the increase from May 1980 to May 1981 was 30 percent for consumer prices, 56 percent for wholesale prices according to official figures,[45] more realistically to be estimated at about 100 percent. For May 1981 to May 1982, consumer prices were reported to have risen 84 percent, wholesale prices 108 percent.[46] Many essentials shot up, and there were sometimes shortages, especially of such necessities as sugar, flour, beans, and milk. The government was pulled between economic demands and consumer needs. For example, in July 1982 the price of rice was suddenly more than doubled. In the face of a storm of protest, the government announced that rice in stock had to be sold at the old price while the new harvest would sell for the new price. "Old rice" tended to disappear despite denunciations of speculation; it was decided to keep the price low for the consumer and high for the growers, the state paying the difference.

GNP per capita decreased about 4 percent in 1980, 9 percent in 1981, and 9 percent in 1982.[47] Construction came almost to a halt except for dollar-financed projects. Real earnings declined July 1979 to March 1982 by 33 percent, low wages apparently falling most. In July 1982, 55 percent of wage earners reportedly received less than ¢3,000 per month, then equivalent to $50 at the free-market rate.[48] At this time the "basic basket" of necessities cost ¢3,800 per month. The Social Security Administration (Caja Costarricense de Seguro Social; CCSS), formerly proud of having virtually abolished serious malnutrition in children, saw new cases multiplying. The budget of the Ministry of Health, charged with disease prevention, was slashed (in terms of rapidly shrinking colones) from ¢385 million in 1980 to about ¢250 million in 1982; many of its centers were closed, and most of the rest were short of medicines.[49] The lack of dollars caused the use of even essential drugs to be severely restricted. Bookstores could no longer afford to import books, and the library of the University of Costa Rica practically ceased purchase of new books and periodicals.

Conjunctural Causes

Several events, 1979–1980, combined against the Costa Rican economy. First, ironically, was the very high price of coffee (36 percent of exports, 1977–1979)[50] in 1977–1978. Coming on the top of the boom, this stimulated overplanting; worse, it encouraged carefree spending and borrowing that became overly onerous when coffee went down as rapidly as it had risen. Then the Iranian Revolution doubled the price of petroleum, 1979–1980, and this pushed the trade balance deeply into deficit. Internal policy compounded the damage as the state refinery sold petroleum products at as little as half their cost, thereby keeping consumption high and forcing the printing of more money.[51] Meanwhile high interest rates made borrowing more costly, and the worldwide recession hurt exports and investment.

Concurrently, the Central American Common Market, which new Costa Rican industries were planned to serve (and which took about a quarter of Costa Rican exports), failed. Civil war and the victory of the Sandinistas in Nicaragua practically ended trade with that country and also made difficulties for overland transportation to other Central American markets. Violence and guerrilla war roiled El Salvador and Guatemala, and the general atmosphere of insecurity cast its shadow over Costa Rica. Whatever remained of the Common Market fell victim to protectionism in the general recession.

Since 1981, Costa Rica has suffered from the general recession of the developed economies, especially the United States, and weak markets for exports, both raw and manufactured. To this has been added the political turmoil and uncertainty of Central America since the Sandinista triumph in Nicaragua in 1979 and the growing civil conflict in El Salvador. Although guerrilla war has had no echo among Costa Ricans, violence has inevitably lapped over the borders and contributed to an atmosphere of uncertainty inhospitable to economic development.

Systemic Problems

It is probably fair to state, however, that unfavorable conditions hastened and intensified a crisis already in gestation. Costa Ricans have often blamed themselves for their troubles, saying that a poor country was trying to live like a rich one. Whether or not Costa Rica has suffered from excess consumption, it has certainly indulged in the unproductive use of resources. The PLN adopted the general policy of having the state provide employment for the educated middle class and benefits for the masses, while supporting nontraditional (especially noncoffee) producers, both agricultural and industrial. The result was not only ambitious social programs, but also growing tendencies to inefficiency and unproductive use of capital that must have overtaken resources in fairly short order even if there had been no deterioration of foreign trade patterns.

The most marked political-economic trend has been toward state interventionism in the economy. Its beginnings go back to Spanish paternalist traditions. In the nineteenth century a national liquor monopoly was established, and the state participated in building railroads to the Atlantic and Pacific ports around the turn of this century. A governmental insurance monopoly was established in the 1920s. The state undertook to help in the marketing of agricultural products, especially coffee, in the 1930s.[52] Trade deficits have been covered by foreign borrowing since the first part of this century. The "new deal" of the 1940s established the social security system. At first limited in scope, this grew steadily to encompass an ever larger percentage of the population. State support for nontraditional producers began with the victory of Figueres, a sisal planter. Figueres's nationalization of the banks in 1948 made it possible to redirect credit from the coffee barons to newer lines that needed help and felt entitled to it. Many Figueristas also favored state intervention in principle as a means to social justice, and they set up a system of autonomous institutions, more or less insulated from the executive (in reaction to the abuses of the Calderonistas), as the means of socializing large parts of the economy while avoiding dictatorship. In the years after 1953, electric power, telephones, the ports, much construction, petroleum refining and distribution, much transportation, and much agricultural marketing, came under state control in the form of autonomous institutions.[53]

Results were in many ways excellent, as already observed. However, the national budget has not been balanced since 1952, the last full year of the conservative administration of Ulate.[54] The assembly has freely used its power to raise outlays, and in the face of multiple pressures on the legislature, the agencies, and the president, expenditures have been difficult to control in Costa Rica as in other democracies. A president desirous of cutting costs can operate on only about 9 percent of the budget.[55]

The percentage of the work force employed by the state grew from 6 percent in 1950 to 20 percent in 1980.[56] Daniel Oduber believed the world was marching toward socialism, a more just order than capitalism;[57] and during his administration (1974–1978), the autonomous institutions, which account for over two-thirds of governmental expenditures, nearly doubled their staffs.[58] Wages of the public sector were 16.4 percent of the total in 1970 and 30 percent in 1979.[59] Until inflation struck, public employees were the best-paid fraction of the work force; they looked to their own interests. For example, when the resources of the social security system were enlarged in 1971, the doctors went on strike to get the new money for themselves instead of expanding the system, as intended by the legislature.[60] Unemployment decreased, thanks to the public sector, which accounted in 1977 for 33 percent of new jobs and in 1978 for 39 percent, while agriculture provided none.[61] Bureaucratization also nourished the growing profession of expediters.

The state-controlled share of the GNP about doubled from 1950 to 1970 and has risen substantially since;[62] estimates run from 25 percent to 50 percent,[63] and one-third may be a fair guess.[64] The skyline of San José came to be dominated not by commercial office buildings but by nationalized banks, the CCSS, and the National Insurance Institute, with their modern and well-furnished offices. The countryside was graced with poorly planned freeways and many unfinished bridges.

The central government hardly grew from 1961 to 1979,[65] but the growth of the autonomous institutions was anarchic. They are partly politicized since ordinarily four members of the directorate are from the majority party and three from the leading opposition party, and by a 1973 law the president gained the right to name the presiding officer.[66] But their policies and budgets have been largely out of control, and some of them were empowered to borrow abroad. They have commonly far exceeded the intentions of their founders. For example, the National Production Council (CNP), set up to stabilize prices of agricultural products, not only built up storage and marketing facilities but went into food processing and retail sales.

Some forty agencies were charged with family assistance and a similar number with housing improvement.[67]

The major forces in the economy came to be the Central Bank; the Corporation for Development (CODESA); the CNP; and RECOPE, which refined and sold petroleum products. As state agencies came to dominate the economy, the way to affluence for the upper class came increasingly to be through dealings with them or at their expense. Directors enjoyed valuable perquisites in lieu of high salaries. Probably at least half of the richer sector of the population depended on the state for most or part of their income.[68] Many of the middle class, thanks to freely dispensed scholarships, could go to the university, where they usually preferred humanistic to technical studies and qualified themselves only for desk jobs; public employment became the prime way to upward mobility and economic security.

Jobs in the public sector usually carried tenure. Some even became hereditary; insurance agents, for example, passed their lucrative posts to their children or relations. To remove public workers was unpleasant and expensive because of benefits owed them, so new administrations would create new jobs for their followers, in filling which civil service rules could be evaded.[69] Most new places were created by the PLN, to which most employees were beholden. It appeared that the expansion of the bureaucracy served to forestall the radicalization of the youthful intellectuals, and there was some tendency to co-opt dissidents with jobs.

In neo-Marxist language, the new bureaucratic bourgeoisie took shape as a class and came to hold the most important positions in the development of state capitalism. Private capitalists, on the other hand, were alienated; whereas the Chamber of Industries was 67 percent PLN-affiliated in 1962, by 1977–1978 it was only 44 percent.[70] The new class was not notably productive. Middle in terms of income, it bore small resemblance to the rising "bourgeoisie" of early modern Europe, an essentially entrepreneurial class. To the contrary, the basic possession of the new class was official position, and it was weak in classic "bourgeois" virtues, oriented not toward industry and thrift but toward consumption and status. Its influence was augmented by unionization; nearly half of public employees were in unions against only 5 percent in the private sector.[71] Strikes, although theoretically illegal, were frequent; the state could hardly defy its workers' unions because they controlled essential services, such as electricity and transportation.

The influence of the political-bureaucratic sector was increased also by state payment of the expenses of political parties. This practice, begun in 1948, was strengthened in 1971 to give parties winning over 10 percent (later 5 percent) of the votes in the previous election their proportionate share of a fund based on a fixed percentage (2 percent) of the national budget. This was intended to do away with the old practice of requiring appointees to turn over part of their pay to their party.[72] However, it favored the ins, made the parties self-sustaining, and gave the whole political community an interest in increasing the national budget. Private contributions were also allowed without limit. Generous financing thus provided a livelihood for a substantial corps of professional politicians.

Among the costs of the enlarged state was the downgrading of local government, traditional functions of which, from education to sewers, were taken over by centralized autonomous institutions operating out of hypertrophied San José. Competition was widely eliminated. The nationalized banks were rather indifferent to depositors and so inefficient as to hinder exports. Various taxes and contributions added nearly 50 percent to payroll costs,[73] considerably reducing the profitability of doing business in Costa Rica. The CCSS, one of the largest businesses in the country, became bureaucratic and wasteful. But it enjoyed full autonomy and even had virtual legislative power, issuing regulations with force of law.[74]

There was little faith in the market; the control of prices of many necessities and state guidance of wages were taken for granted. Almost anything was likely to evoke regulation; for example, export of dairy cattle was subject to prohibition as the government tried to calculate how many were needed domestically.[75] Although the country desperately had to export, exporters were hampered by requirements for many permits and were mostly taxed about 10 percent, in addition to being required to exchange dollars at the official rate. Costa Rica is a traditional sugar exporter, but because of pricing policies it has had to import sugar while failing to fill its quota in the high-priced U.S. market.

Enforcement of rules, however, was slack. For example, it was decreed that taxis must install meters, and some did, but they were never used.[76] Repeated regulations never stopped buses from belching dark and noxious clouds. The adjustment of prices and wages under severe inflation was chaotic; some would shoot up while others remained nearly or entirely static—postal rates, for example, came to represent a practically free service until in September 1982 they were quintupled. Red tape was tangled; to get an auto license required seventeen visits to nine institutions.[77]

The apparatus was not efficient even in its own behalf. A loan extended by USAID in 1976 in the amount of $5.5 million for urban improvements was only about half utilized, not because of lack of potential projects but because of Costa Rican bureaucratic requirements for disbursement.[78] Foreign loans, however desirable, might be held up for months in the detail-ridden Assembly.[79] Not only were commercial loans, which amounted to subsidies in inflationary times because of low interest and easy terms, allocated more or less on political grounds; the nationalized banking system was generally lax in collection. It was sometimes necessary to import commodities readily pro-

duced domestically, such as beans, because export controls and the requirement that dollars be exchanged at a low fixed rate led to clandestine export,
which might give twice the return with less paperwork. Even a slight
acquaintance with business dealings in Costa Rica sufficed to make one aware
that sidestepping the rules was casual and frequent. By the 1970s the idealism
of the PLN had worn thin; more important, the expanded role of the state
vastly increased the opportunities and incentives for corruption. Inflation also
contributed, as civil servants found their pay falling short of their needs, and
the sense of values was undermined.

State-Supported Industrialization

The burdens of the state were greatly increased by the industrialization
policy, directed more to substitution of imports than promotion of exports. It
was entirely understandable to endeavor to make in Costa Rica imported
products in order to employ labor displaced from the rural sector, modernize
and broaden the economy, reduce dependence on a few agricultural exports,
and raise productivity.[80] It was a typical populist program, offering benefits to
all classes;[81] and it was on the agenda of the reformers since 1945, proclaimed
by law since 1959. It was rather successful for some years. The industrial
component of GNP grew to 14 percent in 1963 and 21 percent in 1974.[82]

But helping new and frequently uneconomic industries took resources
from agriculture, the chief earner of foreign exchange. In 1970, agriculture received 70 percent more credit than industry; by 1979, industry received
22 percent more than agriculture; and agricultural production was stagnant
from 1973 to 1980.[83] Industrialization provided disappointingly few new jobs
as new enterprises tended to minimize employment because of labor costs.[84] It
weighed on the budget because of exemptions from taxes, loss of tariff
revenues, free import of raw materials and equipment, and subsidized
financing, both in dollars and colones. It burdened the balance of payments
with raw material and capital imports. Start-up charges tended to become
permanent as the protected industries continued to need help, or at least
demand it. They were generally monopolies and subject to the familiar vices of
noncompetition. They mostly lacked export capability, and industrial exports
lagged far behind the imports needed by industry.[85] The Central American
Common Market was part of the industrialization strategy; so far as the
Common Market functioned, it further reduced revenues because of the
exemption of Central American trade from duties. Import-substitution
industrialization increased dependence on foreign trade and foreign capital,[86]
while domestic consumption was stimulated by rising expectations imitative
of the Western world.[87]

The interventionist-welfare state grew into the entrepreneurial state with the help of CODESA. When it was founded in 1972, a third of its shares were reserved for private subscription, but it attracted almost no private capital. CODESA's board at first had representatives of the private sector, but they were expelled in 1976 and it was put wholly at the service of the state.[88] Its initial capitalization of ₡67 million swelled 60-fold by 1980.[89] Intended to finance undertakings too costly or too risky for private capital and to pre-empt the penetration of foreign capital,[90] CODESA used its access to Central Bank funds not only to make new investments but to gain control of troubled firms, partly by loans and guarantees, mostly (64 percent) by capital shares — CODESA legally controlled any business in which it had any share.[91] CODESA itself was exempt from fiscal controls.[92]

CODESA expanded into dozens of branches, including cotton production, aluminum fabrication, cement, mariculture, and fuel alcohol. Having imported buses, CODESA went on to operate them through its subsidiary, Transmesa.[93] Having undertaken sugar refining, it began to grow cane.[94] CODESA contributed to the pre-emption of credit by the public sector, which by 1980 was taking 62 percent of new internal credit (against 25 percent in 1975).

CODESA produced huge losses, comprising about 20 percent of the entire public sector deficit, which grew to 10–15 percent of the GNP as the crisis came on. Through a mixture of inefficiency and corruption, CODESA became a guarantor of private gain and public loss. Although restricted by bureaucratic procedural norms, CODESA defended state ownership in principle and wanted not merely to participate financially, but to manage its numerous subsidiaries.[95] Corruption was apparently mostly in commissions for deals and in contracts without competitive bidding or on a cost-plus basis. Losses were incurred as CODESA came to the rescue of foundering enterprises. Despite the costs, the promotion of new industry became ineffective.[96] After the manufacturing sector rose from 13.2 percent in 1961 to 21 percent of GNP in 1974 (and agriculture declined correspondingly), it increased only to 22 percent by 1979, and a large part of its capacity was underutilized.[97]

Shortage of exports led to pressure on the exchange rate and to difficulty in imports, and borrowing abroad only briefly postponed and soon magnified payments problems. The turn was the more sudden because the crisis was self-compounding. The weakening of the private sector caused greater pressure on the public, both to keep the economy active and to provide jobs. In 1978–1980 private employment dropped over 4,000 while public employment increased nearly 10,000.[98]

In brief, the political strategy of jobs for many and benefits for all ran out when the public sector became too big and too inefficient and corrupt for the private sector to support it.

Prospects for Reform

The Costa Ricans, being good democrats, looked to a remedy at the polls. They repudiated Carazo's Unidad Party in the February 8, 1982, election and gave the PLN candidate, Luís Alberto Monge, 58.4 percent of the vote against 33.7 percent for the centrist, Rafael Angel Calderón Fournier, son of the Calderón who inaugurated the era of change. Less than 4 percent each went to the conservative and radical leftist candidates. The voters also gave the PLN its largest majority ever in the Assembly—33 of the 57 seats. Then they waited for the new government to fulfill campaign promises and restore prosperity.

Inaugurated on May 8, the Monge administration undertook a series of austerity measures along with a desperate effort to secure financial aid from the United States to stretch out and roll over the foreign debt. Charges for electricity, water, telephones, buses, gasoline, etc., were raised by 60 percent to 90 percent; various other controlled prices were raised; some taxes were raised; and the budget was severely cut. Imports were cut back enough to make a small favorable trade balance for 1980.[99] But belt-tightening increased unemployment and made the crisis more painful, while inflation rapidly made new measures necessary.

To really turn the situation around would be to stop an avalanche. As early as 1978, Rodrigo Carazo in his presidential campaign was attacking the obvious evils of excess government spending, proliferating bureaucracy, corruption, and the expanding role of the state.[100] But during his administration these only worsened. In 1979, a financial reform was begun at the instance of the IMF[101] without results. In the seventeen months to August 1982, there were three agreements with IMF for loans conditional on austerity measures, especially cuts in spending and ending of food subsidies and price controls. All were broken.[102] Carazo several times stated that the demands were inhumane and unacceptable, and the chief action taken was to raise export taxes in December 1981.[103] According to a PLN leader, "we are going to struggle to the end to keep basic social action programs from being halted either by fiscal or budget deficit or the balance of payments or any other reason. It would be the last thing we would touch, not only by the economic imperative of the government but because of the need to maintain peace and social harmony in this country."[104] The welfare of the people, in the words of a deputy, must come ahead of the image of the country in international financial circles; Costa Rica could not pay its foreign debts at the cost of closing schools and hospitals.[105] Urbanization and habits of dependence on the paternalistic state make it ever more difficult to turn back from the welfare state.

The Monge administration was under great pressure not to release the economy to permit readjustments but to attack the symptoms, to impose more price and other controls. Inflation, the shortage of rice, and the depreciation of the colón were attributed to speculators. According to a March 1982 poll, 68 percent thought the new government should give priority to freezing prices. A small majority wanted to see government expenditures reduced, but without firing employees.[106] The measures recommended by the International Monetary Fund (IMF) are politically unrewarding—cutting deficits (and staffs), freeing or at least unifying exchange rates, liberalizing export controls, ending subsidized consumption, freezing wages, and putting credits on a commercial basis (while the government instead lowered rates to agriculture in June 1982 from 25 percent to 18 percent, a virtual gift when inflation was about 100 percent).[107] As the poor suffered more than the rich, the popular reaction was for the state to do more for the needy and to squeeze the rich. But even if the government could enact the demands of the IMF, this would only reduce or postpone the need for basic change, not touch the underlying causes of trouble. Having prospered through the state apparatus, the political leadership can hardly cut off its own feet.

The right to a job is part of the prevalent ideology.[108] Although 4,000 new employees were hired by the CCSS during the Carazo administration while use of health services were decreasing, staffs were to be reduced only by attrition, a slow process in hard times when few wanted to give up even a poorly paying job (which probably did not preclude moonlighting). The very fact that for a long time public service has drawn most persons with a liberal or social science education gives the public sector articulate, informed, and well-organized defenders. No state-controlled enterprise has ever been returned to the private sector, although it was the stated objective of CODESA to withdraw when its assistance was no longer necessary.[109] CODESA, with a statist philosophy, had no inclination to divest prospering enterprises, and no one wanted the failing ones. Indeed, it was legally difficult for CODESA to dispose of holdings.[110]

Conclusion

Costa Rica has an exceptionally well-ordered democracy with quite honest elections, prohibition of re-election, balancing powers, and responsiveness to popular needs. Its politics since 1948 have not been seriously complicated by the Marxist issue, by racial or regional divisions, by the influence of the military establishment, or even by exceptional riches, as in the Venezuelan case. The leading party has been rather typical of Latin American populisms—leader-oriented, polyclass, reformist, welfare-minded, and pro-industrialization.[111] Costa Rica is therefore a clear test of the viability of popular democracy in modern Latin America.

In comparative perspective, the Costan Rican outlook is not favorable. Chile, Uruguay, and Brazil, among others, at one time enjoyed prosperity under democratic government only to become unstable for causes more or less like those afflicting Costa Rica. Costa Ricans have been most troubled by the parallel with Uruguay, where the very democratic state, under pressure for benefits from people and bureaucrats, became too costly for the productive sector.[112] From 1950 to 1978, Costa Rica grew economically while Uruguay was in a long-term decline, but the recent slide of Costa Rica has been much steeper. Costa Rica takes pride in civility and democracy, but so did Uruguay, which was also pleased to compare itself to Switzerland.

Costa Rica has suffered from correctable errors, such as the follies of the poorly considered industrialization program and the excessive resort to borrowing, and the recent bitter experiences may bring correction. But errors cannot be dismissed as being the fault of the PLN because the PLN adopted policies that were winning strategies in the democratic game. In the underdeveloped society, the democratic state lacks not only money but skills and management to fulfill the wants of the people.

Costa Rican democracy has the dual aspects of seeking to serve the people and limiting the power of the leadership. The state enlarges, but nobody in particular manages it; the state, with its many agencies, to a large extent runs itself. The public employees are as well positioned as any group, but they press no particular policy except the security or increase of their pay and places. The state then becomes a sort of grab bag into which many hands reach, or a conglomerate of feudal domains (a characterization often used by Costa Rican critics), all fighting for budget shares. It is hard to formulate a strategy to get away from deficits, inflation, imbalance of foreign exchange, and economic uncertainty.

Moreover, it is more difficult in the politically democratic but socially and economically unequal society to roll back state controls because of the widespread feeling that the rich and powerful will take advantage of license and profit excessively. In the hard times, resentment of class privilege and the conviction of the rascality of the wealthy evidently grew, as sacrifices seemed to fall mostly on the vulnerable lower strata. There was little faith in the free market when it was generally believed that the capitalists could manipulate the market. Problems brought on by statist policies seemed to propel the populist state to more intervention, just as benefits sharpened appetites for benefits. No one has suggested a plausible answer.

It is a further difficulty that "free enterprise" to a large extent means foreign interests. The question of foreign penetration or domination of the modernizing economy complicates the effort to check the growth of the state.

A major reason for the role of the state is to prevent foreign pre-emption of industrialization. In the 1960s, the bulk of new industrial investment was foreign;[113] and recently it seemed that a large majority (perhaps nearly all) of the new enterprises, at least in the technologically more advanced sector, were foreign-backed if not completely foreign-owned. The obvious way to keep a fair share of the economy, especially its infrastructure, in Costa Rican hands is by state action. But this has led to ill-managed investment and reduced the capital potentially available for the Costa Rican private sector, which finds itself in a weak third place.

Nevertheless, Costa Rican democracy should not be blamed for all the problems and called a failure. Authoritarian regimes have done quite as badly, or worse. Chile and Argentina, for example, sustained an overvalued national currency more irrationally and more disastrously. Mexico and many other countries less democratic than Costa Rica have spent more extravagantly with much less benefit to their peoples. The Costa Rican bureaucracy is less hypertrophied than many another and is probably more responsible than those of Brazil, Mexico, etc. Mexico's excessive borrowing was less excusable than Costa Rica's, at least less justified.

It is also possible that the Costa Rican democratic system is at least as capable of straightening out the economy as more authoritarian regimes, which, in Argentina, Chile, Uruguay, and elsewhere, have not coped very competently with economic disaster. The Costa Ricans have shown an extraordinary capacity to absorb a decline of the standard of living, probably in part because of the high legitimacy of the government and its acceptance as representative of the nation. Painful conditions have brought remarkably little extremism of the Right or Left—the latter suffering from widespread repugnance for the turn of the Sandinista revolution to ideological authoritarianism. The Costa Ricans have a critical and informative press that can be trusted to give a reasonably objective, or at least wholly uncensored, account of conditions and needs. With the general attachment to legal ways, patriotic sentiments, tradition of nonviolence, and good understanding of the problems on the part of many persons, Costa Rica is perhaps as well equipped as any Latin American nation to confront its problems and plan its future in a difficult environment.

Notes

Many of the data and ideas of the preceding essay came from conversations with Costa Ricans, who generously gave of their time and knowledge. They were numerous, but special mention should be made of (and gratitude expressed to) Rodolfo Cerdas,

Claudio González Vega, Constantino Urcuyo, Eduardo Lizano Fait, Víctor Hugo Cespedes S., Carlos José Gutiérrez, Victor Pérez, and Mavis Biesanz.

1. John Patrick Bell, *Crisis in Costa Rica: The 1948 Revolution* (Austin: University of Texas Press, 1971), p. 65.

2. Ibid., p. 112.

3. Jacobo Schifter, "La democracia en Costa Rica: Como producto de la neutralización de clases," in Chester Zelaya et al., eds., *Democracia en Costa Rica?* (San José: Editorial Universidad Estatal a Distancia, 1979), p. 204.

4. Bell, *Crisis in Costa Rica*, p. 55.

5. Charles D. Ameringer, *Don Pepe: A Political Biography of José Figueres of Costa Rica* (Albuquerque: University of New Mexico Press, 1978), p. 50.

6. Ibid., p. 32.

7. Bell, *Crisis in Costa Rica*, pp. 138–41.

8. Ameringer, *Don Pepe*, p. 71.

9. Mavis Hiltunen de Biesanz, Richard Biesanz, and Karen Zubris de Biesanz, *The Costa Ricans* (Englewood Cliffs, N.J.: Prentice-Hall, 1982), p. 29.

10. Schifter, "La democracia en Costa Rica," pp. 200–202.

11. Daniel Oduber Quiros, "Las etapas del cambio," in idem et al., eds., *Los problemas socio-políticos del desarrollo en Costa Rica* (San José: Editorial Universidad Estatal a Distancia, 1981), p. 17.

12. Biesanz, Biesanz, and Biesanz, *Los Costarricenses* (San José: Editorial Universidad Estatal a Distancia, 1979), p. 590.

13. Bell, *Crisis in Costa Rica*, p. 161.

14. Oscar Barahona Streber et al., *Los problemas económicos del desarrollo en Costa Rica* (San José: Editorial Universidad Estatal a Distancia, 1980), annex, p. 214.

15. Jorge Corrales, *De la pobreza a la abundancia en Costa Rica* (San José: Universidad Autónoma de Costa Rica, 1981), p. 37.

16. Biesanz, Biesanz, and Biesanz, *Los Costarricenses*, p. 12.

17. *Anuario Estadístico de Costa Rica, 1977* (San José: Dirección General de Estadística y Censos, 1979), *passim*; USAID, *Costa Rica Project Paper: Private Sector Productivity* (Washington, D.C.: Government Printing Office, 1981), pp. 1–2.

18. Biesanz, Biesanz, and Biesanz, *Los Costarricenses*, p. 312.

19. Biesanz, Biesanz, and Biesanz, *The Costa Ricans*, p. 117.

20. Ibid., p. 129.

21. *Anuario Estadístico de Costa Rica*, p. 206.

22. *América Central frente a la década de los 80*, Informe Final, Simposium, 19–23 Octubre 1981, Escuela de Relaciones Internacionales, Universidad Nacional Autónoma, Heredia, Costa Rica, Table 7.

23. *USAID*, p. 54.

24. *Anuario Estadístico de Costa Rica*, p. 218.

25. Ibid., p. 134.

26. *América Central*, Table 24.

27. Biesanz, Biesanz, and Biesanz, *Los Costarricences*, pp. 312, 423.

28. Data of Dirección General de Estadística y Censos, San José.

29. Information of Mitchell Seligson, July 1982.

30. Oduber, "Las etapas," p. 30.

31. Mark Rosenberg, *Las luchas por el seguro social en Costa Rica* (San José: Editorial Costa Rica, 1980), pp. 173–74, 180.

32. Oscar Barahona Streber, "Algunos conceptos sobre la seguridad social en Costa Rica," in idem et al., *Los problemas económicos*, p. 21.

33. Oduber, "Las etapas," p. 25.

34. Biesanz, Biesanz, and Biesanz, *Los Costarricences*, p. 664.

35. Helio Fallas, *Crisis Económica en Costa Rica* (San José: Editora Década, 1981), Table 18.

36. Ibid., p. 97.

37. *USAID: Costa Rica Project Paper, Private Sector Productivity* (Washington, D.C.: Government Printing Office, 1981), p. 51.

38. *New York Times*, December 9, 1981, p. 34.

39. *América Central*, Table 16.

40. Ibid., Table 19.

41. *La Nación*, July 20, 1982, p. l-B.

42. JPRS, *Latin American Report*, April 28, 1982, pp. 36–37.

43. Information of Claudio González Vega.

44. Information of U.S. Embassy.

45. Information of Claudio González Vega.

46. Ibid.

47. *La Nación*, June 20, 1983, p. 14-A.

48. Ibid., July 12, 1982.

49. Ibid.

50. *América Central*, Table 15.

51. *La Nación*, February 13, 1982, p. 2-A.

52. Rodolfo Cerdas, "Costa Rica: Problemas actuales de una revolución democrática," in Zelaya et al., *Democracia en Costa Rica?* pp. 148–49.

53. Geoffrey Glatt, "Don't Cry for Costa Rica," *Barron's National Business and Financial Weekly*, May 24, 1982, p. 22.

54. Howard J. Blutstein et al., *Area Handbook for Costa Rica* (Washington, D.C.: Government Printing Office, 1970), p. 185.

55. Frederico Vargas Peralta, "El problema fiscal en Costa Rica," in Barahone et al., *Los problemas económicos*, pp. 58–68.

56. *USAID: Costa Rica Project Paper*, p. 4.

57. Oduber, "Las etapas," p. 23.

58. Biesanz, Biesanz, and Biesanz, *Los Costarricenses*, p. 207.

59. Corrales, *De la pobreza en la abundancia en Costa Rica*, p. 94.

60. Rosenberg, *Las luchas por el seguro social en Costa Rica*, p. 177.

61. Fallas, *La crisis económica*, pp. 52, 57.

62. Oscar Arias Sánchez, *Quién gobierna en Costa Rica* (San José: Educa, 1976), p. 245.

63. Biesanz, Biesanz, and Biesanz, *Los Costarricenses*, p. 566.

64. Information of Eduardo Lizano.

65. Fallas, *La crisis económica*, p. 30.

66. Mylena Vega, *El estado costarricense de 1974–1978: Codesa y la fracción industrial* (San Jose: Editorial Hoy, 1982), pp. 41–42.

67. Information of Víctor Pérez and Constantino Urcuyo.

68. Denton, *Patterns of Costa Rican Politics*, p. 23.

69. Biesanz, Biesanz, and Biesanz, *Los Costarricenses*, pp. 605, 628.

70. Vega, *El estado costarricense*, pp. 135–42.

71. Ibid., p. 224.

72. Ibid., p. 568.

73. Glatt, "Don't Cry for Costa Rica," p. 22.

74. Biesanz, Biesanz, and Biesanz, *Los Costarricenses*, p. 317.

75. *Tico Times*, July 18, 1982.

76. Ibid., December 1981–January 1982, p. 6.

77. Biesanz, Biesanz, and Biesanz, *Los Costarricenses*, p. 630.

78. Information of U.S. Embassy, San José, July 1982.

79. Biesanz, Biesanz, and Biesanz, *Los Costarricenses*, p. 613.

80. Fallas, *La crisis económica*, p. 22.

81. Paul W. Drake, "Conclusion: Requiem for Populism," in Michael Conniff, ed., *Latin American Populism in Comparative Perspective* (Albuquerque: University of New Mexico Press, 1982), p. 218.

82. *USAID: Costa Rica Project Paper*, p. 3.

83. Fallas, *La crisis económica*, p. 47.

84. Biesanz, Biesanz, and Biesanz, *Los Costarricenses*, p. 193.

85. Fallas, *La crisis económica*, pp. 36, 44–45.

86. Ibid., p. 24.

87. Ibid., p. 38.

88. Vega, *El estado costarricense*, pp. 58, 155.

89. CODESA, *Memoire, 1980* (San José, 1981).

90. Oduber, *Las etapas*, p. 27.

91. Biesanz, Biesanz, and Biesanz, *Los costarricenses*, p. 627.

92. Vega, *El estado costarricense*, p. 58.

93. Ibid., p. 77.

94. Rodolfo Cerdas, "Del estado intervencionista al estado empresario," *Anuario de Estudios Centroamericanos* 15 (1979): 96.

95. *La Nación*, July 26, 1982, p. 4.

96. Fallas, *La crisis económica*, p. 41.

97. *USAID: Costa Rica Project Paper*, pp. 3–4.

98. Ibid., p. 4.

99. *La Nación*, October 24, 1982, p. 3-C.

100. *Time*, February 20, 1978, p. 38.

101. *USAID: Costa Rica Project Paper*, p. 7.

102. *Time*, September 28, 1981, p. 42.

103. JPRS, *Latin American Report*, April 26, 1982, p. 31; and *La Nación*, March 8, 1982, p. 6-A.

104. Jose Miguel Alfaro R., "Transición hacia la democracia participativa," in Oduber et al., *Los problemas socio-políticos*, p. 89.

105. Radio Reloj, August 17, 1982; in FBIS, LAM, August 19, 1982, p. P-1; and Fallas, *La crisis económica*, p. 26.

106. *La Nación*, March 28, 1982, p. 4-A.

107. *Latin American Weekly Review*, October 15, 1982, p. 10.

108. Denton, *Patterns of Costa Rican Politics*, p. 57.

109. CODESA, *Memoire*, 1980.

110. *La Nación*, July 26, 1982, p. 4.

111. As characterized by Paul W. Drake, "Conclusion," p. 218.

112. Biesanz, Biesanz, and Biesanz, *The Costa Ricans*, p. 112.

113. Jose Luis Vegas Carballo, *Hacia una interpretación del desarrollo costarricense* (San José: Editorial Porvenir, 1981), p. 236.

Conclusion

Robert Wesson

The most obvious conclusion to be drawn from the preceding studies is that it is difficult to draw any firm conclusions. The interrelationships of politics and economics even in the relatively limited ambit of Latin America are enormously complex and dependent on numerous factors, internal and external, many of them poorly knowable or unpredictable. Judgments should be tentative at best. If this book had been written in 1978, many of them would be different. But the Iranian revolution multiplied oil prices in 1979–1980 and started a cascade of problems, beginning with a heavy burden on the foreign exchange balances of most Latin American countries. The dislocation would have been much less serious, however, if the international banks had been less eager to lend from their overflowing stores of petrodollars and the Latin Americans less avid to borrow beyond their capacities for repayment once interest rates rose and inflation subsided. Such diverse countries as Chile and Costa Rica, which seemed in 1978 to have earned high marks for economic management, by 1982 could be deemed failures.

Yet the causes of the worst depression in Latin America since the 1930s were not merely external. Many countries, such as India and Japan, underwent the shock of rising fuel costs without being overwhelmed. And the remarkable fact is that Latin American countries more or less self-sufficient in oil, Argentina, Peru, and Brazil, and subsequently exporters of oil, Mexico and Venezuela, all suffered similarly.

This suggests that factors shared by Latin American republics are for some purposes more important than their differences and that political institutions, particularly the central question of authoritarianism versus democracy, may be sometimes less decisive for economic outcomes than intangible social or psychological factors. Very dissimilar polities—military regimes (Argentina, Chile, Peru, Uruguay, and Brazil), a one-party semi-democracy (Mexico), a two-party semi-democracy (Colombia), and democracies (Venezuela, Costa Rica, and Jamaica)—all fall into similar morasses for mostly similar reasons. They all have a weakness for overspending, especially in financially abnormal conditions, and for deficit financing, which leads to inflation. They have large or overly large bureaucracies, the political weight of which, in dictatorships or in democracies, makes retrenchment difficult. They share the apparently uncontrollable urge to maintain grossly overvalued exchange rates in the face of loss of value of the national currency from domestic inflation, reduced export prices, or both. Such states as Mexico, Venezuela, Jamaica, and Costa Rica, as well as Brazil, Colombia, Peru, and Uruguay to varying degrees, have succumbed to this temptation, as have Chile and Argentina. The reasons have been similar—to enable the state to profit from undercompensated exports, to make necessary and unnecessary imports cheaper, to keep up prestige (devaluation is a confession of failure), and to ease the debt load on firms owing dollars. It may also be important that cheap dollars enable the elites to purchase foreign luxury goods and to travel abroad. The foreseeable results of artificial exchange rates have been disastrous: to injure exports and subsidize imports, wrecking national producers as well as the balance of payments, to promote capital export and foreign spending, to consume reserves, and eventually to contribute to unemployment, inflation, and the shrinkage of production.

Democratic and authoritarian states alike are subject to demands for jobs in government, in state enterprises, and in the private sector; and both categories are pressed to undertake grandiose works and expand the public payroll. There are never enough places for the expanding work force or for the crowd coming out of the burgeoning universities with diplomas but commonly without productive skills. The two kinds of state are also equally prepared to borrow for presumably but not necessarily worthy ends beyond realistic estimates of the capacity to repay. The international bankers, eager for high interest and fees and confident nations would not be permitted to default, added to the pressures; and politicians naturally found promises to pay in future years a small price for money in hand today. Thus debts, the charges on which are comparable to total exports, are about equally horrendous as seen from Mexico City, San José, Lima, Brasília, Montevideo, Buenos Aires, Santiago, and Kingston (and Quito and La Paz as well), and only slightly less so from Caracas.

More basically, authoritarians and democrats alike face the problem of managing somewhat fragile economies in adverse conditions of dependency on external markets, shortage of domestic capital, an indifferent work ethic, frequent preferences for shortcuts to wealth, a usually important degree of corruption, and scarcity of competent management. Highest-level decision-making has obviously been poor, especially in regard to exchange regulation, in Mexico, Venezuela, Argentina, Chile, and other states; and it has not been obviously much better in one class of government than the other.

It is easy to forget that authoritarian states, like democratic ones, depend on political supports or civilian collaboration. Although relations of leaders to led are organized differently in a democratic and a nondemocratic regime, the differences are not overwhelming in the Latin American context. Even a strictly military state requires the backing of the administrators (many of whom may be of the military, or retired officers), industrialists, bankers, foreign investors, and others; and politics carries on the contest for shares of the pie, albeit behind a screen. Brazilian President Geisel, after 1974, was watching public opinion as though he depended on it, and his economic policies may not have been grossly different from what they would have been had he been democratically elected. Perón had to satisfy his unionized workers as though he were a democratic politician.

Differently stated, it would seem that institutions on the surface are less decisive than customs, values, traditional power relations, and political culture beneath. Much of the business of government is carried on in a day-to-day fashion with little reference to highest authorities, while the way leaders confront problems may depend more on their general culture, the ideas and currents in the atmosphere, and prevalent modes of action than on the manner of their selection.

Most notably, Latin American presidents have shared or gone along with the inclination to expand the intervention of the state in the economy—a tendency that has been, indeed, worldwide, especially among less developed states. This takes many forms such as controls over banking and credits, production controls by the state or official entities, price controls, and regulation of wages and labor relations; most notable has been the expansion of the state-owned productive sector.

Colombia is an outstanding holdout; in most of the rest, the growth of the state sector has been seemingly unstoppable, nationalization always being much easier than privatization. In Mexico, for example, the expansion of state enterprises has been steady and accelerating. In Costa Rica, the state sector has crept steadily ahead without plan, in response to a multitude of needs and opportunities. The military government of Brazil, having ousted a leftist regime, proceeded to expand the state sector well beyond what the leftists had achieved or perhaps intended. Even the fiercely anticommunist, pro-market regime of Pinochet *de facto* extended state control of the economy. In the crisis of 1981, the Chilean state took over major firms and banks to save them from bankruptcy, and 85 percent of credit came to be in government hands.

Conceivably a major reason for the increase of state ownership is the need for patronage. More respectable reasons, persuasive for democratic as for authoritarian governments, include: to prevent foreign entry into important areas of the economy (as Brazilian state mining and petroleum), to keep failing enterprises in operation (especially utilities and transportation, whose prices are kept artificially low), to make investments beyond the reach of private enterprise (as Brazilian steel and hydropower), to compensate ravages of nature (as Peruvian fishing), to keep control of industries held vital for security reasons (as in Argentina, Chile, and Brazil), to build industry of strategic importance, and to give political leaders levers over the economy (as the nationalization of banks in Mexico and Costa Rica). Ideologically speaking, state intervention is sought to put order in the anarchic economy and to end the class struggle of workers against native or foreign capitalists.

Yet overall national planning is generally futile,[1] and government operation has usually proved inefficient in governments both authoritarian and democratic. The state is hardly equipped to manage very well or to do without the guidance of the market. Public enterprises are inevitably subject to other than economic criteria to some degree, and bureaucratic considerations often take priority over considerations of production. They are generally unprofitable despite including big revenue producers such as oil monopolies. State enterprises are relieved of the discipline of failure; if they lose money, they are not liquidated but rescued by state subsidies. They are ordinarily overstaffed and vulnerable to patronage at all levels, political considerations at times outweighing more productive qualifications. Like other large economic organizations, state enterprises have political clout; they may be the tail that wags the ministry on which they are theoretically dependent. For efficiency, state enterprises should be autonomous, but in their autonomy they are likely to escape control, use their usually monopolistic position for their own benefit, and make investments and borrow money independently of the desires of the central government.

The share of the state enterprises in the national economy does not prevent rapid growth, as demonstrated by Mexico and Brazil. On the other hand, chronically deficitary state enterprises have been very burdensome for the economy of various countries. The losses of Argentine state corporations, especially the grossly inefficient railroads, fueled inflation and weakened both the first and the second Peronist governments, and the deficits of the state sector have been a major factor in the economic ills of Costa Rica and Peru. State enterprises pre-empt much of the national credit markets, and they have contributed heavily to the indebtedness of such countries as Argentina, Brazil, Costa Rica, Mexico, and Venezuela.[2]

A democratic state may have better possibilities of checking the misuse of nationalized enterprises through criticism and modes of exposure in the assembly and the press. Venezuela has managed its petroleum production rather well, much better than less democratic Mexico; and Costa Rican state enterprises have proved moderately efficient. But state firms have functioned equally well in military-run Brazil. The state enterprises in a democratic country are less free to set prices economically when many persons are affected (as by utilities) or to prune staffs.

A different situation arises when political leaders use, or try to use, state enterprises for purposes of political-social transformation as in Allende's Chile or Manley's Jamaica or the Peru of Velasco Alvarado. Results have been very negative. To make an enterprise an instrument of change inevitably undermines, perhaps destroys, its productive capacity as political criteria replace economic ones and political mobilizers replace business managers. The shortcomings of political national enterprises were an important cause for the problems of the leftist regimes in all of these countries.

Several countries have made some effort to divest state holdings, but it is not easy. The authorities usually want to be rid of the most unprofitable, and for these there are no takers. Domestic capital is lacking to buy major enterprises, and there is abhorrence of selling to foreign capital. Buyers are wary, fearful of renationalization or severe regulation. It may be difficult to discharge supernumerary employees. There are probably fears of monopoly if, as usually is the case, there is little or no competition in the state-dominated branch.

Brazil has promised to reduce the number of state enterprises for several years, creating special organs for that purpose, but very little has been achieved. Despite his commitment to the free market, Seaga, in Jamaica in 1983, had sold only three small state enterprises and leased out four hotels. Where public sector employment is the base of the leading party, as in Costa Rica, there is not likely to be much enthusiasm in the government for privatization. There is a temptation, in both democratic and authoritarian societies, for the state to undertake more than it can do efficiently; to reverse this, a strong, virtually revolutionary drive seems to be necessary.

Major tendencies and problems are thus rather similar in quite different states, as the preceding case studies make clear. However, there are some broad differences of inclination. In particular, the nonmilitary regimes, including populist dictatorships such as the Peronist, seem much more inclined to policies of import-substitution industrialization (ISI), the effort to advance modernization primarily by promoting production for the domestic market and thereby replacing imports, partly by means of subsidies of various kinds, mostly by protection. This approach, which was most prevalent in the 1950s and 1960s,[3] appealed as a means not only to national power, wealth, and independence but also to the creation of jobs—blue-collar, white-collar, and managerial. It seemed all very logical, sensible, and politically appealing.

Yet ISI has been a limited success. It is often stated that ISI is exhausted after a relatively brief time, but exhaustion is not to be understood as the using up of possibilities of the replacement of imported goods by national production. Exhaustion rather means tiredness, as costs come to outweigh benefits. ISI commonly generated expensive and inefficient industry based more on the level of state aid and protection than on economic rationality, serving often quite inadequate markets. It cost the economy import revenues (commonly the main reliance of the treasury). It deprived the nation of benefits of international trade, discouraged exports, and usually contributed to the neglect of agriculture. It fueled inflation because of direct costs and because of the higher prices of its products. It has proved a disappointment as provider of jobs because of low volume.

Populist governments have hoped to solve political as well as economic problems by ISI with benefits for urban workers, the middle classes, and capitalists, but they have been regularly defeated or at least checked. ISI had its best possibilities in Brazil because of the relatively large market—in return for access to which planners could require foreign firms to produce for export as well. But even there it prepared the way for the breakdown of the democratic state in 1964. In Colombia, Costa Rica, Peru, Jamaica, Mexico, Chile (prior to the Pinochet government), and Argentina, ISI and related policies contributed to the severity of crises. ISI was a major factor in the paralysis that overtook Uruguay, leading to stagnation, prolonged decline, and political breakdown.

Military regimes taking over from populist or semi-populist democratic governments have regularly gone in the opposite direction. In Chile, Argentina (under both Onganía and Videla), Uruguay, and Brazil, the generals have reduced barriers to foreign trade at the cost of injuring domestic producers, promoted exports, cut down subsidies, reduced deficits, and thus checked inflation. They have also, whether intentionally or not, increased unemployment and reduced real wages. Forcing the nation to swallow this bitter austerity medicine has been possible, of course, only by ignoring public opinion. They have frankly claimed this virtue of being able to act in ways necessary for the health of the economy as a democracy could not.

This seems logical enough, but one should be careful of overrating the importance of the type of regime for the turn of policy. The military regimes in question were able to impose austerity not only because they were legally unrestricted, but because they rode a wave of reaction to the economic failure of the preceding more spendthrift populist-democratic government. In fact, elected constitutional governments are capable of rather vigorous austerity programs, as that of Belaúnde in Peru has shown. Perhaps a better example is Costa Rica; the Monge government in 1982–1983 was able to gain a reasonable degree of acceptance for rigorous belt-tightening. Jamaica has likewise shown the capacity of a democracy to absorb without violence economic setbacks that might lead to disorders in an authoritarian state. Taking power after a leftist episode, the Seaga government had a program not unlike that of the Chilean or Brazilian military (although implementation proved difficult). But not many democratic leaders are able or motivated to sacrifice present popularity for uncertain benefits in the fairly distant future, and a regime firmly based on organized force undeniably should be able to pursue whatever measures it deems proper.

With their ability to take strong unpopular but presumably salutary measures, authoritarian regimes have shown excellent results for a few years following a difficult transition period. With reduced inflation, confidence has returned, national and foreign investors have put capital to work, trade is improved, graphs of national product turn upwards, and the country enjoys something of a boom. This occurred in Brazil in 1968–1974, the years of "miracle," and in Chile in 1976–1981. The Argentine military government appeared for few years, 1966–1969 and 1976–1979, to have found the keys to prosperity. The Peruvian military regime also enjoyed three to four good years. And prosperity brings, apparently, a considerable degree of acceptance.

But an authoritarian government functions best when it is fresh. The officers take power with conviction and self-confidence, and they are able to repress particularist demands from workers and capitalists alike. But with the passage of time the new power settles down, the machine becomes stiff and loses the ability to take decisive action against vested interests, corruption creeps in, and the political struggle resumes whether in the open or behind curtains. A regular cost of the economic stimulation is increased inequality (except in Peru, where the trend was reversed by reformist policies, 1970–1973). The rich get much richer while the poor gain much less or may even suffer, at least for some years, a dramatic decline in their low standard of living. Basic tensions are thereby increased. The generals, ceasing to be regarded as saviors of the nation from anarchy, lose much of their sense of direction, and the power they took away from the elected administration tends to slip out of their hands and to the bureaucracy.

It is doubtless because of loss of ability to direct the state, as well as because of the failure of prosperity, that soldiers think of returning to civilians responsibility for managing the increasingly unmanageable state, in effect confessing their inability to formulate and carry out rational policy. Thus since 1979 military governments have renounced power, or at least the direct exercise of power, in Ecuador, Peru, Bolivia, and Argentina. Since 1974 the armed forces have been edging backwards in Brazil, although it has been a slow march, whether because of reluctance to lose perquisites or a calculation that constitutionalism has to be built up carefully, or because of fears at any stage that the next stage might lead to a populist reaction. In Uruguay it appeared, in 1984, that the generals would like to give back to civilians the economic mess they have made or come into, but were deterred most of all by fears of being called to account for violations of human rights and determined to retain a veto over the civil power.

Another reason that the military men are prepared to yield and open up the system is the need for more information, and this is precisely the advantage of a more democratic system. The democracy is better prepared to consider choices. A freer Argentina would hardly have thrown away the nation's reserves in keeping up a ridiculously high rate for the peso, and it would probably not have blundered into the Falklands/Malvinas misadventure. Lack of criticism made it possible for Chile to stick to its stubborn exchange policy when it was generally obvious that it was leading to disaster. Peru's slippage toward economic ruin in the 1970s was largely the work of a small band of officers without responsibility to civilians. The authoritarian regime, moreover, may lose an important share of its intelligentsia by emigration or repression; this has occurred in the three Southern Cone countries. On the other hand, informed decisionmaking had much to do with the good growth record of Colombia, 1968–1980.

A genuinely democratic system likewise has freedom of criticism and so can check corruption.[4] If there is broad popular interest in public affairs and a free and inquisitive press, abuses of power can hardly be so frequent or shameless as they are likely to be in a closed system. Yet tendencies to use political positions for personal advantage are endemic throughout the region, with variations in degree from Costa Rica to Mexico or Bolivia.

If the democracy is less likely to permit misuse of executive power, it is subject—like the nondemocratic state—to the distortions arising from interest group pressures. The democracy especially suffers a different sort of corruption, the use of the government for the benefit of votes. In quite unequal societies where a large part of the population feel they have no stake in the system, it is very easy for politicians to make it their business—a profitable business—to promise benefits and to use the state to provide jobs and special privileges for their supporters. This implies an excessive number of government positions filled by often poorly qualified persons. The extravagance of Costa Rica has probably been much less the providing of welfare benefits to the masses than overemployment in the bureaucracy and inefficient use of resources in the public sector. Uruguayan democracy suffered from a similar problem, the choking of productivity of labor by a mass of supposedly beneficial protective measures. The democracy may become a government not by the people—who are poorly informed and unorganized—but by, and consequently for, the politicians.

This turn is by no means inevitable, but it is the more likely as the masses are separated from the prestige classes. If the people are mobilizable, a populist turn to using the government for the immediate benefit of the people, or in practice of the organized political following, would seem sooner or later inevitable. For example, Chile under Allende, Brazil under Goulart, and Jamaica under Manley suffered similar problems of the politicized economy: accelerated inflation, social tensions, loss of confidence, an exodus of capital (and, in the Jamaican case, of skills). If the populist-leftist state follows its natural inclination to move toward ideological radicalism or shows signs of following the Cuban example, as the countries cited did, its economic troubles are compounded. There may be generated something of a revolutionary atmosphere frightening to the middle classes, not so much because of popular demands as because of the enthusiasm of leftist leaders for the reordering of society. The expectable outcome in Latin America is a military coup and rightist dictatorship.

Obviously democracy, or an effort to establish a democracy, is no cure-all for economic needs of Latin America; it has failed too many times. Neither does dictatorship offer a solution; the modernized corporate military regime has not turned out much better than its less sophisticated predecessors. It must be recognized that no political constitution can be expected to function very well in adverse circumstances. Institutions do make a difference, but the best have a high failure rate in conditions of poor public morality, lack of common values, social division, and widely divergent and narrowly promoted interests.

No Latin American government (except possibly Cuba) really goes very deep to engage all the main forces in society, and a military regime, however heavy-handed—as in Argentina—is somewhat superficial. Formally democratic governments (with the possible exception of Costa Rica) likewise fail really to bring the people together. Societies that are essentially ungovernable consequently tend to swing, pendularly, between alternatives. It is an old story in Latin America that dictatorship fails after a time, and people call for constitutional rule and democracy; the constitutional rule becomes a sterile contest or leads to disorder, and people welcome or accept a military intervention. There are spurts of economic development and growth as the nation, for a few years, comes close to utilizing its capacities, and there are setbacks partly caused by external market conditions, but much deepened by misguided policies. There is obviously no clear-cut political answer to the problem of underdevelopment.

Some political formations, however, are obviously more favorable than others, and the more democratic probably have on balance more credits. They are more elastic. Jamaica, for example, shows how a democracy can swing within the same political system from a socialistic to a free enterprise approach (although the contrast has been stronger in ideology and rhetoric than in concrete practice, and Seaga has had to compromise with statism). Economic development should have freedom of innovation, openness to criticism, legality, and stability (characteristics that made it possible for Britain to inaugurate the industrial revolution).

Intuitively one may suppose that the government favorable to economic development should be responsive to producers—that is, economic policy should not be in the hands of soldiers or demagogues, but of persons with primarily economic concerns. It may be, of course, that generals want productivity and modernization for national strength and that politicians want prosperity to furnish benefits for their followers. But military or political leaders, even if their intentions are good, are likely to be poorly informed regarding the needs of the economy, and neither authoritarians nor populists want to let power go to the producers. Productive sectors can be influential in either a democratic or a nondemocratic state, but it is a good guess that their chances of making themselves heard are better in the more open society.

The other obvious condition for building a modern economy, at least in reliance on private enterprise, is security with stability. One does not rationally put money into an enterprise unless there is confidence that one can enjoy the fruits of the undertaking in the future. On the contrary, in conditions of uncertainty investors, both national and foreign, will endeavor to safeguard their equity so far as possible, disinvesting and probably taking capital out of the national economy and into a safer refuge abroad. Neither democracy nor dictatorship can guarantee stability and security forever. Conceivably the qualified systems, as in Mexico or Colombia, have the advantage.

It is thus probably fair to state that the most essential factors for economic growth are input from the producers (in Latin America, generally private entrepreneurs and managers) and an atmosphere of security and confidence. Unhappily, however, the influence of entrepreneurship is likely to increase inequality, both because the advancing sector of the economy leaves many persons behind and because of pressure to lower labor costs. Moreover, governments best situated to provide security, qualified democracies and military regimes, have usually promoted inequality, if only by neglect.

But increase of inequality means allowing the health of the society to deteriorate, widening the fearsome gap between possessing and nonpossessing classes. The egalitarian cause is taken up in authoritarian regimes by radicals; in democratic states by populists. Growth may be impressive, but it never suffices to ameliorate much the ills of the unequal society. Dissatisfactions rise, and tensions and social maladjustment undermine the economy. If no state form gives a firm promise of economic development, much less does any really offer a cure for the social problems, the solution of which is ultimately prerequisite for modernization. The one that tries, or seems to try, the populist democracy, has been in Latin American conditions ultimately injurious to the economy and consequently unstable.

This is a gloomy note on which to end a study that, it was hoped at its inception, might shed some useful light on the relationships indicated in its title. But pessimism should not be overdrawn. More or less authoritarian and more or less democratic states in Latin America have both had their better and their worse times, but overall there has been improvement by ordinary standards of progress. Whatever the remaining poverty, Latin America has far more wealth than a generation ago, far more schools, many times as many universities and students, higher levels of communication, and much more sophistication. There is also a stronger basis for democracy. It is probable that the present trend toward democratization will be reversed sooner or later, like previous such trends, but the long-term tendency is in that direction, and the democratic form is clearly the more promising. It is by no means impossible that Latin Americans will be able increasingly to find answers to the political problems of economic development.

Notes

1. *World Development Report, 1983* (Washington, D.C.: World Bank, 1983), p. 69.

2. Ibid., pp. 50, 74.

3. See Robert J. Alexander, *A New Development Strategy* (Maryknoll, N.Y.: Orbis Books, 1976).

4. As observed by William A. Douglas, *Developing Democracy* (Washington, D.C.: Heldref, 1972), p. 2.

Contributors

Werner Baer, professor of economics at the University of Illinois at Urbana-Champaign, specializes in Latin American development problems, including the industrialization process, inflation, state enterprises, and employment. The second edition of his *Brazilian Economy: Growth and Development* appeared in 1983.

Bruce Michael Bagley is associate professor of Latin American Studies at the Johns Hopkins School for Advanced International Studies. With a Ph.D. from the University of California at Los Angeles, he spent four years in research and teaching at the Universidad de los Andes in Bogotá. He has published many articles on Colombian politics.

W. Raymond Duncan is professor of political science at the State University of New York at Brockport. He has published numerous articles on Latin American politics, especially in the Caribbean area. His recent books include *Soviet Policy in the Third World* and *Soviet Policy in Developing Countries*.

William Glade is professor of economics at the University of Texas at Austin and director of its Institute of Latin American Studies. He has focused professionally on the history of Latin American economic development, with particular attention to the role of the state.

John D. Martz is professor and head of the Department of Political Science at Pennsylvania State University. He is author or editor of a dozen books on Latin American politics, plus numerous articles, particularly on the Andean republics. From 1975 to 1980 he edited the *Latin American Research Review*.

David Scott Palmer is chairman of Latin American and Caribbean Studies at the Foreign Service Institute of the Department of State and also lecturer at the School of Advanced International Studies of Johns Hopkins University. Among his numerous writings on politics of the Andean countries is *Peru: The Authoritarian Tradition*.

Paul E. Sigmund is professor of politics and chairman of the Latin American Studies Committee at Princeton University. He has written many books and articles on political theory and Latin American politics, including *The Overthrow of Allende and the Politics of Chile, 1964–1976; Multinationals in Latin America: The Politics of Nationalization*; and *The Political Economy of Income Distribution in Mexico* (coeditor and contributor).

Martin Weinstein is professor and chairman of the Department of Political Science of William Paterson College of New Jersey and also visiting professor at New York University's Center for Latin American and Caribbean Studies. He has published numerous articles on Uruguay and *Uruguay: The Politics of Failure*.

Robert Wesson is senior research fellow at the Hoover Institution and professor of political science at the University of California at Santa Barbara. Among his recent books are *Democracy in Latin America* and *Brazil in Transition* (with David Fleischer).

Gary W. Wynia is professor of political science at the University of Minnesota. His books include *The Politics of Latin American Development, Politics and Planners: Economic Development Policy in Central America*, and *Argentina in the Postwar Era: Politics and Policy-making in a Divided Society*.

Index